The Executive Job Market

Other Books by Auren Uris

How to Be a Successful Leader

Developing Your Executive Skills

The Efficient Executive

Discover Your Inner Self

Techniques of Leadership
(Paperback edition of *How to Be a Successful Leader*)

Working with People

The Management Makers

Mastery of People

THE

EXECUTIVE

JOB MARKET

An Action Guide
for Executive Job Seekers and Employers

AUREN URIS
Research Institute of America

 McGRAW-HILL BOOK COMPANY

New York
San Francisco
Toronto
London
Sydney

THE EXECUTIVE JOB MARKET

66108

3 4 5 6 7 8 9 – M P – 9 8 7 6

Are you interested in a new job?

Or, are you looking for a capable man to fill a critical gap in your executive staff?

The executive job market is of vital concern to every executive, either as a job seeker or as a recruiter for executive talent for his company.

The executive job market is a real-life arena in which career-minded executives look for jobs, and talent-hungry companies seek executives. How successful these searches are depends largely on the familiarity of the individual job seeker, and those doing the company recruiting, with the workings of the market. Strangely enough, there exists very little general knowledge of this important area of corporate life, and of its numerous facets.

Knowledge of the executive job market is becoming increasingly important. The reason is, executive turnover is continually reaching new highs. And every job change, and job opening, creates new problems and opportunities.

At the executive level, jobs are vacated for a number of reasons:

• An executive feels he is in a dead-end job, and seeks to move ahead by affiliating with a new company.

• Jobs are eliminated by acquisitions, mergers, or other organizational changes.

• Disagreements or unsatisfactory relationships with others in management make an executive's continued tenure impossible.

Whatever the motive for exploring the job market, the executive finds himself at a disadvantage, and one that his own subordinates may never experience. An employment-agency head, who has helped hundreds of top men find jobs, explains why:

"Many executives have looked for a job only once in their lives—when they started out to work. They have to adjust to a whole new world of job-hunting techniques and concepts, one in which they are on the *other* side of the interviewer's desk. It can be an unnerving experience. And I've seen it happen repeatedly; the higher up the executive is, the more difficult it is for him to work out an effective plan for marketing his own services."

For the company trying to hire an executive, the choice is made more critical by competitive pressures, scarcity of top talent, and the knowledge that the wrong selection may be extremely costly in both cash and human terms. Here, too, the mysteries and unexpected aspects of the job market can be baffling. This is one area where even the individual expert can be wrong. Often, the best hedge against failure is a broad knowledge of the workings of the market place in which executive talent is bought and sold.

This book was conceived to fill the gap between the scant practical information available, and what's needed to help executive and company operate succesfully in the executive job market. It was suggested by M. Joseph Dooher, McGraw-Hill business book editor and a long-time friend of the author, who perceived the need for a book that would give the executive job seeker the information he requires to understand the job market, its organizations, institutions, and—more important—the unofficial practices and procedures that operate below the surface. With such information, the executive can appraise his job situation more objectively and, if advisable, take steps necessary to conduct an effective job-hunting program. He would be able to answer such questions as these, *before* going through the mill:

Should he go to an employment agency? . . . How does an employment agency differ from a firm that does an executive search? . . . Are job counselors worth the considerable fees they charge? . . . How do "body-snatchers" actually operate? . . . What are the chances of getting a good job by responding to ads? Should I seek counseling—and what kind?

Another equally important purpose of this book is to place in the hands of the company hunting for executive talent, information that can substantially speed the recruiting process.

In almost every case, the executive's problem is never to find *a* job, but to spot *the* job—the one that's best in terms of material and psychic rewards. And to find that job *quickly*, to minimize emotional and cash costs.

Similarly for the company, the problem is never to find *a* man. In the highly competitive atmosphere of our time, the success of a company depends on the capabilities of its management group. A merely adequate executive in a key spot may doom a company's chances for growth, or may even cause its failure. This puts a high premium on being able to find candidates who can not only fill immediate job needs, but also provide future management leadership. Where to look, what kinds of help to use, how to assess job candidates—few of these questions can be safely answered by hunch and intuition.

Times are changing. A decade ago, executives typically looked for the development of their careers within the framework of their present companies. Similarly, companies depended heavily on promotion from within to fill openings in the executive staff. Today, as a result of many pressures, including a rapidly accelerating technology and the ever-more-demanding standards of effective performance, it is becoming more and more usual for companies and individual executives to look to the executive job market for a satisfactory means of advancing mutual goals.

It is hoped that the information in this book, gleaned from interviews with numerous practitioners in the executive job market, will help facilitate the objectives of the executive job seeker and the company seeking executive talent. The contributions of experts from many fields have, by and large, been acknowledged throughout the book. In addition to those whose names are mentioned in the text itself, the author wishes to acknowledge the assistance of the many laborers behind the scenes. These esteemed colleagues at the Research Institute of America are especially worthy of mention:

For editorial assistance, Marjorie Noppel, whose outstanding editorial skill was applied generously throughout the writing process, from the planning to final copy stages.

For information in the personnel field, Mae Fleming Link proved a vastly helpful and unfailing source, both as to how things are done, and how they should be done.

For library services, Carrie Hirtz and Susan Morris, who repeatedly were able to supply appropriate references or news items that added substantial weight to the development of individual chapters.

For secretarial services, Charlotte Braunhut, Angela Rapuano, Louise Ligato, and Margaret Ahn, whose ability to interpret what was meant as well as to copy what was given, frequently saved the day.

The author's family—wife Bette, and Mary, Victoria, Bettina, and Daniel—deserves special mention for its understanding acceptance of difficult schedules, and for encouragement from the sidelines.

Finally, this book has been written with the recollection of an act of kindness performed many years ago by Loire Brophy of the Brophy Employment Agency. Miss Brophy, unhappily gone these many years, listened sympathetically to the job ambitions of an unemployed young man caught up in the grinding mill of the great Depression and, by her understanding, helped him retain his self-esteem, and hope for a brighter future—that eventually came.

Auren Uris

Contents

1

Dynamics of the Market

Harvey Hamilton, University of Pennsylvania 1940, sixteen years of business experience (the last ten in management), self-consciously enters the portals of the Acme Fabricating Corporation.

Company president George Lake, after a genial greeting, escorts Harvey to his new office, introduces him to his secretary, and points to the fresh lettering on the door: "Harvey Hamilton, Director, Marketing." An executive has begun his first day in a new job.

The Costs of Placement

For president George Lake, Harvey Hamilton's arrival marks the end of a six months' search and the expenditure of about $12,000 in fees to an executive-recruiting firm. Not included in direct costs are the hours of high-salaried time spent with the consultant from the search firm and interviews with the applicants. Lake has, in fact, "bet a pile" on his new marketing director. It is counted not only in time and money already spent, but in breaking-in costs yet to come.

Says William Brennan of Brennan Associates, management consultants: "An intangible expense in launching an executive into a new position, particularly when he changes company, is his 'start-up cost.' This is the total of his training cost, i.e., the extra time required of his boss and other executives in briefing him on the problems he will handle, as well as the man's own education period before he is able to make a full contribution.

"The time for this may vary widely. But the cost to the company I would estimate as 50 to 100 per cent of the executive's compensation during his first year."

For Harvey Hamilton, this first day represents a milestone. It signals the

1

end of one important phase of his career, the start of another. He has staked his hopes and ambitions on his future with Acme Fabricating—and at his age, he doesn't lightly face the prospect of another change.

The process of executive search and selection in which Hamilton and Lake have participated is crucial to the vitality and growth of American business. Harvey Hamilton is one of an estimated 1.5 million individuals who, each year, enter an executive office, hang up their hats, sit down behind an unfamiliar desk, and prepare to pit their brains and abilities against a new set of problems.

These 1.5 million are executives who have "made it." Whether promoted from within the company, or recruited from outside, they have started as one of a number of contenders for a job. They have survived a screening and selection procedure that has scrutinized everything from their haircuts to their college grades, the size of their families to their club memberships.

And, as Victor H. Pomper, executive vice-president of H. H. Scott, Inc., Maynard, Massachusetts, manufacturers of quality hi-fi equipment, points out: "Success by executives in new jobs is not a matter of sheer chance. On the contrary, perhaps 90 *per cent of the outcome will have been predetermined*—through the skill and intelligence brought to bear in the preliminary stages, by outside recruiters, if any, the hiring executive, and the successful candidate."

The Executive Market

The processes by which executives such as Harvey Hamilton are recruited, tested, evaluated, and placed, and the ways in which they themselves further their fortunes—in short, the "buying" and "selling" of executive talent and all the procedures related to it—make up the "executive market." "Executive" is used in a broad sense, to apply to anyone in a position of management responsibility in a company, from just above the supervisory ranks to the top salary range, $9,000 to $100,000, and even higher.

In its complex workings, the executive market involves millions of Americans, in hundreds of varying capacities. They range from industrial psychologists who seek to eliminate some of the unknowns from executive selection, to the "go-betweens" who make a profitable living by counseling, recruiting, and placing executives, to the company executives who make the final selection.

Taken all together, the executive market acts like a gigantic heart, pumping its lifeblood of executive talent throughout the body economic.

A few generalizations can be made about this market.

It is the means by which the economy maintains its supply of business leaders. Companies use it to quickly find men qualified to manage their resources. At the same time, it affords the outstanding individual who desires a career in management a channel for seeking and making his fortune.

It follows an inner logic and pattern. No individual, whether as job seeker or recruiter, can hope to succeed in his aim if he does not thoroughly understand the peculiar rituals involved in executive search and placement.

It is in a continual state of flux and flow. A company goes under. Result: Dozens of executives scatter for the marketplace. For example, when *Collier's* magazine closed its doors, hundreds of editors and managers suddenly fanned out into the publishing world. A company merges. Again, dozens of executives in every category are suddenly on the available list, as the acquiring firm consolidates activities—purchasing, engineering, and so on. A firm opens a new plant, and the word goes out—"United Corp. is hiring"—and as the pull of opposite poles, the vacancies start attracting the talent, and men from all over the map move toward the jobs.

The demand for executives—and the willingness of potential candidates to look outside their present jobs for better opportunities—also varies with the health of the economy. During recessions, men who are otherwise "move-minded" become less venturesome; companies too are less willing to take aboard new men when the sales outlook is poor.

But underlying the continual ebb and flow day in and day out are the countless changes taking place in thousands of businesses, some stemming from fundamental management decisions, others from trends in the economy itself.

The Executive Ferment

Within a few months, Du Pont, Prudential Insurance Co., Union Oil of California, Dow Chemical, and many other companies announced the appointment of new top executives. Behind each new appointment lay a chain of events, often known only to a small corporate "in-group."

Normal demands for executives arise in every firm, from time to time. A company must replace a president who has died or retired. A key position is left vacant when a financial executive leaves to head a company division in another state.

In other cases, the appointments represent a "changing of the guard," perhaps a painful reorganization, because management wants to infuse fresh thinking into the corporate body by bringing in younger men with different points of view. Behind the confident executive photograph on the business page reporting a change of job may lie a case of "executive failure" —that is, failure of a top man to deliver the earnings record sought after by stockholders and directors.

A piece in *Dun's Review and Modern Industry,* "The Big Management

Shake-up," by Jack B. Weiner, uses the changes of Pittsburgh's Westing-house Electric Corp. as symptomatic of a general management trend:

> The reorganization of Westinghouse is part of the top-to-bottom manage-ment shake-up—a quiet, but violent movement that has been sweeping American industry. During the last few years, in fact, the tempo of this movement has accelerated. Not only have the upheavals been coming faster, they have been of increasingly greater magnitude. Indeed, and per-haps most noteworthy of all, upheavals have now become such an accepted fact of life for industry that they draw no more than casual notice. Nevertheless, the prognosis is that more and more executives can expect to be caught in them as time goes on.

In addition to executive reshuffling and replacements, the executive market is kept active by the demand for men to fill newly created positions. A new company is formed. Or a president decides that his firm must take a more sophisticated approach to its markets and hires a marketing director to set up a new unit, coordinating product development, advertising, sales. Perhaps a corporation opens a branch to tap a new market.

Three Underlying Factors for Change

When the entire executive search and hiring process is viewed from an even broader perspective, however, three other factors appear that have a major influence on the dynamics of the executive job market.

1. *Technological advances.* These accelerate, and a company finds that its old-line executives lack sufficient engineering or scientific knowledge to take advantage of the new concepts, equipment, or processes. Says J. Benton Vandegrift of Vandegrift Associates, an expert in the area of operations research:

> A company's very survival in today's competitive climate may depend on hiring new executives who *do* understand the new technology and tech-niques. Decisions on manufacturing, administrative and financial matters are made with the help of new techniques bearing such names as "opera-tions research" (OR), "program review and evaluation technique" (PERT), "value analysis" (VA), and so on.

Dun's Review recently pointed out:

> American management has changed more over the past ten years than in all its previous 150-year history. The computer alone has created a vast and far-reaching revolution in management, and one which is still con-tinuing. New marketing techniques are being replaced by others almost as soon as they have been developed and production has passed the get-it-out era for one of incredibly complex technology.

Result: Just as in the sports world, executives seeking to fill a vacancy on a "management team" find that standards get stiffer from year to year.

Where earlier an engineering executive may have been adequately qualified if he had electronics experience, now he may be out of his depth unless he is familiar with lasers or microwaves or thermoelectricity or some other highly specialized area. And this same increase in qualifications, educational and technical, is required for every management function, from production to finance.

2. *Competition.* The activities of competitors may cause an organization to decide on basic changes in its products or sales strategy. The quality of its product, its advertising concepts, or its distribution channels may all be involved. The carrying through of such plans is likely to set up a long chain of executive separations, hirings, and replacements.

3. *Executive specialization.* Older executives, who expect to get a job on the basis of past experience and general skills, are often jolted when they enter today's job market. The demands are often more specific than they ever dreamed of, for traditional functions are being broken down or "splintered" into new subfunctions, each requiring its own special competence.

For example, consider personnel administration. According to *The Conference Board Record*, "In addition to the more usual personnel functions, activities such as organizational planning, management development, manpower planning and behavioral research have become major interests of today's personnel executive." The executive is now expected to develop an environment for high motivation and productivity. Even as traditional a function as finance now has distinct fields including budgeting, new acquisitions, profitability accounting, and so on.

Moreover, the demand for any given kind of executive experience doesn't remain fixed. Heidrick and Struggles, a Chicago consulting firm, has charted the trends in newspaper ads for executives, by category, over a period of years, and the figures provide an interesting insight into changes in the American economy itself.

For example, this was the pattern of demand for executives in the first quarter of 1964 compared to the same period in 1963. Note the sharp changes for all except personnel and general administration.

Note: Figures are based on a count of newspaper display ads in eleven big metropolitan areas throughout the United States.

Category of Skill	% of Demand for All Categories	
	1964	1963
Engineering and science	24	16
Engineering and science—defense work	26	7
Marketing	15	30
Finance	14	22
Manufacturing	12	17
Personnel	6	4
General administration	3	4

Significantly, too, in the first twelve weeks of 1964 there were 5,969 openings, advertised in the eleven cities charted, compared with only 3,460 in the first thirteen weeks of 1963.

As Heidrick and Struggles pointed out, the resurgence of demand for executives reflected the optimism which prevailed in the high-level economy of 1964. In this case, the overall figures also represented a sharp rebound from the severe drop-off in hirings which occurred after the death of President Kennedy. Demand for executives in the first quarter of 1964 was 24 per cent above the last quarter of 1963.

How Things Look to the Company That Is Hiring

As the elephant who was described as six different animals by six blind men, the essential character of the executive market depends on your point of view.

To the company with a vacancy to fill, the executive-hunting process is important but largely impersonal. If no one on the premises fills the bill, it is assumed that somewhere outside there is an individual with the precise skills and experience needed. Very likely he's making a substantial contribution to the success of another company, and, hopefully, he's dissatisfied.

In theory, the hiring company's problem is simply to decide which of various channels is most likely to lead to the target—ads in the classified sections of newspapers? Executive-search firms? Psychological testing services? Management consultants? The bank? Perhaps several facilities will be used.

But in practice, the executive who carries responsibility for selecting and hiring the new man won't approach the task as impassively as the textbooks might have it. First, he realizes that the man who's to sit behind the now-vacant desk must become an integral and personal part of the company. And the executive, if he's a good organization man, may feel like the young man contemplating the advisability of taking a mail order bride: It would be nice if there were a less "commercial" means of selecting the executive mate.

The fact is, there's a great deal at stake, as Harold Mayfield, director of personnel relations of Owens-Illinois, indicates in an article in *Management Review:*

> When we bring a new employee into the fold, we are probably going to be living with him a long time—for better or worse. If we have picked wisely, the payoff continues over the years, and we have made a fundamental contribution to company success. On the other hand, if we have not picked wisely, we have taken on a liability that may be with us a long time, and no amount of modern machinery or managerial skill will make up for this weakness at the source.

Also, as the hiring executive knows, his own career may be at stake. This is decision making at its most crucial. Even if not involved personally in the situation, he may feel that his judgment of people is on the line, in the eyes of his president or board of directors—and *he needs to be right.* There is also his responsibility to the man he will select. He may hire a top executive away from another job where he was secure and content. Suppose he doesn't like the new company or his assignment; suppose he doesn't work out? It's a tough load to carry on one's conscience.

Emotions of the Job-hunting Executive

The state of mind of the prospective employer, however uncertain, is calm compared to that of the average job seeker. Consider the executive who holds a successful job and receives an offer "too attractive to refuse." He appears to be in an enviable position. Yet even he faces doubts and uncertainties. Will he like the new firm? Is the position compatible with his life's goals and ambitions? Will his wife like the new location if he has to move? And the $64 question: Would he do better, long range, to stay where he is? A new job, particularly for the man over the age of thirty-five, means laying not just his career but the very substance of his life on the line. An executive's work very often *is* his life.

Now consider the executive who has been fired, or the one who quits without having another job in immediate sight. The state of mind that is most likely to arise has been called by some observers "executive panic." The executive looking for a new affiliation often has his self-confidence shaken to the core. There are various explanations for this. For one thing, the unemployed executive, as a fish out of water, is completely out of his natural element. The foundation of his financial and emotional security has been yanked out from under him.

Being unemployed carries a stigma for many people, and for the executive even more so. At one stroke, he has been deprived of status and his means of support. He may even feel ashamed, as a medical man who has had his license revoked or a lawyer who has been disbarred. "I felt *no* one wanted me," says one executive in bitter reminiscence of a brief period of unemployment. "It was hard to take."

Perhaps this sentiment is overstated for some executive job seekers. But the evidence from most sources suggests not only that "executive panic" is more the rule than the exception, but that it is frequently a serious handicap to the man looking for a job. One executive job hunter I talked to recently said, "It took me two months just to recover from the shock of having been fired." "It was ego-bruising," reports another. Certainly a man with any degree of insecurity, and that includes most of us, is bound to experience some degree of discomfort.

Underlying the ego-damaging effects of executive unemployment are additional factors. Undoubtedly *guilt* is one of the more important ones. The executive who has hired dozens of managers himself remembers, perhaps too well, his own "objectivity" and impersonal feelings toward the job applicants who walked into his office. Now he is in the same situation, and it's easy to read into the reversal of his position a kind of Satanic justice.

As one executive put it, "I can't help remembering the pity I felt for the poor S.O.B.s I had coming into my office when I was hiring." A man who thinks *he's* considered a poor S.O.B. by a person whose goodwill he must win to get back into the system understandably faces an interviewer with mixed emotions.

These first reactions of shock and guilt generally wear off, of course. In anywhere from a few days to a few weeks, the average executive job hunter shows the same aggressiveness and self-confidence that he exhibited as a working manager. A certain percentage of job seekers, usually in the lower-age group, may even approach the business of finding a new position with a sense of adventure. Optimistic in their outlook and buoyed up by a healthy sense of their own worth, they fear the future not at all. "Every time I've quit or been fired, I've got a better job," reports a well-placed advertising-agency art director. Job hopping is his means of making professional progress.

Nevertheless, the underlying tensions are there, and it's no accident that the "middlemen" in the executive job market are often referred to in emotion-tinged terms. Note this executive-market jargon, and the tensions and emotionality from which they arise become clear:

Blood suckers. Firms and individuals who perform job counseling, guidance, and other services for the out-of-work executive—short of finding jobs—for a fee. (Also may counsel the employed but "looking" man.)

Flesh peddlers. Employment agencies that place job-seeking executives and professionals.

Body snatchers. Recruiting firms who act for the company seeking to fill an executive vacancy. Not infrequently, they raid competing firms to get suitable candidates. (Also sometimes referred to as "head hunters" and "personnel pirates.")

Add Competition

In the ideal case of executive placement, the two parties grope toward each other and eventually meet. The company discovers that the man is indeed the right mate, and joyously hires him. The job seeker is similarly pleased. In reality, of course, it's much more complicated. There is competition, often fierce, between companies for particularly desirable candidates. There is also competition between individuals for given job openings. It is not unusual for an advertisement in Sunday's *The New York Times*, for example, to produce 700 or 1,000 applications for one job opening.

The executive job market is not a neat system. It is subject to inequities and error; it has its capable and serious practitioners, and its quacks. It *could* work better; it could be easier on anxiety-ridden job hunters and harried talent seekers. Systematization of needs and skills, working through computers, may simplify the mechanism in the future. Already there are some successful applications of computers to executive recruiting.

But meanwhile, both the executive looking for a job and the company looking for an executive can boost their chances of success immeasurably by understanding the market. They must know not only its obvious aspects, but the behind-the-scenes, below-the-surface factors that actually determine the outcome when man seeks prospective employer, and recruiter seeks man.

2

The Hunt for Executive Talent

Look at a company organization chart, and you'll see a number of neat, static boxes. The position of the boxes may change little, if at all, over a five- to ten-year period. But it would be wrong to assume that the occupants were quietly tending their bailiwicks—year in and year out. In the average company, the true picture of the organization chart could only be taken by a movie camera, for it is constantly changing. It is the ebb and flow of executives coming and going (in and out of countless organization charts) that feeds the executive market.

To both the man looking for a job and the company looking for a man, an understanding of the events leading to a job opening is highly important. The causes can be many and varied, from something as subtle as a president's hidden dissatisfaction with a staff member to the frazzled chief who bellows, "I'm going to get myself an assistant!"

Whatever the particular needs, it helps if the company is aware of them, in order to select the appropriate candidate. The job applicant must also know, so that he doesn't make the same mistakes as his predecessor, or take a job where he'd be unhappy.

The following pages describe some of the factors that are likely to be hidden behind the ad "Top Executive Wanted," or the phone call that starts, "We'd like your help in finding. . . ."

Company Structures Change, and Vacancies Open

There's a lot of "rubber" in the structure of the average company. Without it, businesses couldn't make the adjustments to inside and outside pressures that are necessary to survival, such as:

Business growth. Company A opens a sales branch in the Southwest to be nearer a lucrative market for its outdoor furniture. Company B builds an assembly plant in Cleveland, to keep up with the demand for its new infrared oven in the Midwest. In both cases a call goes out for executives to fill newly created vacancies. Expansion almost invariably brings the need for fresh executive talent to handle the newly created responsibilities.

The nature of the openings may vary. In one case the company may need an "assistant to" for an executive whose job has developed a case of elephantiasis. In another, the job may require a man to head up a brand new plant, such as the Cleveland assembly operation.

Speed of growth may vary too. Some companies grow slowly, adding executives here and there over a number of years. Others "explode" overnight as some special market opportunity makes it imperative to take action on a crash basis. But whatever the nature of the expansion, more executives are needed. And each time, the wheels of the job market take a few extra spins.

It's important that the candidate being interviewed for a job in a growth situation realize this fact. He can make or break his chances according to the impression he gives the interviewer about his hopes and ambitions for the future. The interviewer may subtly lead the conversation so as to find out where the candidate wants to go, how responsible he is to educating himself for greater responsibilities, how quickly he wants to forge ahead, and so on. Tip-off to this kind of situation often lies in the ad that reads "Wanted: man who is anxious to grow with company."

Promotions from within. Many companies follow a policy of filling key positions by advancing present employees. But even these go outside for executives from time to time. And the reason often is the "promotion chain," which works as follows:

The president of the company moves up to chairman of the board. The executive vice-president is made president, and the general manager moves up into *his* job. The head of the fabricating division is promoted to general manager, and so on. In theory, the chain reaches right down to the lowest management level, leaving no position unfilled. In practice, a neat line of advancement is seldom maintained. While executive B may be able to take A's place, and executive C to take B's, chances are there's no one qualified to step into C's shoes. Result: The call goes out, and a search is started for a new executive C.

Reshuffling of responsibilities. Management may relieve an executive of certain duties and responsibilities and parcel them out among others on the staff in order to make better use of available brainpower. Or an older man may be shifted to a less-demanding spot, to open up a job for an up-and-coming younger person, as well as to take the pressure off him. A production executive nearing sixty, for example, may be unable to meet the accelerated pace necessary as his company expands. The personnel director leaves, and the production man is given the vacant position with the idea that his familiarity with the company and his experience in handling people will make it possible for him to function in this new spot.

Another common occurrence: The job specification may be changed because no one is available inside *or* outside to handle the job as originally envisioned. For example, the president of a paint company decides it's time to bring all sales and advertising functions under one head. In the organization chart, the job might look like this:

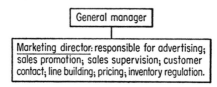

But the president soon learns that no one within the organization can fill the bill and no one outside is willing to, at the salary he's offering. Result: He divides the responsibility between *two* men, like this:

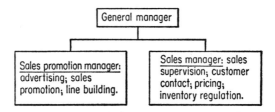

This type of job splitting often takes place when a company cannot find one person with all the desired qualifications. And then, the company usually tries to hire a man who has the growth potential to fill the bigger job later on. This is why applicants applying for a specific opening may be asked about their familiarity with some apparently unrelated field—such as research and development when they're being interviewed for a purchasing manager's job (the company plans to do extensive materials research), or information retrieval systems when the job calls for an office manager.

Future needs. "You can slice the future any way you like," says Richard S. White, president of Automation Engineering Laboratory, Inc., Stamford, Conn., designers and builders of special automatic equipment, "one-year periods, five-years, or short-range–long-range. However it's done, you've got to staff for tomorrow in hiring your executives for today. Otherwise you're gambling with your company's future."

The different ways in which companies "slice the future" for planning purposes are described by Prof. Edith Sands in *How to Select Executive Personnel.*

A number of manufacturing companies determine their needs for executive personnel three to five years in advance. The banks and insurance companies studied required a longer lead-time of five to ten years. Public utilities projected their needs ten to fifteen years into the future, while merchandising companies, dealing as they do with consumer products, apparently plan no more than three years ahead, many even less. One company, for example, reported six months to one year as its planning-ahead period, based on "knowing in advance the number of new stores and new districts to be created, and also knowing what executive changes will be made due to retirements, transfers, promotions, or demotions." The extreme in long-range planning was found in one manufacturing company which said its needs for executive personnel have been projected 30 years ahead. This is not too far in the future for a company whose expansion plans involve maturation of trees.

In staffing for the future, one of the biggest problems is to achieve the right "age mix" of executives. Individuals must be carefully dovetailed to make sure that all key men won't hit retirement age at the same time. Many presidents also like to be able to feel that they can keep their firms on the growth curve—and maintaining a young, aggressive executive staff is one way to do it. This accounts for the cadet programs, the hiring and training of young college recruits, the setting of maximum age limits in hiring. It also explains why an experienced applicant may be told, not unkindly, that while he's satisfactory for the present job, he doesn't qualify for the position because he'd be ready for retirement just when the company would really need him most.

Executive Obsolescence

If we lived in a static world, old age and ill health would be the main reasons for replacing executives. But an economy that can give rise to thousands of new products in just a single year has created something else—the young but obsolescent executive.

Human obsolescence is hardly new on the work scene. Hand turners, blacksmiths, harness makers—hundreds of occupations have vanished under the wheels of progress. But it has remained for our era to tap the working *executive* on the shoulder and wave him off the field. Two trends have contributed to the shortening of the executive's job life:

Introduction of new processes. John Black, head of bookkeeping for a toy manufacturer, does a good job of supervising the work of his twelve clerks, doing manual calculations. However, since his employer and a management consultant reorganized the billing-bookkeeping routine around a new electronic accounting machine, John Black, at age sixty-two, has been out of a job.

Sudden obsolescence also struck Henry Simon. Henry rose from the ranks to become head of an important production unit in a metalworking company. A skilled machinist, he knew his machines so well that he could have taken them apart and reassembled them in the dark. But Henry lacked the experience and technical know-how to adjust to the new electronically controlled units that must be left to the care of their own new maintenance engineers.

Not even executives with broadest overall knowledge of their companies are exempt from the effects of "progress." More than one financial executive, for example, has burned the midnight oil trying to keep up with the new terms of computer programing, operations research, and so on.

Computers, new chemical or metalworking processes—the new technologies make strict demands not just on the operating people who run the equipment, but also on those at the top who have to control the entire plant economy. This results in a second area of change causing shakeouts in company organization charts.

Management skills. Managerial methods have changed drastically in the past ten to twenty years. The bull-of-the-woods type of manager, gruff and often tactless, wouldn't fare too well on the executive ladder today. The typical executive recruit approaches his task not only with greater sophistication but with a new outlook and a new kit of manager's tools.

Take decision making. Ten or fifteen years ago, a man could feel superior if his decisions were good more times than they were poor, and he could attribute his skill to "hunch," intuition, or "feel." Now, even the greenest graduate from a business school knows that the solution to a tough problem may require calling in the boys from OR, EDP, etc. And woe betide the executive who doesn't speak—or at least understand—the language of the experts.

Consider another important activity of the executive—handling people. Some radical changes have also occurred during the past fifteen years in our ideas about human relations. Not so long ago, personnel people preached a doctrine of employee relations that was a peculiar compound of amateur psychology and half-baked semantics. Supervisors were supposed to ask for "cooperation" when they wanted obedience. They were taught to get results by letting employees "participate in decision making," even though it was often obvious that employees couldn't care less.

Today's manager is far more realistic in his approach to people. He's more aware that people have different motivations for working. Researchers in the behavioral sciences have given him many valuable clues on how to get results without expecting people's personal loyalty. And he's geared to achieving objectives if his men show moderate interest in their work; he no longer expects complete dedication.

Executives trained in the old school of human relations can find the going pretty rough when they try to achieve results with the "new employees." Today's typical college graduate works because he must, has few illusions about the company's interest in him, but he will usually respond well to an intelligent no-nonsense approach.

Executives, Too, Grow Old

Imagine yourself in the richly carpeted office of the president of an old established firm. Two men are talking:

COMPANY PRESIDENT: Bob, I've been looking over our organization chart lately. . . . PERSONNEL DIRECTOR: Yes, J. B.? PRESIDENT: I think we need to beef up our executive staff. (He *really* means, "I tire more easily now than I did five years ago.") DIRECTOR: I think you're perfectly right, J. B. (He thinks, "That recommendation I sent him a few years ago is now 'his idea' "!) PRESIDENT: I'd like you to study the situation and report back to me at the end of the month. DIRECTOR: It's a challenging assignment, J. B. I'll be glad to tackle it. (He's thinking, "I'll just dust off that old report, change the date, and send it along.")

The sentimental aspects of executive aging have intrigued many writers, for there is pathos in the spectacle of an executive firebrand being slowly dragged down by the old man with the hour glass. The economic reformer, too, finds plenty of ammunition at hand in cases of esteemed executives who have devoted their best years to their companies, only to be shunted off on the retirement track because they cannot keep up with the younger men.

Poor health, declining mental faculties, or failing physical powers create the need for fresh talent within the company. Moreover, the social reformers have increasingly less to rail against, for business, in general, has faced up well to the problems of its aging employees. It isn't unusual for a company to change job content, for example, so that superannuated executives can continue in less-demanding activities. In the average company, retirement programs and liberal separation and pension plans are standard operating policy.

Company Politics

Power plays and skirmishes within executive ranks create a certain percentage of job openings too, though this is hard to measure. Executive X may create a job in order to bring an ally into the company. Executive A may establish one to weaken the power of executive Y. An officer in his fifties may leave to "seek a better opportunity" when he's actually been forced out by a hostile colleague (more valuable to the president) who has issued the ultimatum, "Either he goes or I go."

The executive pyramid gets mighty narrow at the top, and competition for the choice positions generates some fancy infighting. In the process, new jobs are created and old ones are vacated.

"Greener Fields"

Given good and sufficient cause, executives, as everyone else, will bite the hand that feeds them. Here are some of the most common causes for resigning:

Lack of recognition for superior performance
Advancement opportunities blocked by poor retirement policies
Inadequate compensation
Lack of challenge
Disagreement with company policy
Disagreement with a superior
Offer of a better job—more lucrative, more challenging, etc.

Push for Profits

Last but not least, competition and the need to produce profits for owners and stockholders create executive turnover:

Share of market. In any industry where research gives contending companies a fairly good idea of the share of the market they enjoy, there is a constant pressure for a greater share. The company that has 5 per cent wants 10; the company that had 10 and now has 9 knows it must reverse the trend to survive.

Profits. An annual statement in the hands of discontented stockholders or owners can become a lethal weapon used to beat a company's management about the ears. It often creates a decision, "We've got to get some good men in here to improve our position."

Sometimes it's the competition's profit and loss statement that becomes the prod. If competitor A shows a fat return on investment and company B's is slim, B is going to have to perform better to measure up. This also may lead to the resolve to recruit executive talent that will make such improvement possible.

Six Steps a Company Must Take before Entering the Executive Job Market

Before a company makes the first phone call to the employment agency or recruiting firm, six questions must be raised and resolved if the executive hunt is to move ahead, best foot forward. All concern the job, and all have a direct bearing on how successfully the company bags its quarry. The questions must also be settled for the sake of the new executive; otherwise, life in his new position may be hardly worth living. These are the six problem areas:

1. *"Replace the man or fill the job?"* "We kid about the irreplaceable man," said a personnel executive, "but sometimes we discover there is such a species—when the man dies."

The first question a company must consider is whether to look for a reasonable facsimile of the former executive or redesign the job to fit the manpower available. More often than not, at the top of the executive pyramid, jobs shape around the capabilities of the men who hold them. In cases of replacement, a company can waste countless hours, dollars, and tempers if it goes looking for a "second Mr. X."

Taking the other course—altering the job—of course raises another question, "Which executives should get which chunks?"

Next question: Even if the job can be filled without changes in the content, *should* it be? If the company has plans for growth which involve new responsibilities, for instance, a job vacancy may give the president a chance to make changes that he couldn't put through during an executive's tenure. Or take the case of the publishing firm that lost the director of its important mail-order division. The president observed that the first big decision he had to make was whether to hire a man who could continue the operation as is, or look for someone who'd take an entirely fresh dynamic approach.

Obviously the type of man a company seeks will differ, depending on how it answers such questions. And the pros and cons of *all* alternatives must be weighed carefully before making a commitment.

2. *"Is everybody happy?"* A whole different set of problems arises from the need to keep existing employees satisfied. An executive recruiter recounted: "We found the perfect man to head up manufacturing operations for a pen company. The guy was hired. His first day on the job, we received a distress call from the president. The engineering vice-president, who hadn't been consulted about the hiring, was threatening to quit. He was furious because he had not been rung in on the decision. He also felt that the new man should be reporting to him instead of to the president."

An even touchier situation can develop when a company passes over an executive who has set his sights on a promotion into the vacant job. The disgruntled man may take out his resentment by doing everything he can to wreck the new incumbent.

The wise company head will follow an absolute rule: Before a new man even crosses the company's threshold, his future colleagues, subordinates, and superiors will be fully briefed on the rationale behind his hiring. Anyone who is upset will get a chance to question the hiring, sound off, or ask questions. All uneasiness or resentment may not be eliminated. But it does give the top man a chance to say: "I'm sorry you feel it's an unwise decision, Frank, but the new man is coming in at the beginning of the month. All of us involved in the decision think he's capable and qualified. Of course, he'll need your help, and I'm sure that it will be forthcoming."

Worry and insecurities tend to arise in every hiring situation, and a company must allay the anxiety one way or another if the job is to go well.

3. *"But is he our type?"* "I'm considering two candidates for the plant engineer's spot," says a top executive. "Both men have the education and experience we want. Applicant A is a sure bet; it's obvious that he'll do the job well—but that's about it. I'm not so sure that this is the case with applicant B, but he certainly expresses far more imagination. Should I take a chance on the unknowns in B's makeup, and hire him, or play it safe with A?"

One president describes this as a choice between "a plodder and a plunger." He personally favors the risk taker over the man who goes by the book.

Other companies may use different words to express the same problem, namely, does the candidate fit the company "image," to which all executives, consciously or otherwise, must conform? Is he an "IBM man," or a "GE type," and so on. Occasionally, a top executive may have to ask himself, "Even though he's an offbeat candidate for us, should we hire him?"

Sometimes the choice is made deliberately, for obvious reasons. The institution that advertises, "You have a friend at the X New York bank," can be expected to seek executives who *look* amiable. A conservative Wall Street brokerage house, with some logic, will avoid hiring anyone who resembles a beatnik (unless he is the nephew of the senior partner and fresh from the Wharton School). On the other hand, the advertising firm that needs a man to head a creative department may positively welcome the flamboyant man. (Even a normally conservative client might not be favorably impressed by an Ivy League type if he's paying for a far-out campaign to sell false eyelashes or soap with "caress appeal.")

4. *"What qualifications are essential?"* Says one employment agency official: "Qualifications can be ludicrous. A small firm asks for a man who, if we could supply him, would be suitable for a top job at GM or Du Pont. You'd be surprised how often we hear a job description that runs like this: 'And it would help if the man knew something about information retrieval, had a good marketing sense, and knew his way around machinery.'"

This doesn't mean that the company should settle for a bare minimum. There should, however, be some reality to the list of qualifications. The campany hiring a financial executive is perfectly justified in looking for a man who can set up financial controls, direct long-range planning, and make recommendations on acquisitions, for instance. But these talents form a logical whole. What often happens is that the executive in charge of the job description starts thinking, "And while we're hiring, we might as well try to find someone who can do A, B, C, and so on."

5. *"Generalist or specialist?"* "Companies often say they want generalists, when the only man they'd really hire must be a specialist. Sometimes what they mean is, they want a specialist who can tackle every job in the book." Be one executive recruiter's disenchantment what it may, companies often have the problem of deciding how broad-gauged or how specialized is the man they need.

The merits of the man who "knows a little about a lot of things," over the one who "knows a great deal about one thing," have been argued with especial vehemence through executive suites these days. The fact that the arguments pro and con seldom succeed in changing anyone's preconceptions adequately proves the pointlessness of the debate. This is inevitably the result of arguments in the abstract about concrete situations.

Certainly, to the company with a job to fill, and future executive requirements to think about, it's tempting indeed to look for a specialist to fill the immediate job need, and hope the executive also has the capability of assuming broad managerial responsibilities. But in specific cases, often the best a company can do is make a firm decision to straddle the issue. Accordingly, it looks for a specialist with a fair potential for general management performance. Or, it looks for a generalist with the ability to perform satisfactorily in a somewhat specialized function, perhaps with the reinforcement of a supporting assistant or staff.

6. *"Should we agree to an employment contract?"* Executive employment contracts that bind a company to retain a new man for a stipulated period, at a stated salary, and so on, though not frequent, are sometimes used as a final inducement for an executive who wants evidence that he's not giving up a sure thing for a venture that may not pan out. The written contract underlines the company's commitment to a course that will largely be determined by the presence and activities of the new executive.

These contracts more effectively protect the employee than the employer. A company may desire to hold a man such as a head of research and development with a long-term commitment. But if the executive really tries, he can usually break the contract far more readily than the company.

More to the point is the unwritten but nevertheless ethically binding agreement between employer and employee. The company, when it finally makes its choice of candidate, owes the executive full cooperation and backing. And the newly inducted executive, similarly, owes his new employer and colleagues unstinting availability of his mental and physical energies.

It is when these implicit commitments are honored by both parties that the success of the placement, from the viewpoints of both executive and company, have the greatest chances for success.

3

The Executive Job Seeker

The executive job seeker has been talked about, written about, argued about, and worried about. Yet he's seldom been identified, and in the minds of many people, he is a faceless abstraction, with as many identities as there are personalities to visualize him. In the pages ahead we'll take a look at *who* he is, *why* he's entered the job market, *how he feels* about seeking a new position, and *what he can do* to get better results, faster.

Fifty Job-seeking Executives—Some Vital Statistics

Is the typical executive on the job market old or young? A self-educated man or an academic whiz? Married or single? To get a better picture of prospective clients, a New York City job-counseling firm queried a random sample of executives who came into its office seeking information. The findings are set forth below. Although this survey was informal and some executives undoubtedly shaded the truth in answering uncomfortable questions, such as "How long have you been unemployed?" the findings do throw some light on one group of executive job seekers in a big-city market.

THE EXECUTIVE JOB SEEKER—A PROFILE

1. "He" is predominantly male:
    Sex: 49 Men   1 Woman
2. He is almost always married:
    Marital status: 43 Married   7 Single
3. He's most likely to be young, as executives go—thirty to forty years old—but older men make up a substantial percentage:
    Age:

21-25: 2	36-40: 10	51-55: 4
26-30: 4	41-45: 4	56-60: 1
31-35: 17	46-50: 6	61-65: 2

4. He's well educated; a college degree plus an MA is common, but he seldom has a Ph.D.:

Education:

High School: 11   BS or BA: 28   Masters: 10
Ph.D.: 1

5. Length of time on the job with his old company is short, five years or less being most common:

Years with last or present company:

0-2: 23	9-11: 2	18-20: 2
3-5: 11	12-14: 5	Over 20: 1
6-8: 3	15-17: 2	No response: 1

6. Most men recognize the importance of looking for new jobs while they're still employed (or say they are):

Present job status: Working—35   Not working—15

7. Average time they'd been looking was not too long, reflecting the good economic climate when the survey was made:

Length of time looking for work:
Average: slightly over a month and a half (1.6 months)

8. By and large, the executives seeking jobs were in the middle- to lower-executive salary brackets; thirty-seven out of fifty were making $20,000 a year and under:

Salary:

$ 7,500-$10,000: 14	$20,000-$22,500: 5
10,000- 12,500: 10	22,500- 25,000: 1
12,500- 15,000: 2	25,000- 27,500: 1
15,000- 17,500: 8	27,500- 30,000: 0
17,500- 20,000: 3	30,000 and over: 6

The group of executives interviewed represented a pretty fair sample as to the size of companies they worked for. Eleven were from small companies, twelve from medium-sized firms, and twenty from large companies. But the findings obviously aren't representative of all times and cities.

At any given time and place, of course, the makeup of a job seekers' group will vary, depending upon the general economic climate and events or developments in specific regions or localities. The merger of one company with another, relocation of a plant (such as the textile companies' moving to the South), a company closing—all can turn scores of top administrative executives loose on the job market. When major defense contracts are canceled or cut back, as periodically happens, the market is temporarily glutted with engineering executives.

Seven Basic Types of Displaced Executives

The executive profile that emerged from the job counselors' survey is purely a statistical creation, of course. Of more practical value to the prospective employer and the executive recruiter is an understanding of the differences in *outlook and attitude* when executives enter the job market, resumes tucked in their attaché cases, looking for a new employer. These differences are important to recognize because they determine three things: (*a*) how executives tackle job hunting, (*b*) how they behave during their search, particularly in interviews, and (*c*) the degree of success they achieve.

Studies of actual situations indicate that most men fall into one of seven categories, which can be briefly sketched as follows:

1. The *"happy"* executive. He's fully employed, but he can always be tempted by a more attractive job offer.

2. The *job hopper.* He's working, but to him, one job is merely the way station to another. He's always looking around for the chance to climb to a higher rung on the success ladder.

3. The *"unhappily employed."* He's dissatisfied in his job, is actively seeking a change.

4. The *"half-and-half."* This man is nominally employed; actually, he and his employer have agreed that he should be looking.

5. The *"confident unemployed."* He's out pounding the carpets of a variety of executive suites—sure that he'll find what he's after.

6. The *"worried unemployed."* He's putting on a front, fighting panic.

7. The *"punchdrunk unemployed."* He's still looking (usually after an excessively long time), goes through the standard routines, but feels that his position is almost hopeless.

That each of these seven types may behave differently at crucial stages of the job hunt, such as during a job interview, seems obvious. Certainly, the man who tests the job market while he's still a satisfied employee, drawing down his $30,000, will behave far differently than one whose nerves are raw from months of fruitless searching. Yet company interviewers often *do* fail to recognize the differences, and where the man being interviewed is well qualified, perhaps extremely good, this is unfortunate on two counts: The man being interviewed, if he's tense and overanxious, will leave a poor impression. The company will miss a chance to hire a topnotch executive.

How Executives Are Fired—the "Resignation" Tradition

Very few executives are ever fired. One reason is simple. Whereas employees below management level are still, in a sense, "hired hands," executives are "family."

But there are other reasons: "A firm with any sense at all," explains the president of a California engineering firm, "can't see itself putting an executive out on the street. It's bad public relations. And it's hardly a good advertisement for the judgment of the management that hired him."

Such reasons lead to the traditional "executive resignation." In this connection, Winston Churchill's words are singularly appropriate: "There are always two reasons for doing something, a good reason and the real reason."

The "good" reasons behind executive separation are as many as ingenuity can create. Here are some standard face-savers:

"Our vice-president is leaving us to fulfill an old ambition. He has always wanted to go into consulting," reads part of an announcement in a dairy company's house organ.

"J. D.'s wife needs a change of climate because of her health," announces the company president at a staff meeting.

"An opportunity he couldn't afford to pass up was offered to Tom," explains Tom's boss, "and as of the end of the month, he'll be hanging his hat on the rack at the XYZ company." Interpretation: After months of searching, Tom, with his boss's help, finally landed a job at XYZ.

Some executives are subjected to such round-about firing tactics, report the editors of *Fortune*, that they're not aware of what's happening—until they're out. The head of a department store, for example, told a vice-president, "I think you're the best damned trouble shooter I've seen, and I want you on my personal staff as a consultant." When two weeks passed without the vice-president's having been given anything to do, he asked the president about it. The president suggested he take a month off, to rest and relax. When he returned from vacation, his original job was filled by a new man, the president himself was on vacation, and the executive's consulting office had been turned into a filing room. He did the only thing he could—he resigned, and turned to the executive market for a better answer to his job needs.

Fortune also notes the popularity of the "bypass" technique. For example, the man to be fired finds that his name starts being omitted from important memoranda, or he's excluded from conferences. Or top management uses a personal habit to break an executive. The production manager of a cosmetics firm, for example, made it a rule never to work on Sundays, although some of his colleagues did. The president and general manager deliberately scheduled meetings on Sundays. When the production executive continued to refuse to attend them, he was told that the company had to let him go, because of his lack of interest in his work.

Generally, firings are done verbally because the executive responsible can soften the blow to the man's ego more effectively than in a curt dismissal notice. But not always. One president who was embarrassed to fire a certain subordinate because he was also a friend put a dismissal note on the man's desk without ever mentioning it to him. The subordinate, fully aware of the president's discomfort, retaliated with a brilliant ploy: He never acknowledged receiving the missive, and the president didn't dare write another. The vice-president then went on to do a good job for the company. (Few misfirings turn out as happily as this.)

Executives may even resort to downright trickery to remove a man. *Fortune* relates the story of a clothing manufacturer who suspected that his sales head was looking for a better job. He placed a blind ad in the newspaper for a sales manager, asking for the exact qualifications his man possessed. The latter rose to the bait, answered the ad by letter, and was instantly given the heave-ho for his "disloyalty."

There are many and varied ways of getting rid of a man when management decides he's no longer "right for the team." But from the bluntest to the most kind, no technique can alter the fact—the executive has lost a major prop in his life, and he must find another, as rapidly as he can.

"Why Terminated?"

However he leaves a company, there's one hot potato that every executive job seeker must soon learn to handle, for it appears on every application blank, arises in every job interview and comes up *ad nauseam* at various points in the job hunt. "*Why* did you leave (or, why are you thinking of leaving) your job?" A simple question, yet it's seldom easy for an executive to answer, and the answers are rarely dependable.

It is not simply that people tend to distort facts that show them up unfavorably. Sometimes a man was let out who really doesn't know why. Or there are several causes. Or, as noted before, employer and employee agree that it's best to cover up a job failure with an arranged "resignation." (Such a resignation may actually indicate a failure of the *employer* to develop the man.) Even if the man quits on his own initiative, the real reasons don't necessarily favor him.

Clues to the real reasons why executives quit, "resign," or are fired lie in the problems they have on the job. One list of "career problems" is shown below. It was compiled by Saul Gruner, director of Executive Job Counselors, New York City, and it is of particular interest because of the dearth of reliable information in this area. (Outright failure on the job isn't included, although this is, of course, an important reason for terminations.)

Typical Executive Career Problems

1. *Underplaced.* The executive's capabilities are largely unused, resulting in dissatisfaction with the job, salary, status, etc.

2. *Personality clashes.* An executive encounters difficulties in working with colleagues or superiors due to personality problems—either his own or another person's. Insecurity may cause him to be suspicious that, for example, subordinates are after his job. On the other hand, he may find it impossible to work with a certain colleague, whose cooperation he must have, because the man is deliberately out to knife *him.* In any case, the executive ultimately fails if he cannot perform his job in these situations.

3. *Organizational dead end.* The man sees no chance for advancement because of the nature of the company's ownership, management policy, or organizational structure.

4. *Company politics.* The power structure of the company is such that the individual, as an "out" member, faces an arbitrarily determined dead end.

5. *Lack of recognition.* A capable executive gets lost in the shuffle because his company has no machinery for reviewing executive achievement. Or he started in early with the firm as a "local boy," and his special abilities have come to be taken for granted. There are all kinds of reasons for a company's "recognition lameness." A company may deliberately withhold recognition because it doesn't want to grant any salary increases, and it follows the theory that "If old Jack isn't satisfied here, he can take a job elsewhere. He's not irreplaceable."

6. *Job "disappearance."* A $50,000 executive job may literally vanish with the scratch of a pen if that pen has signed a merger agreement, a purchase order for equipment of advanced design, or a contract with a management consultant in labor-saving methods. Cutbacks in defense spending and the spread of automation in clerical operations have also accelerated the turnover of managers at both middle and top levels.

Executives' Reasons for Wanting New Jobs

It would be unfair to assume that all executives leave more or less involuntarily. A goodly percentage take off in search of greener pastures when their companies would very much like to keep them. From a company's viewpoint, the reasons behind such bona fide resignations are of utmost importance. And a study made by Richard D. Gleason Associates, Chicago career consultants, indicates that many job changes could have been prevented rather simply had the companies had better communications with their executives. Here's what Gleason found, as reproduced from the pages of *Sales Management:*

"Why do you want to change jobs?"

This question was asked of thousands of executives and junior executives over the past nine years. The answers and observations fall into seven basic categories. Percentages indicate frequency of mention and a general comment follows to describe how those questioned feel about each category. Highlighted under each comment are typical reasons—33 in all—for job changing. The astute employer will see in these a checklist of things to investigate for possible improvement. The restless employee, on the other hand, will note that he is not alone in his problems relating to job changing.

UNSATISFACTORY BOSSES (19.1%): "The right kind of boss wants you to grow so that he can get ahead himself."
• I don't respect his abilities or leadership.
• He gives responsibility without commensurate authority.
• Toughness is okay if it's fair and without favoritism.
• I can't get decisions, assistance, or support when needed.
• Communications are poor; he keeps me in the dark.
• He never follows channels; goes around me to my subordinates.

ADVANCEMENT IS LIMITED (16.7%): "Give me the right opportunity— then money and position will take care of themselves."
• I want work that really challenges my ability.
• Opportunity seems blocked by blind adherence to seniority, favorites, or relatives.
• I was passed over for advancement, so my future is blocked.
• Being in a secondary department or a subsidiary prohibits my getting into the main stream.
• My boss still thinks of me as the boy I was when I started years ago.
• Too much deadwood in the organization impedes my own progress.

POOR PAY (15.3%): "I'm in my most productive years, but my income doesn't show it."
• My income hasn't kept pace with inflation.
• Outsiders are brought in at higher scale.
• Company-wide bonus doesn't reflect my extra contributions to profits.
• Taxwise, I'd rather have some of my income deferred.
• Flat salary gives no reward for added effort.
• Company emphasizes security, but I'd rather have the pay and arrange my own security.

LACK OF RECOGNITION (14.2%): "You have to be respected as a person to do your best."
• I only get criticism; there's never any recognition for things well done.
• You never know where you stand; it's like sitting on a powder keg.
• Status symbols, such as title, office, clubs, car, or reasonable expenses, are overlooked.

UNSATISFACTORY WORKING CONDITIONS (13.6%): "Money isn't everything —poor job conditions take the pleasure out of working."
• Too much travel—too little time at home.
• Inadequate staff makes me the highest-paid office boy.
• Equipment is insufficient to do a good job.
• Comfort factors—like heat, noise, or odors—are neglected.

UNCONGENIAL ASSOCIATES (12.2%): "My best waking hours go into the

job—a little more friendliness and teamwork could make things better for all."
- Cutthroat rivalries take the fun out of one's normal desire to excel.
- Personality conflict with fellow workers kills team spirit.
- Unethical or immoral practices cause unpleasantness.
- Strict adherence to protocol stifles friendliness.

SECURITY THREATENED (8.9%): "Perfectly happy with the job, but concerned with the company's future or my future with the company."
- Fear of merger, acquisition, or closing causes concern.
- Influx of owner's family or outsiders threatens security.
- Company seems complacent about the inroads of competition.
- Aging management no longer seems to take an interest in the business.

How Do Executives React to Joblessness?

Ideally, what happens to a displaced executive is this: Shortly after the word travels around that he is "available," a blue-chip company offers him the exact position he wants. It pays more money, offers better chances for advancement, and provides more challenging and compatible work. And, give or take a few months, this happy experience *is* enjoyed by many men.

But considerably more often, *this* is closer to what happens: Week after week goes by, and no prospective employer calls to announce the magic words, "You're hired." Self-confidence, gradually eroded by anxiety, turns into despair and perhaps even panic. Then comes a kind of emotional second wind, a psychological callus forms, and the executive renews his attack on the job market. But now he is acting automatically and from weakness, because there's nothing else to do but continue looking. He seeks a job without any real hope that he'll find one. Of course, he almost always does. But when he looks back, the experience is recalled as a nightmare.

What accounts for the difference between the success story and the near-failure? Luck? Outstanding personality? Special skills and abilities? All these factors play a role, of course. But they don't explain why so many personable, highly competent men whom you would expect to be sure bets to turn their executive skills to the problems of job finding have gone through harrowing experiences. And why others, far less deserving, have literally stepped out of one executive suite into another, and often a far more luxurious one.

The plain fact is that the average executive becomes like a lamb in the jungle when he leaves the snug harbor of his company and steps out into the employment arena. There's a simple and often ignored reason: With some exceptions, to be described later, there is no source of ready help to which the executive job seeker can turn. He's strictly on his own, and he's singularly ill-equipped. Schools don't give any courses in how to find a job. Company management-development courses certainly don't treat such negative subjects.

In fact, as the inexperienced young bridegroom on his wedding night, the executive job seeker faces a strange situation. His circumstances have been celebrated in song and story. The lore of job hunting is sufficiently widespread for him to have all kinds of bits and pieces of information, opinion, second-hand experience. But this web of knowledge applies to other people, other places and times. Now that *he* is in this fabled situation, everything he has heard tends to confuse rather than guide him.

Career Indecision

There is, in addition to general ignorance of how to find a job, another major obstacle that faces many executives who enter the job market. And this handicap, strangely enough, exists at all echelons and age levels. It may have hampered the executive in performance of his previous job, but when he joins the ranks of job seekers, it becomes an ever-present obstacle to a satisfactory pursuit of his job search.

"Mr. X," the counselor said, "you've had considerable experience in two areas, as a salesman and as a sales manager. You've described how, in your last job, you actually started from scratch and organized a fifty-man group of salesmen for a textile-products company that was entering a new field. Now, in your next job, would you like to continue as a sales manager, or get back into selling?"

The sales manager thought for a moment, then said: "Neither."

"But if you could have any job you wanted. . . . "

"I just don't know," was the reply.

This man, at forty, still had not come to grips with a basic career question: "What do I *really* want to do?"

Eventually after considerable thought, the sales manager did clarify his feelings. He had always been interested in sports. It wasn't the function that he was dissatisfied with—selling, or sales managing—but the industry. He wanted to get into the sporting-goods field. With this clarification, his job problem, while not spontaneously solved, at least could be stated in specific terms. He went all out for a selling job in sporting goods, and landed one—first as a salesman, later as a regional manager.

Believe it or not, such career indecision is far from rare. Furthermore, it is *not* confined to the lower-age brackets. Men of forty and fifty, after years of apparent success, have still harbored major doubts about what they were doing, or the kind of job they should be looking for. The obstacle this unresolved question poses for the executive job seeker is obvious. Settle it he must, either on an *ideal* basis—"This is what I really want to do, above everything else," or on a *practical* basis—"This is what I can do best," or "This is the skill that brings the highest financial returns." One way or another, the job seeker must make a firm decision as to his career goals if his efforts are to be effectively directed.

Five Demoralizing Influences

It is very important that those interviewing an executive understand his special problems, both inner and outer, in order to evaluate him properly. The executive job seeker himself will also find that some insight into his problems can be enormously helpful, so that he's not too surprised or disturbed by the normal vicissitudes of the job-hunting process. There are five threats to the executive's peace of mind.

Few executives ever face all of the problems and pressures described below. Yet almost everyone can benefit by being aware that job hunting has its seamier aspects. It's like peacetime soldiers staying in combat-readiness. If a conflict ever breaks out, they are able to cope with it and to act appropriately on a few moments' notice.

1. *Deterioration of role as head of family.* "The better my wife behaved, the worse I took it," confides one vice-president, looking back to his job-seeking days. "I just couldn't stand to see her being so darn brave. . . . "

The executive who crosses the line from employed to unemployed status almost inevitably undergoes a shift in his family situation. Instead of being the confident breadwinner, he is now a job seeker—a man touched by misfortune. As weeks of joblessness drag on, his position of authority within the family may be undermined.

Work is very important to the male role in our society. This is how Dr. Harry Levinson of the Menninger Foundation explains it: "In Western societies, work enables a man to meet another definition of manliness: the head of the family. Most men take this role for granted, and most can do so until they have no work. Then the meaning of work for this aspect of being a man becomes all too painfully clear."

But even when there is no actual change in the treatment he gets from others, the man may develop a new sensitivity and interpret innocent acts in an almost paranoiac way. When John Jr. misbehaves, for example, the supersensitive father may couple his changed job status with Johnny's seeming lack of respect for paternal authority. Normally he'd simply chalk Johnny's behavior up to youthful high spirits. Result is that family tempers shorten; feelings become edgy.

Unusual understanding and expressions of security and affection from inside the family circle are needed for a job-seeking father to operate without fear that he's "let the family down," or that he has somehow become declassed in their eyes.

2. *Dwindling savings.* "I've remortgaged my house, spent every cent I have, but I can't hold out any longer. I'm going to take that $15,000 job. It's ironic, because I *know* that if I could hang on for another month, I'd be offered one at $25,000." So spoke an accounting manager of our acquaintance, after the seventh month of unemployment.

Where the job hunt drags on, and the job seeker lacks substantial savings, dwindling funds are an obvious demoralizing influence. It's not a case of starvation, or anything as dramatic as that. Quite simply, the bills start to pile up, and the job seeker, in his home community, shifts from a valued customer to a credit risk. He either gets, or thinks he gets, fishy-eyed stares from the gas-station operator, the grocery-store manager, the candy-store owner, and even the milkman. A man has to be made of iron to withstand this kind of pressure.

3. *The stigma of joblessness.* But the major threat to an executive's equilibrium is often not some outside problem, but his own loss of a sense of worth. (Obviously, we're not talking here about the category of happy, career-minded men who find zest in every new job hunt, or about the calculating job hopper.) Most jobless executives find themselves either actually or emotionally without a career mooring, and many can't take it. In a society as success-oriented as ours, the very need to change jobs suggests a major failure. In fact, among some people, joblessness carries a stigma, as divorce. It is their *own* sense of failure and even shame that causes many executives to become near wrecks before they meet with success.

4. *Sense of failure.* Only a small percentage of job seekers find what they're after in less than two or three months. Most go through a long trial period of experimenting with various approaches. For example, in the executive sample described earlier, most of the fifty managers had used personal referrals from friends, registered with employment agencies, and had both placed and answered newspaper ads.

Among this particular group, efforts to find a job might be said to have failed. There had been contacts made, job interviews undergone, in some cases jobs had even been offered but were unacceptable, for one reason or another. Such failures, if repeated over and over, are a major source of lowered self-confidence and optimism. A man starts thinking, "Perhaps I'm too old." Or, "My education isn't good enough by today's standards." Or, "I'm up against impossible competition from better qualified men. I guess I just can't make it." And so on.

5. *Dependency.* "I think it likely," states Dr. Lloyd Hamilton, New York psychiatrist, "that executives who suffer most in the jobless situation have undergone some kind of severance from a figure on whom they were emotionally dependent. It may have been an esteemed superior, a mentor within the company; in some cases, perhaps the company itself played the role of protector. With this prop gone, a host of fears are mobilized."

For a small percentage of job seekers, Dr. Hamilton's analysis is probably revealing and, therefore, helpful. Awareness of this situation may explain to an overly upset executive that there is a clear psychological basis for his exaggerated feelings, and that his troubles are *not* rooted in hard realities of the outside world but, to some extent, within himself. With this insight, he may be able to adopt a more realistic view of his problems.

Dr. Hamilton goes on to describe the brighter side of the coin: "For many men, job hunting can be a tough but ultimately worthwhile experience. By facing up to the personal and career problems involved, and solving them by the direct means of winning a position despite the competition, they have increased in self-confidence and maturity."

The Favorable Factors

Having looked at the worst, we can now consider what the executive job seeker has going *for* him. We find a number of factors as compelling on the helpful side as the destructive ones were on the negative. They may not all apply specifically to a given individual. But together, they create a general environment that makes the process of job hunting considerably less of an ordeal than it might be otherwise.

1. *The growing economy.* Aside from some minor recessions, the post–World War II era has been one of tremendous expansion and economic growth. New businesses, plants, and branches have been as hungry for executive talent as for buildings, equipment, and capital.

2. *The managerial shortage.* The fact that relatively few people, the "hollow generation," as the Research Institute of America has called them, were born in the 1930s is another factor favoring the job hunter in the years immediately ahead. Moving toward 1980, "this small generation" will produce a shortage of persons in the forty to fifty-five age group. "Management," according to the Research Institute, "is not only the most urgent calling of the future but the most critically short resource of all." By 1980, the United States will have to get along with roughly three potential leaders to do the job that four are doing today.

3. *The "Good Samaritan" spirit.* Almost every job hunter discovers one heartwarming fact: "People are really helpful!" It's true—complete strangers often go far out of their way to lend a helping hand.

"After a few minutes of the interview," reports B. H., an unemployed production manager, "I realized that the company had no job opening. But the president continued our conversation, told me he knew one or two people who might be interested in my qualifications, actually telephoned them while I sat in his office and volunteered that I'd be getting in touch with them. What a boost that was!"

4. *Greater job-hunting know-how.* The average executive today tends

to be somewhat more sophisticated about job hunting than his predecessor of fifteen or twenty years ago. (He's likely to have read more discussions on the subject—or been asked for advice by more job-changing friends.)

For example, he knows that the time to look for a new job is while he's still employed—that this puts him in a vastly stronger bargaining position. He's usually aware of the various avenues of executive recruitment. He may be poor at writing a resume of his professional education, training, and experience, but he knows that one *must* be developed.

5. *Business's respect for management talent.* Every business publication from the *Harvard Business Review* to *Fortune, Business Week, Business Management, Dun's Review,* and *Nation's Business* has published articles on the crucial importance of top executive talent to the success of an enterprise. Intentionally or otherwise, the business press, magazines, and books have done a selling job for executives, with the result that a picture of the scarcity and worth of top executive talent has sunk deeply into the thinking of most business managers and owners.

6. *Increasing turnover rates.* "Faster In and Out in Top Jobs," reported *Business Week* of November 26, 1960, and this trend has been helpful in an interesting way. It's not that greater turnover necessarily means better job prospects for the individual: that can cut two ways. The point is, rather, that there's less stigma attached to job changing. Twenty years ago, a man who was let go was suspect: "What's wrong with him?" Today, everyone knows that mergers, reorganizations, and marketing shifts can tumble personnel needs about, and the "looking" executive is almost an accepted phenomenon.

Twenty years ago, too, the man who quit, or looked for another job while still holding one would have been suspect. But in today's turbulent business climate, the ambitious executive looking for more challenging ladders to climb is not only accepted at his own face value, but usually admired.

The Avenues Ahead

With the conclusion of this chapter, we start to look into that aspect of the executive job market dealing with the institutions and procedures by which job and seeker come together. Chapter 4 now takes up the five basic avenues of recruitment that may be used by a company seeking an executive, or by an individual looking for an executive position.

4

The Avenues of Recruitment

As the company sees it, here's how the "bad news" may appear: "He's just handed in his resignation. A competitor offered him the number 1 sales job at a 50 per cent increase in salary." "The heart damage is severe. His doctor says he won't be able to return to work for at least a year." "His performance has been slipping ever since December. We'd better start looking for a replacement. . . ."

Regardless of how a vacancy develops, a company faces the same problem: matching a man to a job.

It's not so very different from the job-seeker's point of view: "Next week the boss's son takes over the spot I've been working toward for the past five years. I'll have to start looking around now." "The new owners are bringing in their own staff, Jim; there's no rush, but it might be a sound idea to put out a few feelers. . . ."

Regardless of how the blow falls, the problem is the same: A man must take steps to find a new job.

Whether a man is looking for a job, or a job is "searching for" a man, there are five traditional paths along which the ultimate meeting can take place. This chapter tells briefly what they are and the relative value of each to both the company with a job to fill and the executive job seeker.

This distinction is important because although the five paths may be approached from either end, they don't hold out the same degree of promise in both instances. When a company is seeking an executive, for example, a recruiting agency is an excellent starting place, because eight times out of ten the recruiter will produce a satisfactory applicant. If you're hunting for a job, however, recruiters are almost always a waste of time. Even those who keep extensive files of resumes just don't welcome job applicants; they depend on other sources for their supply of manpower.

"Files on individuals are our stock in trade," asserts one recruiter, "but we seldom find a man that way." Another executive searcher says, "We get two or three hundred unsolicited resumes coming in here every week. Maybe one in a thousand ever gets placed. The timing of the submission and the vacancy we're trying to fill rarely match."

Comparative Evaluation of the Five Paths

The chart on the next page highlights the relative cost, popularity, and effectiveness of the five most commonly used methods for recruiting executives and for getting a job, namely,

Promotion from within the company

Employment agencies

Personal referral

Space advertising in newspapers and magazines

Executive-search firms

As the chart indicates, most companies prefer to fill executive job vacancies by promoting people from their own roster. (This is also the commonest form of that popular sport, executive ladder climbing.) But since internal promotions have little *direct* effect on the executive job market, they'll be considered here only briefly, as background for understanding the other avenues of recruiting.

Why Companies Recruit from Within

"In six cases out of ten," says William Hertan of Executive Manpower Corporation, New York recruiting firm, "an executive job will be filled from within the company." This makes a good deal of sense, according to Hertan, for at least three reasons:

The promotee is a known quantity. He's been on the payroll for a number of years, his good and bad points have been exposed. As one executive puts it: "The devil you know is a safer bet than the devil you don't." And certainly, many companies have had outsiders come in all "shiny and new," only to discover later that they had weaknesses, just as the deserving but all too familiar employee who qualified for the spot but was passed over.

Morale. The desire to maintain or build morale may be the most important reason for promoting people already with the company. In order to hold good men, an employer must make them feel that there is a personal future for them with the company. Each promotion represents needed reassurance, not just to the man moved up, but to all employees, that good performance and loyalty will be rewarded.

FIVE METHODS OF RECRUITING EXECUTIVES[1]
(A comparison of use, efficiency, and cost)

Recruiting method	Per cent of total hiring[1]	No. of applicants screened to fill one position	Cost of recruiting, dollars	Time spent by company processing candidates, hours	Time to find the man, months
1. Promotion from within company	63	(Depends on company situation)	No direct cost	(Depends on company situation)	(Depends on company situation)
2. Employment agency	41	Dozens by agency, 10-20 by company	No cost if man pays fee; if company pays, $2,000	30-60	5
3. Personal referral from outside source	37	2-3	Disbursements	10	Indeterminate
4. Newspaper ads placed by company	35	200 through resumes and 20 in person, by company	Cost of ad : $100-1,000	100-200	5
5. Executive-search firm	34	15 by agency, 4 by company	$4,000 plus disbursements	30-50	2-3

NOTE: Executive jobs at the $20,000-a-year level are used.
[1] Figures based on a study by Executive Manpower Corp., N. Y. (Percentages add up to more than 100 because some companies use two methods simultaneously, i.e., advertising and employment agency.) Figures in other four categories are taken from a group of typical cases and averaged out.

Opportunity to move upward is also essential to keep good executives stimulated and challenged. Each higher rung in the management ladder represents more power and responsibility as well as more money. According to one management consultant, what the creative, dynamic executive wants from his job most is a voice in running the show. To hold such men, a company must groom them for openings at the top echelons of management, then see that they are placed in jobs for which they qualify, as they become available.

Low cost. Inside recruiting has a zero cost, if you leave out the indirect expenses of "bringing along" employees, executive-development programs, and the like. No fees are paid to an executive recruiter or employment agency. Company officers and department heads don't have to spend hours interviewing candidates sent by the recruiting firm. And often the candidate for the opening is an obvious choice, so management can fill the job almost immediately.

What Causes Companies to Look Outside

Yet, even companies that take pride in moving employees up the ladder must go outside for executives from time to time. Notes Edward Raisbeck, Jr., partner in the executive recruiting firm of Thorndike Deland: "Promoting from within is sometimes a poor decision; at other times it is plainly impossible. Businesses often grow faster than they can develop their own executives."

Companies are impelled into the outside job market by a variety of factors, some logical—others quite irrational. These factors are the most frequent:

Lack of a qualified candidate. Obviously this is a universal (and logical) reason for hiring an outsider. Company growth, invasion of new markets, addition of new product lines or services, and so on, may create the need for specialized executives that the company didn't need, or couldn't justify, before. When an industrial-tool manufacturer branched out into the home-workshop market, for example, no one within the company was qualified to head up the marketing activity. Needed was a man experienced in consumer packaging, one who knew merchandising to hardware stores and who could write advertising copy in a pinch. The existing staff was highly competent but was oriented to industrial markets and sales channels.

A sudden breakthrough in machine or materials technology may leave a company vulnerable to inroads from competition, if no one in the company is conversant with the new methods, processes, or techniques. As one company head emphasized, "When change comes to a business, it can come fast . . . and the need to find a man with high talents in fields not previously occupied by the company can be pressing indeed."

Lack of depth, especially in functions such as purchasing and engineering, is another reason why companies forsake their policy of "promote from within." When the man managing the activity moves up or leaves, there's no one to take his place. Medium-sized companies often don't have more than one specialist of a kind, and there is no neat chain of successors as there may be in line jobs.

Fear of inbreeding. Companies sometimes go outside for executives, even though they have qualified men at hand, because they fear that "inbreeding" will weaken their corporate strength. It seems to be true, particularly in rapidly changing industries, that only the periodic infusion of new blood can ensure the flow of new ideas and fresh viewpoints a company must have to survive.

Desire to avoid personnel problems. The only man qualified for an executive job opening may be so unpopular with his colleagues or the men he'd supervise that management cannot risk promoting him. This often gives rise to a delicate situation because the man himself may be loyal, hard-working, and very good at the technical aspects of his job. He may also be confidently expecting to step into the vacant office. An astute manager will handle such a situation by a simple expedient: He will write into the job specification a special qualification which no one within the group can satisfy. An outsider can then be brought in without creating strife.

Desire to avoid a difficult decision. A top executive may face the problem of choosing between two men:

Executive A—He's the better man, but he's a political "out."

Executive B—He's politically "in," perhaps because he wears the right school tie or has some other personality or background asset that makes him particularly acceptable.

It's no secret that the latter man wins out at least as often as the former. But when an executive faces a choice in which the advantages and disadvantages offered by two or more candidates tend to balance themselves out, he "can't make up his mind" and seeks to resolve the problem by bringing in an outsider.

Personal considerations also may stymie the promotion-from-within process. Executive friendship for one man may balance the capabilities of another. And a top executive, unwilling to hurt the feelings of a close companion, unwilling also to do an injustice to a deserving colleague, will go outside.

"We'll Have To Go Outside . . ."

When a company decides to tap into the reservoir of executive talent lying outside its gates, the executive doing the recruiting can take any one of four approaches. He can call up an employment agency, advertise in the newspapers, ask help from friends, colleagues, officers in the company's bank or accounting firm, or put the entire problem into the hands of a professional recruiting firm. No one approach is best; each has its own advantages and disadvantages measured in terms of cost, time, and quality of job applicants it is likely to turn up.

At least three factors play a role in determining a company's choice of one method over another, or one combination of methods over another:

Scarcity of qualified individuals. "There's no point in our advertising for a scientist to head up our new research lab in Arizona," said the president of an electronics firm. "There are only a handful of men in the entire country who qualify."

The recruiting methods that work for popular job categories would be an utter waste of time for this executive. He'll turn to an executive-recruiting firm, possibly even one that specializes in the kind of research skill being sought. And chances are an even 50-50 that the recruiter will already know the names of that "handful" who are eligible. He may even have been in touch with some of them already, on other placement quests.

Whether the order to be filled is for a hard-to-get scientific skill or for some unusual *combination* of qualities, such as "left-handed sales manager who knows Renaissance music," the executive recruiter is likely to get the business. His stock in trade is knowing where to look for the hard-to-find individual (if he hasn't spotted him already).

The converse is also true. If you're trying to fill a job that has easily defined specifications, for which many people qualify, the natural medium to use is newspaper advertising.

"Local boy" preferred. "We want a sales manager for our Southeastern district who can talk to country storekeepers," said the sales vice-president of a large paint company. "They account for a substantial chunk of our business in that territory in the South, and being 'in the family' is a big help in selling your product." Obviously, this company isn't going to recruit all over the United States, or use the expensive services of an executive recruiter. "The man we want will be a native of the South and a local employment agency or newspaper ad should find him."

And, in general, when a company decides to hire locally, employment agencies and newspapers *are* the best bets.

The do-it-yourself type. The degree of confidence felt by the executives in charge of hiring is another determinant of what method will be used. If he (or his colleagues) believes that no one understands his needs as well as he, chances are that he'll advertise for the new man or call up an employment agency. On his own, he'll undertake the job of screening three or four dozen resumes, culling the most promising men, then selecting the final winner.

On the other hand, the executive who feels the need for professional assistance in filling a critical job is likely to recommend that his company employ the services of a recruiter or management consultant.

Strengths and Limitations of the Five Recruiting Methods

The chart on the next page spells out some of the pluses and minuses of the traditional avenues, as seen from two viewpoints: the recruiting company and the job-seeking executive.

Unusual Job-hunting Gambits

It goes without saying that most companies stick to the traditional recruiting methods when they're looking for an executive. For one thing, in this area the tried and true usually works. For another, most businessmen want to project a dignified and solid picture of their companies; unusual recruiting approaches just don't fit in.

But the job seeker is bound by no such restrictions. If he's aggressive and/or creative, and feels he has nothing to lose, he may be tempted to try an unorthodox approach. If he's looking for a job in advertising or selling, he may even go to great lengths to plan an offbeat campaign because imagination and "creativity" are what he's selling. In any case, there are a number of turnings off the beaten path that some job seekers may take:

"Spectaculars." Everything from sandwich signs to a blimp trailing a man's key qualification has been used to let the world know of the job seeker's existence. In the case of the sandwich boards, the man who had been hired to carry them about was instructed by his employer, "Walk back and forth in front of 5 Broad Street at lunch hour. That's where the company is I'm aiming at."

Direct mail. An executive who is either job hunting in a specific industry or knows companies likely to be interested in a man with his particular professional background can often, to good purpose, develop a mail campaign. Depending on the effectiveness of his mailing piece, he will get a certain percentage of appointments.

"Social" contacts. Some farsighted executives make it part of their long-range career planning to join organizations—social, political, fraternal, country-club organizations—at which they will be likely to meet men who can help them advance their job objectives.

By-line articles in trade publications. A head of plant engineering spends evenings and weekends writing articles on plant maintenance. He hopes that by having articles under his by-line appear in leading trade journals, he will impress the men whose okay is needed to hire him for a better job elsewhere.

Partial investment. Executives, particularly those who may find the

	Company seeking executive		Executive seeking job	
	Advantages	*Disadvantages*	*Advantages*	*Disadvantages*
Promotion from within	A minimum of dislocation, fast, cheap, morale-building	Results in inbreeding and diminution of fresh ideas; limited by quality of present roster.	Builds job security; a welcome payoff to loyalty, superior performance, and so on.	Politics may interfere; salary may lag behind status.
Employment agencies	Often may have resumes of 20 qualified applicants on hand within hours; can depend on agency to make preliminary reference checks.	Agency is geared to do a volume business; often cannot take time to do a satisfactory service job.	Agency may take the initiative in contacting a local firm; company pays fee in 80% of cases; no fee unless placement is made.	Less-qualified applicants, those with unimpressive work records, older individuals may get short shrift from some agencies
Personal referral	Usually refer well-qualified people. Often a personal knowledge of applicant eliminates guesswork on habits, social capability, etc.	At best is haphazard; lacks broad quantitative base from which a selection may be made.	Enters interview situation under favorable circumstances. No fees involved.	If referral is made by "wrong" person or to executive at wrong level in company, success is unlikely.
Newspaper ads	Traditionally successful; usually brings in large response including acceptable percentage of qualified individuals; cost reasonable.	Large number of responses requires careful screening.	Blind ad hides identity and makes job hunting possible while still employed.	Costly; generally a shotgun approach where a rifle is needed.
Executive search	A good firm acts almost as an outside "staff" department; concentrated effort can bring results within 90 days; can pinpoint executives with highly specialized skills.	Fees are high and are payable whether search is successful or not.	In rare case where the recruiting firm has a call for the man who seeks them out, entree is assured and under good auspices.	Firms seldom keep resumes on file. Chances of getting a job by this means are extremely small.

going rough because, for example, of advanced age, may decide the best way for them to develop satisfactory job prospects is to offer a certain amount of capital in addition to their services.

These specialized approaches will be treated in greater detail in separate chapters, 10 and 11. The following five chapters will take up in turn each of the more common means by which a company finds an executive, and an executive a company.

5

The Employment Agencies—
Brokers of the Marketplace

"Let's suppose," said Robert Half, president of Robert Half Personnel Agencies, New York City, "that you're a company president looking for a key executive. Write out a description of the man you need, and we'll see if he exists." The following specification was quickly scribbled:

> Man over 40, with knowledge of electronic data processing and finance; background in the paper products industry; manufacturing and marketing experience. Married. College graduate. Willing to relocate.

Robert Half gave the description to an assistant at 1:15. At 1:45, the resumes of twelve men who filled the prescription were placed on Half's desk.

Admittedly, Half's demonstration was a tour de force. It illustrates a major strength of an effective employment agency—the ability to produce suitable candidates from existing files. The typical agency has other capabilities, of course, as well as some drawbacks. This chapter will look at both from two viewpoints: the job seeker's and the company recruiter's.

This much can be said at the outset. For the executive, registry at one or more qualified agencies should definitely be included in the job-finding program. For the employer, the agency may very well be the best—that is fastest and cheapest—method of finding certain categories of executive personnel at low- to medium-salary ranges.

Types of Agencies

There are about four thousand employment agencies in the United States. (This figure remains unchanged from year to year, but the turn-over rate is a high 50 per cent. About two thousand firms drop out each year to be replaced by two thousand new entries.) These may be broken down into about thirty categories, according to the type of personnel they handle. You need only pick up a newspaper with a sizable amount of agency advertising to spot some of the categories—domestic, secretarial, industrial, engineering, and so on.

Only a small percentage of the four thousand agencies handle executive personnel. There are about three hundred agencies in this category in New York City and vicinity, and another three hundred scattered across the map, clustering in Chicago and Los Angeles.

The employment agencies that place executives—acting as brokers between the "buyer" and "seller" of executive talent—are further specialized, either as to function or industry. Robert Half, for example, specializes in accounting and financial personnel—accountants, controllers, treasurers, credit and office managers. Dunhill Employment Agency, operating nationwide in major cities, specializes in marketing and sales executives. Other agencies that specialize in certain types of business—insurance, advertising, metal trades, for example—work at all levels, including the middle and upper echelons.

A helpful tool for the job seeker and the company looking for executive talent alike is the directory of private employment agencies published by the National Employment Association. Agencies are listed according to state, city, and their functional specialty. The breakdowns include these categories: technical and engineering; advertising and sales; management and financial; professional (medical, legal, scientific). To get a copy of the directory, write to the National Employment Association, 2000 K Street N.W., Washington, D.C., 20006. There's no charge.

In addition, whether you're an employer or a job seeker, you can get guidance as to which agencies serve your particular needs by inquiring at almost any agency. There is sufficient sense of service and trade loyalty among the agencies to motivate the large majority to furnish helpful answers to reasonable inquiries. The agencies, as most other enlightened businesses, realize that helpful service to the public at large eventually creates goodwill that feeds back to the entire industry.

How Employment Agencies Work

The brief demonstration put on by Robert Half actually contains the essence of the employment-agency approach when it seeks candidates for a potential employer:

1. The "looking" company submits a description of a job and the man who can fill it.

2. The agency searches its files for people that fill the requirements.

3. If none are available, the agency usually runs a newspaper ad, de-

scribing the job. From among those answering, qualified candidates are selected.

4. The resumes of qualified candidates are sent to the client, usually with some minimum sorting or screening. It's up to the executive in charge of the recruiting to evaluate the resumes and select the candidates that best satisfy company needs.

Employment agencies differ from executive-recruiting firms in that their fee is contingent and is collected from either the firm or job seeker. The executive-search firm is always retained by the company. The agency collects a fee if it makes a satisfactory placement, otherwise not. Although the fee may be paid by either the applicant or the company, in most cases it is the company that pays. In the Eastern part of the country 80 per cent and in Chicago up to 90 per cent of the companies pay the agency fee.

For the job seeker, the agency operation consists of these steps:

1. The job seeker is "qualified" as quicky as possible, either on the basis of a resume or a brief interview. If the agency feels it has a chance of placing the job seeker, he's asked to fill in an application blank that is standard with the agency.

2. In addition to the information on the blank, the applicant is interviewed, to fill in special experience or "selling points" his background, education, experience, or native abilities may offer.

3. One of two things may happen next. (a) If the agency knows, through its contacts, of a company that might be interested in the qualifications of the applicant, it phones or writes the company, acquainting it with the facts of the man's capabilities. (b) The man's application is placed in a "current" file, to be pulled and submitted when an appropriate job requisition comes into the agency.

4. When the applicant is sent out on a job interview, he is usually given a short briefing, to prepare him for what he'll find. This may include background of the company, a recital of the history of the job, or of the company's man-seeking experience, a description of the executive doing the interviewing, and any other pertinent aspects of the situation.

Legal Restrictions on Agencies

To get perspective on the agencies, it helps to go back a bit in time, and review the development of the industry over the years. The private employment-agency business in the United States was officially born at the turn of the century, during the great immigration waves. Rapidly expanding industries needed workers of all kinds. It was an era of robber barons, sweatshops, and exploitation of child labor . . . and practices of the agency people were often downright unsavory.

In 1905, to correct matters, state governments entered the picture and passed laws to regulate the operation of the agencies. Subsequently, the agencies themselves formed the National Employment Association to further elevate and maintain ethical standards and business practices.

State laws regulating agency operations vary considerably, but in general the objectives are the same: to protect the job seeker from exploitation and to make it impossible for an agency to enter into any activity that might affect its objectivity, or might lead to exploitation of its applicants.

Besides fees—which will be discussed shortly—there are five practices employment agencies must avoid:

1. Discrimination
2. Kickbacks, or fee sharing with company representatives (Fee splitting among participating agencies is legal and frequently done on a cooperative basis.)
3. Prohibited activities, such as counseling on a fee basis, although some states, such as New Mexico, permit the practice
4. Misrepresentation of services and job opportunities
5. Referrals for illegal, immoral, or questionable business enterprises

Agencies must be licensed in almost every state, and this means keeping detailed ledgers of placements, billing, etc. In New York, a license is *not* necessary, however, if a firm handles only jobs paying $9,000 or over and *all* fees are collected from the employer. This is why executive-search firms don't go below this figure. They don't want to be governed or considered as employment agencies. Because New York City and Boston are such large employment centers, the state law is enforced by the city license bureau rather than the state government, as is customary in other areas.

The Matter of Fees

Every state has its own rules about employment-agency fees, and they are usually stated in the employment contract. In New York, the fee schedule operates on a sliding scale based on a percentage of yearly or monthly earnings. The top fee cannot exceed 60 per cent of a month's salary, i.e., 5 per cent of annual pay. (On an $8,000 job, the maximum fee would be $400.)

Under New York law also, if a job is salaried at $9,000 or more and the *employer* pays the fee, the sky is the limit; any payment agreed on by employer and agency is okay. Some agencies charge 10 per cent at $10,000 and up, point by point, to 15 per cent at $15,000 . . . and some go as high as 20 per cent. This accounts for the varying fees paid in the executive brackets.

Employees and agency both are protected in various ways by state law. Some examples from New York (regulations may differ in other states):

If an applicant reports for work and loses his job through no fault of his own, the fee can't exceed 10 per cent of his gross earnings, and may never be more than he would have paid had he stayed on the job.

If he quits his job or is fired for cause, the fee may not be more than 50 per cent of the salary received.

If an employee accepts a position and changes his mind before reporting for work, the agency is entitled to 25 per cent of the maximum fee. But if he remains with his present employer, New York law entitles the agency to 50 per cent of the maximum.

Anyone interested in knowing the state laws on employment-agency fees should check with the local Better Business Bureau, or the local licensing bureau. Many of the BBB's have prepared excellent leaflets as a public service. Bulletin 209 of the U.S. Department of Labor, "State Laws Regulating Private Employment Agencies," is available from the National Employment Association in Washington, D.C. It is also informative on many aspects of agency operation across the country.

Agencies Offering Extra Help

A handful of employment agencies located chiefly in Philadelphia and Chicago, with a few in New York, perform full-fledged executive searches in addition to their normal services. Thus, if a company needs a man who is hard to find because (*a*) his skills are scarce or (*b*) the job is complex, such an agency puts on its other hat and sallies forth as an executive recruiter. Few firms do this sort of recruiting, however, except on an occasional basis.

A number of agencies do more than the cut-and-dried matching of applicant to job order, however. Harper Associates of New York is typical of this group. Here are some of the methods that set the more effective agency apart:

"If necessary, we'll sit around and brainstorm a job specification or a man's requirements to diagnose a problem," says Maxwell J. Harper, president. "We'll circulate a promising resume or a synopsis among ten to five hundred companies. And we do counseling without any charge."

Also, like other top-drawer agencies, Harper will refer job applicants to other agencies in the field if it feels that they could be of greater help in turning up the right job. "This is not pure altruism on our part," says Harper. "An applicant today may be an employer tomorrow." Harper tends to specialize in upper executive levels—financial, marketing, engineering, and manufacturing—and doesn't claim to be equally effective in the lower echelons.

National Personnel Associates—Clearing House for Jobs

An organization that greatly aids Harper and similar agencies in placing people outside of their immediate locales is National Personnel Associates.

NPA complements the activities of the National Employment Association, and it is a potent factor in agencies' success with executive placement. Formed in 1957 in Chicago, because of agencies' need to transfer applicants around the country, it has a membership of about 110 agencies in ninety-odd cities throughout the United States. There's also one NPA member in Toronto and another in Mexico City. Additional members are expected, as the organization expands its activities.

Through the NPA network, an employer in Tampa, Florida, for instance, can find an executive candidate in San Diego, California. Similarly, an executive with narrowly specialized experience may find a job through an NPA member even though no opening exists in his present area.

NPA members use two means of communication to inform each other of job openings: direct phone calls and listings published in the NPA monthly *News*. Here, chosen at random, are two sample job listings:

ASSISTANT TREASURER
Degree required. Should be Vice President of bank in the short-term investment area. Prefer ivy league school.
Salary: $18,000+.
FT. WAYNE, IND.—TOWER PERSONNEL SERV. INC.
Att: Sam Armstrong

SUPERVISOR PROCESS DEVELOPMENT
Ph.D. organic Chem. 10 years experience in industrial Res/Dev involving synthesis and plant process development. Will supervise new process section in Res/Dev in organic chemistry.
Salary: To $17,000.
ERIE, PA.—MUSSINA PLACEMENT SERVICE

The *News* listings are broken down into four categories: Accounting/Financial; Sales/Marketing; Technical Engineering; Miscellaneous.

NPA's nationwide network obviously offers benefits to both employer and job seeker. It provides a nationwide "universe" from which a company may draw candidates for executive positions. It presents the job seeker with an opportunity to match his resume up against job openings almost anywhere in the country.

The fee is usually paid by the employer who hires a man through NPA channels, the "standard" being 10 per cent of annual salary. The fee is divided three ways: NPA gets a service fee of 3 per cent; the remaining 97 per cent is divided evenly between the agency to whom the job order was submitted and the agency that supplied the successful candidate.

National Personnel Consultants

In addition to NPA, there is another organization that acts as a clearing house for jobs for a group of agencies. National Personnel Consultants was founded in Milwaukee in 1937. Organized originally to help Milwaukee firms get salesmen from other areas, it soon became active in the executive-personnel field.

Milo M. Haffner, executive secretary of NPC, says, "We put out a publication, the 'Employment Counselor,' that lists jobs and people available in areas all over the country. The organ is mailed on a weekly basis, so that the information is current." Haffner also points out that the agencies belonging to NPC are among the pioneers in the private employment-agency industry.

One measure of the successful activity of NPC: Somewhere between 250 and $300,000 worth of service charges were shared by the participating members of the association in 1964.

For further information about NPC and its member agencies, write NPC, Suite 806, Guaranty Building, Indianapolis, Indiana.

The Enemy—USES

The most serious long-range threat to the private employment agencies in the executive area might *seem* to be the executive-recruiting firms. But although agencies and executive searchers do carry on a silent and, at times, intense feud, the real battle is between all private placement services and the United States Employment Service.

Although in existence before 1933, in that year the USES was expanded to help unemployed persons find jobs during the great depression. The private agencies bitterly claim the government service has since strayed far afield. Specifically, they charge the USES with the following "foul plays":

• *It seeks to build a manpower monopoly* which could lead to control of employment in the United States. Actually, in 1962, USES began cultivating a new look under then Labor Secretary Arthur Goldberg. It moved aggressively into the professional-placement field, setting up fancy new offices separate from its unemployment compensation and blue-collar employment divisions. In some localities, such as Dayton, Ohio, the new facilities include conference rooms, testing rooms, and counseling facilities.

When USES started recruiting on college campuses in 1962, taking surveys of imminent grads, the agencies were hardly reassured. And the situation became even more strained when the California USES linked up seven of its professional-placement offices by teletype in a pilot project aimed at testing the feasibility of nationwide computerized employment services.

• *It is unfairly competing with private employment agencies.* Agencies point to the fact that some of the state employment offices have taken ads calling themselves the "no-fee agency"—when they're really paid for by taxpayers. They also claim that USES is concentrating more on finding better jobs for those already employed than on helping those on the jobless rolls. It is said that in 1962, 60 per cent of the jobs USES filled went to people currently employed rather than to those out of work. But reliable percentage figures are difficult to obtain.

The rift has been further widened by such practices as the following:

• In Toledo, a USES office put a mobile unit on the road to seek out job changers.

• In Washington, D.C., USES placed a retired Army general in private employment at $35,000 a year, and in the Midwest, a local office advertised for a steel-mill superintendent willing to move to Argentina, at $23,754 a year. (These two cases are repeatedly quoted by private agency representatives as examples of USES incursion into the executive-placement area.)

There's little question that USES will get deeper into the picture with higher-skilled white-collar people, professionals, and technicians, if only because of shortages in these skills.

Yet there are no signs at present that the state employment offices are, or will get, involved in the placement of executives to any considerable extent. First, the $35,000 general notwithstanding, few executives would think of applying to USES—it doesn't have the proper status connotations. For the same reason, company personnel people would not tend to call this source for individuals at the executive level.

The situation may change in the future, especially if local offices continue to go aggressively after job candidates, and if the coming shortage of managerial talent hits companies hard. Then it seems likely that many would turn to new sources, such as USES, just to be sure of touching all bases.

Friendly Competitors—Executive-search Firms

There is confusion in some quarters as to the differences in operation between employment agencies and executive search firms. The chart below details just what the differences are.

Comparison between Agency and Search Firms

	Employment Agency	Executive Recruiters
Area of operation	Recruits at all levels and categories, from handyman to top executive	Executives only
Represents	The job-seeker, or the company on a contingent fee	The company seeking executive talent
Restrictions	Regulated by state law	Unregulated—except in Missouri and Canada

	Employment Agency	Executive Recruiters
Fees	Sometimes paid by successful candidate, but in 80% of cases, by the company	In all cases paid by company; generally, about 20-25% of job's annual salary, plus expenses
Physical setup	Main elements—interviewing rooms and filing areas, where resumes and personnel records are kept	Fly-by-nights can work out of telephone booth—and sometimes do. But reputable firms have competent staffs, a library of reference books, and usually attractive quarters, where both clients and candidates are met and interviewed.
History	In business for about 60-70 years	Came on the business scene after World War II, and increasingly from late 1950s
Salary levels	Placements cluster around lower executive-salary range—9,000 to $15,000	Placements go mostly from $15,-000 up, with largest cluster at the $20,000 to $25,000 range.

Reasons for Using an Employment Agency

Bernice Jennings, head of Bing-Cronin and Leonard Personnel, Inc., one of the agencies in New York City that handles executive placement, cites six reasons why companies turn to employment agencies instead of hiring on their own:

1. An agency will usually attract far more job candidates, since it has many different jobs in a variety of companies to offer. The employer has a wider range of qualified talent to choose from than if it advertised for candidates on its own.

2. Through special resources and contacts, the agency often knows where to find candidates who are most qualified for particular jobs. Accordingly, a company stands a greater chance of getting the right person for the spot.

3. An agency saves time, which is usually at a premium when new employees are being sought. A good agency will do the initial screening, filter out the poorly qualified candidates, and submit only the names of those worth the employer's attention.

4. The employment agency assumes many of the costs a company would normally bear, such as advertising, long-distance telephone calls, and travel.

5. The name of the hiring company can be kept confidential for as long as necessary. (There are a number of hiring situations where it is important that the name of the company be unknown to candidates during the preliminary stages. Secrecy, of course, is not possible with do-it-yourself hiring.)

6. A good agency, using its broad experience, will act as an adviser to employers, as well as to job applicants, and try to match the needs of both.

All Is Not Beer and Skittles

Bernice Jennings reflects the official attitude of the best people in the employment-agency field. But the agencies have also come in for criticism, and not just from those outside the field. Many people think they're useless for executive placement, for example. And if you talk to some top people within the field, privately they will admit that the agencies have a number of problems.

"Time pressure is our biggest headache," says the head of a well-known Chicago agency. "Sure, we could often do a better job. But we are only paid when we actually place a man. And every dollar that we invest in advertising or traveling to find an executive is almost a pure gamble."

Another expert expresses the same facts somewhat differently: "The agency business is essentially a volume business. Inevitably we must skim the cream and concentrate on placing the surefire candidates. That's why it's not a matter of policy but of expediency that the less-marketable executive job seeker sometimes gets short shrift."

Jobs Vanish

Another fact of life that often causes agencies to cut corners: 20 to 25 per cent of the jobs they're asked to fill disappear. Says one agency head, "We may get a call for a man from a company—a perfectly reputable firm making a bona fide request—and three weeks later have the requisition canceled. The fact is, for every hundred calls for men that are made, only seventy-five to eighty executives actually are hired."

What happens to the other jobs? A number of things. The top executive in a firm may have second thoughts about the type of man he wants. Or he reconsiders the cost, e.g., "We'd have to make over a $100,000 more in sales a year to justify that new executive's salary."

Sometimes the jobs vanish because the company believes, in retrospect, that its original decision to recruit was unwise. Or, the qualifications that were being sought turn out to be unrealistic when they are stacked up against the resumes of people available, and the executive doing the hiring gives up in discouragement.

Which Master to Serve?

Many agencies fall down, in the opinion of a West-coast agency head, because they never come to grips with the basic ambiguity of their function: They're supposed to represent the job seeker, but most of the time it's the company that pays the agency fee.

As the job seeker's representative, the agency might be expected to furnish highly individualized service. But as one agency man observed, "It's easier to fill a job than to market a man." The amount of time and effort required to probe, analyze, and guide a job seeker is usually far beyond the time that may be reasonably invested—or gambled, as the agency officials are more likely to see it.

There's another point, usually missed by the casual observer, but one that becomes clear once the business dynamics of agency operation are understood. Technically, the agency represents the job seeker; but since the typical agency makes its profit by filling jobs and serving an employer's needs, it is the company requirements that are catered to. After all, it's the company that represents the opportunity for repeat business and is the agency's permanent market. In addition, as already mentioned, most agency fees for executive positions are paid for by the company rather than by the executive who is placed.

The Communications Problem

"We want a man who can. . . ." The call that comes in from a prospective employer all too often starts a "groping" match. Seemingly, few companies can clearly identify and put into words the qualifications they seek. Starting with a vague description of what's wanted, communication between company and agency is further complicated by semantic difficulties. The company says, "We'd like to have a man to take care of our marketing." By "marketing," it may mean any activity from simple market research to the planning of sales strategy, advertising campaigns, new products, and counterattacks on competitors. Obviously, a different type of individual would be chosen to fill these two far-different jobs.

"I always like to get together in person with the executive doing the hiring," says one Chicago agency official. "If we don't both try very hard to arrive at an understanding of what we're looking for, I know our chances for success are practically zero."

It is in nailing down requirements, often a weakness of agency operation, in preliminary consultation that the good executive-search firm shows up to advantage.

How to Recognize a Well-run Agency

There are dozens of qualified and expert professionals in the employment-agency field, people of high ethical standards and outstanding capability. But the agencies that lack capable management are likely to be a waste of time for both the executive job seeker and the employing company.

The difference between the good agency and the second-rater is as great as the difference between a Saks Fifth Avenue and a bargain basement. It's important to know the signs, whether you are seeking a job or an executive. The well-run agency not only operates more efficiently, but also maintains higher professional standards, and it will produce better results.

Everything that the average agency does, the superior agency does better. Its procedures are more systematic and businesslike. Interviewers take more pains to make sure they accurately picture a company's needs. The agency will do a better job of screening its files for possible candidates and of screening the answers to ads it may run for a particular job opening. It doesn't try to drown the executive-seeking company with large waves of candidates on the theory that the more people it sends over, the greater the chance that one will be hired, and a fee earned.

By contrast, the poorly run agency tends to cut corners. In its need to hold down costs, it will be less careful about updating files, spend less time in interviewing and classifying job seekers. It will do no counseling. Its personnel may be poorly trained or inexperienced, and they will often lack the maturity and professional know-how to be able to go through the complex and sometimes confusing steps required to mate a job and a man. In any case, the "right" agency is also the one that best understands the job requirements of the employer. And this know-how serves the applicant's objectives as well.

The Agency Counselor—Key Man

Despite all the theories of agency operation, the plain fact is, an agency is only as effective as the counselors who do its interviewing.

These are the people who take the application or resume that is submitted by a job applicant, look it over, and then interview the applicant. The better agencies have specialists with extensive knowledge and experience in dealing with the companies and types of executive personnel with whom they work.

As many job seekers have discovered, there is an enforced intimacy between applicant and counselor that is, in many ways, as close as the relationship between a patient and a psychiatrist. The counselor needs a full and accurate picture of the job seeker's capabilities in order to match him to a job request. This calls for a degree of openness on the executive's part that may or may not be easily achieved.

Certainly, it requires a close rapport between interviewer and candidate. "If a harmonious relationship is not established," says one agency official, "My advice to the man looking for a job is to try to get another interviewer."

The better agencies are fully aware that they don't satisfy their function when they hand a man a slip of paper that says, "See Mr. Smith of the Acme Company." The conscientious operators do as thorough a job of briefing the candidate on the prospective employer as they are able. They will describe the company, suggest material that the candidate might read that will give him a better understanding of the company operation. They will tell the candidate what they know of the company interviewer, his preferences, his background, and so on. They will also tell a man, as well as they can, how to present himself, and how to relate his experience to the needs of the company.

What Agencies Offer a Company

To the company seeking executive talent, a reputable agency offers broad experience in the hiring field, and may have staff specialists in the very field in which the company operates. The agency may be familiar with the business or industrial "in" group. It knows the particular problems of given industries. It knows the business situation in which the company is involved. Further, it may know what the competition has been doing in the way of executive hiring or firing.

Although the agencies differ from executive-search firms in some respects, when the executive position involved is at a salary level of $9,000 or above, the agency has considerable freedom of action. It can, for example, negotiate with the company and arrange to have the company not only pay the agency fee, if and when a man is found, but also pay for such investments as advertising and so on.

One example of agency enterprise: A call recently came to a New York placement service from an English firm about to open operations in the United States. The company official said they were looking for a marketing vice-president. The agency representative met and discussed the situation broadly with the company man. Eventually the agency submitted half a dozen resumes, and as a result of the discussions with the agency as well as a consideration of the resumes, the company decided to hire two men: one as marketing vice-president, the other as national sales manager.

Important Tips for the Employer Using an Agency

William D. Reiff, current president of the Washington Employment Agencies Association, and vice-president of Acme Personnel Service, considers these seven points most important for companies seeking executives through private employment agencies:

1. *Take time to search out the agency best suited to meet your specific needs.* There is an increasing trend for private employment agencies to specialize, i.e., financial, administrative, sales, technical, etc. (As mentioned earlier, a directory, broken down according to state and city, and keyed by function speciality, can be obtained without charge by writing to the

National Employment Association, Washington, D.C.) A personal visit to the agency is recommended. There is never a registration fee for listing either an applicant or a job.

2. *Ask the agency for references from other clients.* Experience and reputation are important in this field, and an agency can be judged by its reliability, integrity, efficiency, and client satisfaction—just as any other business organization.

3. *Agree upon the fee arrangements in advance.* Fees for company and applicant vary, depending upon state law and custom. In accordance with local law, some agencies charge a service fee for an executive search, whether or not it's successful. In other instances, a company pays a fee only if the vacancy is filled. Sometimes, the fee is shared between the company and the applicant; other times, the applicant assumes entire responsibility for the fee.

4. *Prepare a detailed job description for the agency.* Preferably in writing, include personality traits and physical characteristics that relate to the position. If possible, show qualifications and requirements in order of importance.

5. *Agree on advertising copy and address for replies in advance.* All private employment agencies will place advertisements, at their own expense, to help a company find the most qualified candidates in the shortest amount of time.

6. *Spell out your timetable and salary requirements.* Confidential information is mutually respected. Must the opening be filled immediately? Within a month? Or is it a position that may possibly be available sometime in the future? What is the salary range? Minimum and maximum?

7. *Take advantage of all the services available from a good agency.* Professionally trained and qualified executive-recruiting experts are available for consultation at many private employment agencies. There is no charge for this service.

• Private employment agencies specializing in executive selection will provide special services such as depth interviews, testing, credit and applicant validation studies, without charge.

• A private agency can work closely with—and strengthen the efforts of —a major company engaged in a widespread recruiting effort through a field team. This can be accomplished in the strategic cities prior to, during, and after the company's recruiting drive. A network of National Employment Association private agencies offers complete market saturation on a daily basis.

• If executives are needed in a hurry, indicate this clearly. Through automated systems, in which data about job applicants are "filed" in a computer, some agencies can locate a candidate from a grouping of half a million names within a comparatively short time.

Important Tips for the Job Seeker

We asked a number of "agency-wise" people what they considered the most important things for an executive job seeker to observe in using this path to a job. Here is the consensus:

1. *Hold on to your job while looking.* Most experts agree this is a good idea whether you use an agency or not. But particularly for the agency, it's a reminder that the executive's skills are marketable.

2. *Register at the agencies that have experience in your speciality.* Some agencies specialize in particular functions, such as finance, accounting or sales, merchandising and marketing, or science and engineering. You can usually identify such agencies by the newspaper ads they place.

Few agencies handle executive positions only. Even when they specialize, they usually place people at all levels in the given function from trainees right up to top executives. Dunhill Employment in New York City, for example, specializing in the sales field, places anyone from a sales trainee on up to marketing vice-presidents.

Some agencies specialize in certain industries. This is not as common, but prevails in certain areas dominated by key industries such as automobiles in the Detroit area, steel in the Pittsburgh area, petroleum in the Southwest. These agencies become intimately familiar with operations of companies in one field, and their experience gives them unique qualifications to find executives—and place them—in the industry.

3. *Count on quantity as well as quality.* Spread your search to all agencies that indicate their interest in your qualifications.

4. *Cooperate fully with the agency.* It's generally best to be honest, even when you have to reveal what you consider adverse information. The truth may come out eventually and be more damaging than if you had been honest in the beginning. One agency head told us about an executive who falsified his college record, stating that he had graduated from a certain Midwestern university when he'd only attended for a year. Actually, the man's background and experience was so good that this educational record was unimportant. Yet the fact that he had falsified the facts led the agency to recommend another candidate for the job.

Also, agencies say, it's to the job seeker's advantage to let them know the result of an interview immediately. The agency may then be able to tell you the company's reaction and offer advice based on their reaction—essentially, how to emphasize strong points and minimize any weak points.

6

Executive Search— Total Service for the Employer

In the late 1950s, executive recruiting started to make it big on the public scene. Proof: The subject came in for considerable attention at the hands of magazine cartoonists. For example, a *New Yorker* cartoon by James Stevenson shows a worried company president huddled over a king-sized intercom. He is voicing his fears of inroads on his executive staff by recruiters to an executive vice-president, when suddenly from the silence he realizes that the vice-president himself has just been "body snatched."

The Stevenson cartoon graphically illustrates the bewilderment, even fear, with which executive-search operators were first greeted by the business community.

In this chapter, we'll take a look at what goes on behind the scenes; who the recruiters are, how they find executives; their impact on the job market itself. Then, the chapter directly following gives recommendations on how a company can get best results from a recruiter and how an executive can take greatest advantage of a surprise solicitation.

Recruiters as a Turnover Factor

The executive-search firms are a major factor in executive recruitment, particularly in the upper salary brackets. But they deserve special attention for still another reason. They play an important role in *shaping* the entire executive job market.

For one thing, executive search is an attitude-creating operation. Today's business manager has a different—and enlightened—view of the executive job changer, due in part to the recruiters. These days, the man who quits to take another job is less likely to be labeled "disloyal," or, "misguided opportunist" than described admiringly as "a man with plenty on the ball." While the executive recruiters didn't deliberately set out to propagandize in favor of the mobile executive, they created an atmosphere and specific circumstances that tended to bring about the transition. For one thing, the business community was reminded in terms it understood—action and cash —that the executive is worthy of his hire. Second, an active element was introduced into the executive-career field. Even if a recruiter didn't come knocking at his door, the executive came to realize that "somebody out there" might want him. In short, the recruiters greased the wheels of executive turnover.

It is for reasons such as these that the recruiters come in for especially detailed examination here.

Recruiting behind the Potted Palms

In 1961, as executive-search firms were beginning to proliferate over the business landscape, *Life* published an article by Warren R. Young, "The Pirates of Personnel," that was an important factor in forming the image of the recruiter being conveyed to the public at large. In true detective-story prose, *Life* gave its readers a highly colorful account of executive search operations.

Described was a secret meeting of three men behind potted rubber plants in a Cleveland airport lounge. One of the trio, described as a wide-eyed and round-faced New Yorker with the intense look of a professional card player, was Bill Hertan, the "personnel pirate" of the piece. The second man was simply billed as a top vice-president of a California manufacturing concern. The third man, a successful controller of a major Detroit company, was the executive who was being "recruited." The conversation between the three, apparently desultory, actually stuck pretty much to the matter at hand— the job offer being made to the Detroiter on behalf of the California firm. As a result of this spy-story meeting, and the inducements made, the executive resigned his job for a better-paid position in California.

The executive searcher, said *Life*, in depicting the profession, "is a man who specializes in stealing executives from one company and delivering them to another. Wearing Ivy League suits and brandishing depth interviews instead of cutlasses, personnel pirates today annually make off with executive talent valued approximately at $70 million in direct compensation." Of course, the figure has increased considerably since 1961.

They Sail the Ocean Green

In 1963, executive recruiters took in a cool $15 million as fees for their services in seeking out executive talent. (This figure comes from the Association of Executive Recruiting Consultants, a group of executive-recruiting firms formed to oversee and set standards for recruiting practices.)

In number they are about three hundred strong, with one hundred firms concentrated in the New York City area alone. Big or small, high-class offices or something less, the search firms at one time made up a fairly clear-cut category. But this is becoming less and less true, as companies with a peripheral interest in executive recruiting invade the field by establishing formal executive-search divisions. For example, not only have many management consultants jumped into the field, but also banks, accounting firms, law firms, and psychological testing companies. (These "fringe recruiters" will be discussed in a later section in this chapter.)

No matter how respectable the recruiting firm, however, the *activity* itself has come in for some strong censure. This is reflected in the terms by which people often refer to recruiters. *Life* magazine, for example, referred to "personnel pirates." More common, however, are "body snatchers" and "head-hunters." The derivation is all too obvious.

If you want to find "body snatcher" in the classified phone book, however, you wouldn't look under the B's but under Executive Search Consultant (Manhattan phone book). The recruiter's own trade association prefers "executive-recruiting consultant."

Today, of course, executive-search firms have become firmly entrenched as an accepted part of the business scene—despite the occasional poor performer and the fast-buck seeker. All in all, the nature of their function tends to make them the cloak-and-dagger operators of the executive placement process.

Rise of the Recruiters

The phenomenal increase in executive search activity is well-reflected by the following answers, gleaned in the course of a survey of a broad cross-section of industry made by George Fry Associates, management consultants and executive recruiters:

Q: Have you ever used the services of an executive-search firm?
A: Yes—65%
   No—35%

The second part of the question indicates the rapidly accelerating rate at which professional recruiting is penetrating industry.

Q: How recently have you used an executive recruiter?
A: Within the past year—67%
   Within the past five years—35%
   More than five years ago—5%

Various explanations have been given for the mushroom growth of the recruiters. Two major ones that have general acceptance are these:

1. *Economic expansion.* The fifties and sixties ushered in a period of intense industrial activity—mergers, acquisitions, expansion of operations into foreign countries, increased competition—this enormous economic growth created a need for executive talent that greatly exceeded the supply at hand. The only way to acquire enough top men to fill jobs was by raiding other companies. And the "head-hunters" performed this job so well that more and more companies turned to them to fill critical executive jobs.

2. *The demand for more-highly trained managers.* By and large, industry's requirements for executive talent have become more exacting—and difficult to meet. Automation, EDP, OR, "control management," technological advances on a broad front continue to raise the qualifications and lower the number of executives who can make the grade.

Besides these underlying factors, executive recruiting attracted widespread interest for reasons such as these:

• *The cloak-and-dagger atmosphere* in which many recruiters seem to operate intrigued the business world. To the relatively uneventful routines of normal business activities the recruiter brought color, excitement, and a certain amount of Hollywood-type mystery. This image, by the way, is one that the recruiters themselves rather fancied and, for that matter, promoted.

• *The promise of pushbutton recruitment:* "My headaches are over," said one company president at the successful completion of an executive search. "From now on, I'm handing all my executive-personnel headaches to these executive-search people." The effective firm will assume responsibility for every step save the final selection of the winning candidate.

• *Chance to get desirable executives otherwise not available.* The executive-search firm is able to penetrate companies—often competitors—and lure away desirable executive talent. Under the mores of business, this would not be an "ethical" thing for the hiring company to do directly. The recruiter makes "raiding" acceptable.

How the Executive Searchers Work

Executive-search firms function differently from employment agencies. (See chart, page 49, on the employment agencies.) For one thing, the agency represents the *job seeker;* the recruiter is retained by the employer. Another difference: In almost every state, employment agencies are strictly regulated and licensed. Recruiting firms are quite free to operate as they wish, since they are not licensed. (California now insists on recruiters' qualifying under its employment-agency license law. This may, or may not, spread to other states, depending on the ability of the "researchers" to organize and show the legislators the desirability of unlicensed professional service.)

Other differences in operating approach become apparent as one analyzes the steps involved in "searching." There are no mysteries to the process. It's readily described by the searchers as follows:

(1) The request, (2) the consultation, (3) job definition, (4) research, (5) the proposal, (6) screening, (7) final selection.

Less-readily admitted by many searchers, however, are the complications that often interfere. Here are the actual mechanics of the search process and the disruptions that can occur at various stages.

1. *The request.* A company calls upon a recruiting firm to help fill a management vacancy—but it may never become a client. Reason? The recruiting firm itself may decide not to take the job for one or several reasons.

• *Economics* may prove to be an obstacle. For example, the principal of one search firm received a call from a small out-of-town bank, looking for a trust officer at a $12,000 salary. The searcher turned the job down after a brief exploratory exchange, since he knew that in order to fill a job at that salary level, he'd have to approach men making 8,000 to $9,000. Few good young executives in this salary bracket would be ready to change jobs because they'd still have a way to go in their present companies. He also anticipated correctly that the minimum $4,000 fee charged by his firm was higher than the bank was willing to absorb—particularly on a noncontingency basis.

• *Difficult organizational problems* may scare off a search firm. "Just today I turned down a client because the reporting level was wrong," observed one recruiter. "The man they were looking for would report to a division head rather than to the executive vice-president. From our experience, we strongly felt that the arrangement was untenable. Rather than lose the goodwill of *two* prospective clients, we turned down the job."

• *Questionable reputation or history* of a company may lead a search firm to refuse a would-be client. Faced with a record of excessive executive turnover, unsavory proxy fights, difficult internal politics, the astute recruiting consultant may decide that chances for satisfactory culmination of a search are slim, simply because no qualified executive, fairly happy in his present job, would want to leave for a "problem" company.

As Donald E. Wright of Antell, Wright & Nagel puts it, "We must make sure in advance that there will be no unpleasant surprises on either side."

• *As far as the employer is concerned,* the search firm must also pass some preliminary tests. The chief one is proof of satisfactory work done for other clients. This isn't always easy because a big stock in trade of the search firm is its highly confidential relationship with clients. But as Donald E. Wright points out, from time to time search firms are able to use selected clients who are willing to tell other companies of their favorable experience. Often, too, it is possible to describe executive positions they have successfully filled in the past, in somewhat disguised terms.

2. *The consultation.* A representative of the search firm calls on the client company, analyzes its organizational needs, and discusses with top officers the nature of the job requirements. This aspect of the search process represents one of the major functions of the executive-search firm. It is precisely because executive recruiters insist on consultation with the client at *all* stages of the search process that their batting average is so high.

During the initial consultation, the recruiting firm questions the client about all aspects of the job vacancy. He will make sure, among other things, that the company has not overlooked men already in its employ (otherwise a nasty situation may greet the new outsider).

Once the validity of the search has been established, the search-firm representative works with the company executive to pin down a description of the job to be filled and the type of man that will be needed to fill it.

Practical outcome of this meeting is the submission of a proposal by the search firm in the form of a letter, outlining the terms of the search, fees, method of payment, and so on.

3. *Job definition.* Different recruiters have different ways of developing the job description and the related executive specification, i.e., detailed qualifications of the individual needed to fill the job.

Antell, Wright & Nagel use what they call an "executive sketch." This pins down in black and white both a description of the position to be filled and the education, background, and experience a candidate must have to qualify for the job. (See the appendix, pages 248-9, for examples of two executive sketches for positions which Antell, Wright & Nagel successfully filled.)

The Job-Man Specification

Other search firms have their own equivalent of the executive sketch or job-man specification. It's worth digressing at this point to spell out the several purposes it may serve.

A. TO STAY ON TARGET WITH THE CLIENT. The written description is presented to the client to make sure that the specifications developed do indeed represent what he is seeking.

B. TO ALERT SOURCES. The job-man description is sent out to sources that may know of executive material—banks, accounting and law firms, individuals, business contacts, professional associations, and appropriate universities. For example, Harvard Business School will be sent the "spec" if a financial executive is being sought, Purdue if an engineering executive is wanted. Universities are often contacted, too, because a client demands that his executives come from particular campuses or educational backgrounds.

C. TO FLUSH OUT CANDIDATES. Search firms often send specs to individuals who they feel are possibilities for the job, with the note, "Can you recommend anyone?" Another favorite approach by some search firms is to ask the "nominee" to "evaluate yourself in terms of the requirements" of the description.

D. TO HELP THE INTERVIEWER. The job-man description may be used as a *working checklist* during interviews with candidates. The interviewee's qualifications as to education, experience, salary expectation, and so on, are checked against the job description, so that no important factors are forgotten.

E. AS A REFERENCE-CHECK TOOL. The more experienced recruiters realize that their objective is not to check a man's background and history in the abstract. By sending along the job description, the question can then be asked of a reference source, "Do you consider Mr. X a good man for this job?"

How the Executive Searchers Work (cont'd)

4. *Research.* The final objective of this step is to develop a list of names, addresses, and telephone numbers of prospective candidates.

The recruiter and his backup staff engage in a systematic hunt which usually takes from three to ten days. There is considerable variation in the way firms go about it. For example, in one case a recruiter will depend on the firm's personnel files to find suitable prospects, in another on business and trade contacts. Some firms may tend to favor printed sources, registers of professional associations, "Who's Who in Commerce and Industry," and so on.

5. *The proposal to possible candidates.* Once the prospect list is completed, the individuals are contacted and acquainted in more or less detail with the job opportunity. If a man shows interest, he is asked to provide the search firm with a resume and other material describing his qualifications.

Sometimes an executive will not himself be interested in a proposition but he will suggest another man: "Forget about me—but try Bill X—and don't tell him it was my idea."

Communication is often thwarted at this stage by the recruiter's reluctance to divulge the name of his client. He usually withholds this "revelation" until he meets with the small, final group of candidates. However, candidates can expect to get a general description of the company, as well as the nature of the job, job title, and salary level.

At this point, the candidate himself may upset the applecart by asking a key question. Unsatisfactory responses to questions about location of the client, for example, may bring a statement, "I don't want to relocate," and that prospect is scratched.

Recruiters point out that they maintain contact with the client almost constantly during the search period. The average client, not kept posted, will begin to wonder what he's getting from the search firm other than bills. The contact also serves as a safeguard; if the search is going astray, the client can help get the search back on course.

6. *Screening.* Interviews are set up with all qualified executives who have indicated their interest in the job. Psychological tests may be given. At this point, resumes, backgrounds, and current job performance are evaluated against the yardstick of the client's requirements.

Not infrequently, an executive will express interest in a job opportunity, but refuses to submit a resume. If the recruiter feels that the man is particularly desirable, he will humor him and try to worm sufficient information out of him to make up an evaluation sheet. Refusal to participate in the preliminary screening steps used to be quite common. But now, with the increased sophistication of executives in the ways of executive recruiting, it's more usual that once the executive decides to follow up an opportunity, he cooperates in all details.

One recruiter says, "In a typical search we never interview fewer than twenty-five to thirty candidates. And usually where the requirements are complex, we try to have two different people interview the same candidate in order to cross-check observations and evaluations."

To speed things up, a representative of the client company may help the recruiter with the rough screening of resumes. Bringing the company into the evaluation process early accomplishes two other objectives: It prevents the recruiter from selecting the wrong people to interview; it gives the client an idea of candidates and qualifications actually available, and thus helps him make a realistic final choice.

7. *Final selection.* Usually three to five men are submitted to the company for final interviewing.

Significantly, although the search firm stands ready to consult or counsel at all earlier phases of the search, in this final step it generally makes a special effort to stay in the background. The experienced recruiter knows how important it is that the client make up his own mind . . . and live with the result as *his* choice.

Reference Checking or Pre-Employment Investigation

In the typical executive hunt, reference or background checking is an extremely delicate operation. Some of the less-experienced recruiters have learned this the hard way. If references are checked *before* the client has made his final choice, a candidate may find himself in the unenviable position of having tipped his hand to his present employer, only to be rejected by the executive-seeking company. Then he's really out in the cold.

The reputable recruiting firm uses a number of safeguards to prevent background checks from backfiring. For example, the procedure recommended by Antell, Wright & Nagel is that the client send a letter of intent to the final candidate. The letter states that if reference checks are satisfactory, the man will be hired according to the terms that had been finally agreed upon.

At this point, the candidate must agree to open himself to a more or less complete investigation—possibly including a check of his wife and family, and parental ties. It is then up to the man himself to go to his employer and state his intention to accept the job opportunity that has been offered.

One recruiter says, "In our group of five final candidates we try to provide a range of qualifications. For example, we may have men who will expect slightly above the salary level being offered. In some cases, we may have one or two outside the particular industry involved who nevertheless qualify for the job, while the balance may be in the industry."

Somewhat to their sorrow, recruiters find that some clients feel cheated if they're presented with a relatively small number of final candidates. Faced with this attitude, the recruiter will usually do one of two things: produce more candidates, or explain that although additional men could be produced, it is to the client's advantage to trust the recruiter's judgment and select his man from among these hand-picked finalists. Many clients, of course, are perfectly willing to make a choice from among two or three final candidates that the recruiters present.

Recruiters have various problems in submitting reference-check material to clients. One firm is extremely reluctant to put any reference reports in writing: "We can never be sure of the possible fate of such material. In the case of a merger for example, it may fall into the wrong hands, or a secretary or file clerk may see material which is of a highly personal, confidential nature."

Some recruiters solve the problem by submitting favorable information in writing, and conveying questionable information verbally. (Because of the importance of pre-employment investigation, or PEI as it is sometimes called, you'll find the subject treated at greater length in Chapter 17.)

Most search firms institute a follow-up on their placements. They'll check with the new executive every thirty days over a six-month period. This contact ostensibly fulfills the purpose of providing guidance should any unexpected difficulties crop up. But as one outspoken recruiter confesses: "It also gives us a chance to develop a strong 'in' with the client and enlarge our contacts with him."

The Fringe Operators

Besides the firms whose sole activity is recruiting, there is a large and growing group that has developed searching as a sideline. In some cases

they have been attracted to the activity as a source of revenue; in others, as a means of rendering special service to their clients. Types of organizations that fall into this category:
Management consultants
Banks
Law firms
Accounting firms
Psychological testing companies
In a somewhat different category, but still to be included as a kind of fringe operation, are the employment agencies that also perform searches in the same way the professional search firms do.

Why Management Consultants Get into the Act

Almost every general management-consulting firm does executive recruiting to some degree. Remarks one consultant with a smile, "We may proceed rather informally, and with just a touch of professional embarrassment —but most of us do it. Whether a man is discreetly 'suggested' for a key management job or whether someone searches out candidates, there is a close connection between many consulting engagements and the search for executive personnel."

Management consultants got into the recruiting game very early—as far back as pre–World War II days. It was a natural activity for them for two reasons:

1. *Studies consultants made for clients often revealed that outside executive talent was needed* to implement the new programs and organizational structure. Having applied sophisticated procedures to the analysis of a company's weaknesses, the consultant—and his clients—often discovered that the programs were beyond the comprehension of the existing staff. So management simply asked the consultant to find the kind of executive who could handle the more complex responsibilities.

2. *Executive placement was a means of getting business.* In the early days, management consultants had a hard time selling their services because the businessman didn't understand the concept of outside help. So they actively solicited recruiting business in the hope that by placing a man in a key spot, they would gain an "in," and then be invited to study the company's operating problems in greater detail. Such engagements could be not only highly profitable, but also valuable for establishing the consultant's reputation as a proponent of the new "science of management."

If a company, for any reason, decides to use a general management consultant for recruiting, it should choose one carefully. Says Allen P. Burr of the well-known consulting firm George Fry & Associates, "There are general consultants who accept recruiting engagements on a fee basis and approach the work systematically—professionally. But many attempt to recruit in their 'down time,' and they are just not sufficiently involved in the field to perform effectively."

Also, it might be added, consultants face a special problem: They can hardly raid companies for executive talent if they hope to keep or win them as clients later. This tends to narrow the field from which they can draw.

Case History of an Accounting Firm

Consider the case of Price Waterhouse & Co., the well-known public accounting firm. For many years, Price Waterhouse helped its clients find accounting and financial personnel. This was done quite informally. The firm was in a strategic position to perform such service, since its normal accounting activity brought firm members into contact with both ends of the executive-placement equation:

1. In the course of working contacts with client companies, needs for specific executives would become known.

2. The interest of executives who felt ready for a change would also be known. In such cases, if there were no violation of basic obligations, Price Waterhouse representatives could pass information that might, eventually, move a good man into a desirable spot.

As the need for executives expanded, P.W. got an increasing number of requests from clients for "bright young men," or qualified veterans. At this point, the operation was put on a somewhat more formal basis, with the recruiting activity given to an operating executive as a part-time responsibility.

Eventually, the requests for executives came not only from clients, but from a number of companies that had heard of the accounting firm's placement activities. The firm then decided to formalize its recruiting operation and set up a separate department under the guidance of Mathew J. Beecher, whose sole function was executive placement. In the past several years, Beecher has made over sixty placements a year just from P.W.'s New York office. The executive-placement activity has three benefits for Price Waterhouse: it serves clients' needs; it helps establish good relations with the business community as a whole; it enhances the firm's reputation for service and brings in many new friends.

The Price Waterhouse recruiting program is essentially an adjunct service activity, and no attempt is made to have the function profit- or fee-oriented. Although the accounting firm occasionally gets requests for executives outside the accounting and financial categories, the majority of its requests are in those two areas. Accordingly, its regular activity gives it an inside track, a productive proximity to available individuals and sources that can mean quick and effective results in search assignments.

It was—and still is—instrumental in placing those members of its own staff seeking positions in industry.

A *Psychological-services Firm*

Of particular interest to a talent-prospecting company is the possibility of recruiting through a psychological testing service. Although not all testing organizations take on such assignments, those that do perform reasonably well, with costs running less than an executive-search firm's.

For example, The Personnel Laboratory, Inc., with offices in Stamford, Connecticut, and New York City, started taking on search assignments as far back as 1949. Clients who had used TPL only for testing candidates felt that they needed guidance in finding applicants, and asked the firm to help.

King Whitney, Jr., president of The Personnel Laboratory, says that his firm undertakes as many of the recruiting tasks as a client may want: advertising, resume screening, interviewing, testing, and reference checking, for example. Final choice is left to the employer, from a group of recommended candidates.

Although some searches are conducted under the usual percentage or flat-fee arrangements, an increasing number are being handled under what Whitney calls "time-and-step" charges. Acting as an extension of a company's personnel department, TPL staff members carry out the parts of the recruiting process desired by the client company. Charges are on the basis of actual time spent, plus expenses. Working in this fashion, The Personnel Laboratory recently recruited a public relations executive for a client, starting with the placing of an advertisement in three publications and finally recommending final candidates. Cost to the company, says Whitney, was about one-third of what a search firm might have charged. Although the service the client received was not so broad as that furnished by a good search consultant, it apparently was satisfactory, and at a saving.

7

The Executive Recruiters—
Making Them Work for You

Says the president of a watch-manufacturing company, "Blank Associates? They did a terrific recruiting job for us. Found just the fellow we wanted, and helped us reorganize a problem department besides."

Counters his friend, president of a jewelry firm, "Blank Associates are robbers. Charged me $4,000 for absolutely nothing. They didn't turn up a single candidate worth interviewing."

There *are* differences in attitudes toward recruiters on the part of companies who've used them. Generally, the "pros" are clients who feel they've got a lot for their money, the "antis" those who feel they've been "had."

Knowing in advance what services an executive recruiter can provide makes all the difference. Companies often fail to take advantage of assistance that recruiters are well able, and very willing, to give. This oversight can be a major cause of failure.

This chapter tells what steps companies can take to get maximum value from the dollars spent on an executive-search service. It also has some important suggestions for the executive who, as well as looking for employees, may one day himself be the target of a recruiter's phone call.

Waste of Time for the Job Seeker?

Before discussing *employer* use of searchers, a point must be made on what the recruiting firm offers the job seeker who is *not* solicited. If one had to give an evaluation in one word, that word would be, "Nothing." Of the many search-firm spokesmen queried, all agreed that an attempt by a job seeker to gain employment through a search firm almost always fails.

Recruiters tell you they are dismayed when a man looking for a job confuses a search firm with an employment agency. The consternation becomes particularly strong when job-hunting executives—and often those who don't really qualify for the executive category—turn up at the office door.

In most cases, the job seeker is met with courtesy, even a willingness to tentatively offer some off-the-cuff advice. But in the vast majority of cases, the job hunter is wasting his time. The search firms seldom are interested in unsolicited job seekers.

"We get anywhere from one to three hundred letters and resumes a week," says one search-firm official. "We'll have someone skim them, do a rough screening job. It's happened just once in two years that out of the thousands of communications we've received, a resume just happened to come in that suited a search we were making at the time." And this luck in timing didn't get the man the job—merely qualified him to be a candidate.

Most searchers say they don't try to keep comprehensive personnel files of executive candidates. Making an effort to get the "best man" for a vacancy, they will go to more-likely sources to find what they consider their ideal candidate, "the man who is more or less happily turning in a top performance with his present company." The mere fact that a man is "looking" tends to make him unacceptable to some searchers.

Accordingly, for the job hunter, a final suggestion: Don't waste your time on the search firms, since it is much better spent in other job-finding avenues. Two exceptions:

1. If you hear that a firm is actively recruiting for a position for which you're qualified, contact it, and mention the position specifically. That way, the connection won't be missed by some individual who may not be in a position to relate your qualifications to a current search.

2. If you have unique job qualifications—education, experience, skill— in an area in which you know a firm has done considerable recruiting, you may send in a resume, pointing out the special nature of your background.

Although the search organizations prefer to cast a mystical shroud around their sourcing operations, they are not above putting an acceptable candidate found in any fashion in with others uncovered by their more usual methods.

Now, back to the point—how employers can work most effectively with the searchers.

How a Company Can Get Best Results from a Recruiter

We asked three top recruiters—William Hertan of Executive Manpower Corporation, Robert A. Huttemeyer of Thorndike Deland Associates, and Paul H. Kiernan of Kiernan & Company—what steps companies can take to get maximum value from search firms. Their replies provide specific guidelines, a unique and practical assist for any company that deals with such firms.

GUIDELINE 1: *Don't hesitate to use the recruiter as a personnel consultant.*

HERTAN: "In his capacity as consultant, an experienced recruiter will not only identify problems related to the job, but will help clear the decks of difficulties before the job is filled."

KIERNAN: "Take advantage of your recruiter's knowledge and experience to get advice, particularly on these points:

"The salary (and fringes) you should offer to pay for a given job.

"Compromises you should be willing to make on such points as titles, reporting relationships, and so on.

"His opinion as to strong and weak points of specific candidates.

"How to integrate the new man into the company speedily. The recruiter can help the new executive to become a productive part of your organization in the shortest possible time."

GUIDELINE 2: *Analyze the job and pin down your requirements in a good job specification.*

HERTAN: "If there are gaps in your job specification, note down specific questions and put them to the recruiter."

HUTTEMEYER: "Even a detailed and up-to-date job description should be expanded on verbally with the recruiter. Emphasize especially important functions or responsibilities of the job, indicating where other men have failed, what aspects are particularly demanding, and so on."

KIERNAN: "Try to reach a hard decision on the kind of man you're looking for before the search actually begins. Once the search starts, any major change in job specifications means that the recruiter must, in effect, start a brand-new search. This can be enormously wasteful because it usually happens that the candidates already found will not match the revised job specifications."

HERTAN: "Above all, be realistic about the job specifications. Ask yourself whether some of the qualifications you're demanding are actually available, and in what quantity."

GUIDELINE 3: *Assign one person to deal with the recruiter.*

HUTTEMEYER: "It's been our experience that even though several company executives may interview the candidates, it helps if one man is designated as the central clearing house, the liaison man with the recruiter. He should be available most of the time, so that there will be no danger of losing a good prospect because there wasn't anyone around to see him. Rare perhaps, but it's been known to happen."

GUIDELINE 4: *Be frank about all the aspects of your problem.*

HUTTEMEYER: "Treat your recruiter as you would a doctor or a lawyer. Be frank with him even in areas that are not easy to discuss. For example, does the president have any prejudices? One of our clients rejected half a dozen good candidates, before he finally confessed to the recruiter that the company president couldn't stand moustaches or bow ties.

"On the other hand, we've had clients admit to us that they were undertaking a search with the main intention of comparing inside talent with what was available outside. That was O.K. with us—it made possible a much more constructive relationship with the clients than if we'd stumbled onto the fact.

"If by any chance the search has already been attempted either by people within the company or even by another recruiting firm, it will be helpful if the steps taken are spelled out. The precaution can save time, money, and possible embarrassment to all concerned."

GUIDELINE 5: *Let the recruiter know of any good sources of candidates you've found.*

HERTAN: "Suggest candidates, too, if possible. This can save time for both of you."

HUTTEMEYER: "In discussing possible sources of candidates, be frank about industry policies on executive transfers. Specify, if you can, companies you wouldn't want someone from, as well as those organizations you consider good prospecting grounds."

GUIDELINE 6: *Give the recruiter a thorough briefing on your company as well as on the job.*

HERTAN: "Where the man you're looking for is going into a really broad-gauge job, it's highly important that you give the recruiter a clear picture of the company. For example:

"Pertinent attitudes of the company, from within and without, that is, the company image. (Is it conservative, family-owned, the 'hottest' in the field?)

"Existing company political situations: expected or imminent developments (mergers, proxy fights).

"Company history.

"Copies of annual reports that detail the company's operating situations.

"Fringe benefits, bonuses, and so on.

"In short, tell the recruiter everything that he needs to know to do the best job—including any negative facts that may apply to either the job or the company. In my experience, these come out eventually. If they're made known in advance, a considerable amount of grief can be avoided.

"The recruiter also wants to know why the job is open at all, something about the previous holders of the job, why no one within the company has been selected to fill it (or have they been approached and turned it down?), the background, working habits, personality, and prejudices of the supervisor of the position to be filled.

"Be prepared to spell out the working conditions and social obligations of the job (small Southern town, largest plant in town, heavy social obligations; or big-city job, but plenty of traveling and little socializing, etc.).

"Establish the widest possible salary range, and then expect this to be backed up by an industry study by the recruiter to determine what the job is worth."

KIERNAN: "A point I'd like to add is the need for the recruiter to physically visit company premises, and to get to know the firm and the people involved in the final candidate selection, and the co-workers of the new man."

GUIDELINE 7: *Get a clear understanding about fees, in advance.*

HUTTEMEYER: "As in any business transaction, there should be a clear understanding of fees and services, preferably in writing. A letter from the recruiter to the client company is usually sufficient. If details are complex, there may have to be an exchange of letters in which unclear or ambiguous arrangements are pinned down."

KIERNAN: "As far as size of fee is concerned, clients should certainly feel free to question any items on the expense sheet that seem too high. But it's just as important to question expenses that seem too low. These may indicate that the recruiting firm has not worked as hard for you as it should."

GUIDELINE 8: *Stick with one recruiting firm until it gets results.*

HUTTEMEYER: "There is one practice that we, as recruiters, naturally frown on—but it works to the detriment of the client company at the same time. It's the matter of giving the assignment to several recruiters at once, and making a three-ring circus of the search. Word gets around fast, and the company that attempts this type of approach may not only destroy confidence, but also dampen the recruiter's enthusiasm."

KIERNAN: "If you've picked the right recruiting firm, you shouldn't have to tell the recruiter how to conduct the search, as tempting as this type of desk-side quarterbacking may be. And don't compete with him. If by chance you find a good candidate on your own, tell the recruiter about the man, and let him be screened and evaluated along with the other candidates."

GUIDELINE 9: *Follow up on every candidate the recruiter refers to you.*

KIERNAN: "When candidates have been selected for you to see, take the time and trouble to see them. In the press of daily activity, it's tempting to postpone seeing the candidates, since such interviews can be very demanding and time-consuming. Just remember that getting the right man in the right job is probably one of the most important things you can do for your company. It deserves priority attention."

How to Tell a Good Firm from a Second-rater

Naturally, not all of the firms in the executive-recruiting business provide the sort of services mentioned above, nor are all equal in professional competence. The trick is to determine which, of the various names gleaned from the classified phone list or suggested by business acquaintances, is best for a company's purposes.

Unfortunately, you can't judge by the record alone. Even the best of recruiters will admit that he draws a blank in about 20 per cent of his searches. Reasons include everything from the client's changing his mind to failure to find a man at the salary being offered. But although there are no hard-and-fast rules, there are some fairly reliable and easy-to-observe signs that distinguish the good bet from the poor one.

For example, it goes without saying that the better firm operates on higher ethical levels, charges a fair fee without "disbursement" padding, and does a more professional job on all phases of the search, from the original spotting of possible candidates to the final screening, testing, and presentation.

But other factors in the recruiter's operation may also be revealing. For example, the firm that's been in business a longer period of time is usually a better bet than a newcomer; the firm located in attractive quarters in the "good" section of the business district will probably do a better job than one operating from an out-of-the-way hole-in-the-wall office. The personal appearance, manner, and experience of the men on the recruiting firm's staff is also important to observe.

A systematic way of combining all these factors is provided by the check-list below. It was prepared by the Research Institute of America to help companies select a recruiting firm when several are being considered.

A Seven-point Checklist for Rating a Recruiting Firm

To use the chart as an evaluation tool, mark the appropriate box next to each factor. Then add up the numbers next to the boxes and compare the totals for various recruiters. (The numbers weight the seven factors according to their relative importance.) Other things being equal, the firm with the highest rating "wins."

Factors	O.K.	So-So	Poor
1. Physical facilities:			
a. appearance of offices	4( )	2( )	0( )
b. type and size of staff	4( )	2( )	0( )
c. atmosphere—calm, dignified, professional	4( )	2( )	0( )
2. Length of time in business	10( )	5( )	0( )
3. General reputation of firm (or recommendations)	12( )	6( )	0( )

Factors	O.K.	So-So	Poor
4. Intelligence and maturity of the contact man you deal with. (Does he seem to know his business and understand *your* needs?)	8( )	4( )	0( )
5. Intelligence and maturity of the man who will do the actual recruiting. (How favorably does he impress you?)	8( )	4( )	0( )
6. Fees—discussed in advance, and equitable	12( )	6( )	0( )
7. Proximity to your office	8( )	4( )	0( )

Critical Differences between the Good and Poor Recruiter

Beyond all these fairly obvious tests are some more-critical points that stem from situational factors. Various problem situations inevitably arise in the course of an executive search. These situations are handled smoothly and effectively by an experienced recruiter. The less-experienced or incompetent man, however, may either flub the situation or else cope with it by sweeping it under the rug. Needless to say, the client suffers. The following table summarizes the main situations that test a recruiter's capabilities and briefly tells how they'll be handled by a good and an inept recruiter:

Critical factor	*The effective recruiter*	*The poor recruiter*
Job specifications	Tries to make them as clear and tight as possible.	Tries to keep them loose in order to simplify search.
Evaluation of candidates	Checks references carefully, and does a thorough screening job so as to submit as few candidates as possible. In his presentation of candidates, mentions each man's weak points along with his strengths.	Being less expert, does a poorer job of screening and compounds this fault by putting too much weight on favorable factors, toning down weak points of candidates to expedite hiring.
Number of candidates referred to company	Refers as few men as possible, usually no more than five.	Presents a large number of candidates, leaving client to do interviewing and screening.
Reference checks, general investigation	Checks references in depth but carefully so as not to jeopardize candidate's present position.	May do only a perfunctory job of reference checking to save time and expense.

Critical factor	The effective recruiter	The poor recruiter
Primary responsibility	Always feels his primary responsibility is toward client; secondary responsibility to job candidate.	Sometimes confuses priority of responsibility, particularly if he develops an unprofessional interest in pushing a particular candidate.
Induction and training	Works closely with client and new executive to shorten the break-in period.	Probably lacks experience to provide much help.
Dealing with negative elements	Sits down with applicant and the employer to discuss any "negative" aspects—excessive executive turnover, illogicalities in chain of authority, for example.	Glosses over negatives in hope that "things will work themselves out."
Need to backtrack	Occasionally a recruiter makes a mistake, e.g., a candidate whom he has rated high proves to have some blemish on his record. The effective recruiter reveals this fact and, if important, dissuades client from hiring the man, even though he had originally presented him.	In the same situation, says nothing but closes his eyes, crosses his fingers, and hopes for the best.
Salary negotiations	Discourages his client from over-extending a given offer. To go beyond normal or desirable salary levels is frequently short-sighted and may mean eventual trouble. It can, for example, impair the harmonious introduction of a new executive into a corporation, since executive salaries are no secret.	Attempts subtly or otherwise to pressure company to boost salary level to win over desirable candidate, regardless of possible consequences.
Follow-through on details—promises, etc.	Sees that promises made to the newly inducted executive are fulfilled. For example, reminds client at proper time of promises he made to new executive—increase of $X after six months, issuance of a stock option at the end of a three-month period, etc.	Prefers to have these matters be the client's affair.
Continuing consultation	Makes himself available for guidance and counsel at	Usually stays out of counseling situations, which may show

The effective recruiter	*The poor recruiter*
every step in the search from beginning to end.	up his lack of experience or acumen (and thus avoid making glaring errors.) Confines himself to preliminary screening and leaves as much of the decision making and evaluation as possible to the client.

What to Do When the Phone Rings

At least once in his career, every top executive is likely to get a phone call from an executive recruiter. Sample: "Mr. Smith, my name is Jones, with the XYZ Personnel Consulting Company. We're trying to locate an executive vice-president for a leading manufacturing company. The man we're looking for. . . ." (A brief description follows). "Do you happen to know anyone with these qualifications who might be interested in such an opening?" The recruiter, of course, expects the executive to put himself at the top of the prospect list.

But the executive is in a hot spot. He must instantly decide several critical questions before he opens his mouth or he may endanger his current career. Is the phone call likely to be some kind of trap? How shall he respond to this telephone approach? Can he trust the person at the other end? *Would* he be interested? Is his best move simply to utter a curt negative reply, and hang up?

Dealing with the Recruiter—Phase 1

We asked our panel of three top recruiters—William Hertan, Robert A. Huttemeyer, and Paul H. Kiernan—how they would advise an executive who has just been rung up by a recruiter. Here are their recommendations:

HERTAN: "If the caller is known to the person receiving the call, of course, he answers as he thinks best. But if he is a stranger, the executive should always ask whether he can return the call. There are two reasons: first, to avoid any embarrassment if someone is playing a trick or trying to pull a fast one (and it could have serious repercussions); second, to give the executive the time and freedom to speak at his leisure, when his conversation need not be guarded. When the executive returns the call, he should ask the recruiter to call him, the executive, at his home in order to free both parties from any conspiratorial attitudes."

HUTTEMEYER: "The executive should always be courteous but cautious. There's no necessity for the cloak-and-dagger bit, but neither should you expose yourself to a stranger. I, too, suggest that the executive call the recruiter back—just to make sure it's not a bad joke or, even worse, someone from the executive's own company. Then, play just a little hard to get—don't appear too anxious. Recruiters are on the phone a lot and they are extremely sensitive to nuances in voice, delivery, or manner. You probably won't have to suggest lunch, or an outside meeting, or a call-back. The recruiter will often sense your feelings, and will take the initiative. It may be wise, if you've never heard of the recruiting firm, or have reason to be wary, to ask for a letter."

KIERNAN: "Even if you're not personally interested in the recruiter's query, it can't hurt you to listen. You may be able to do a friend a favor by recommending him. And even if you're not interested in the job described, other opportunities may come through this recruiter later on."

Evaluating the Man behind the Voice

The next point to which the Messrs. Hertan, Huttemeyer, and Kiernan addressed themselves was: "What, specifically, should you watch for in the unseen recruiter's story?"

HERTAN: "The executive should be wary of *any* recruiter who, over the phone on the first contact, makes the following *gaffes:*

"1. Gives the executive the name of the recruiter's client. This is either highly irregular, or a sign of a completely inept approach.

"2. Tells too much about the job, its specific details, etc. There's a lot more talking that should take place before this stage is reached.

"3. Mentions, or even hints at, payment of a fee in whole or in part *by the executive.* As is pretty well known by now, the client who hires the recruiter always pays the entire fee."

KIERNAN: "To judge the caliber of the recruiter, ask yourself these questions: Does he use a professional approach—no high pressure, no promises, no selling? Is his manner businesslike? Does he display a knowledge of the qualifications on the job? Has he prepared himself to answer questions about the job? If not, this would indicate that he is not treating you as a serious candidate.

"Next, ask questions about the position: size of the company, organization structure, where the company is located, why they need a new man.

"Such questions do not necessarily imply that you are interested in the job—or commit you to anything. In fact, you should ask the recruiter to send a written specification of the job to your home, so you can study it at leisure.

"After you've evaluated the job specifications, you should call the recruiter back and tell him whether or not you are interested in pursuing the matter further. Remember, too, you can always indicate that while you aren't his man, you know of someone who might be."

Dealing with the Recruiter—Phase 2

Once he decides that he *is* interested in the recruiter's proposal, the executive faces an entirely new situation. In the first stage, he's merely established whether or not there is a common meeting ground, and whether he should investigate further.

This second stage finds the recruiter—and the job-interested executive too—in a much more hard-nosed attitude.

Paul H. Kiernan provides this view of the typical course of development that follows: "If you are interested, the recruiter will arrange a meeting with you. Even during this interview, he may not identify the company for whom the search is being made.

"A good recruiter will be evaluating many candidates for this job—perhaps hundreds. Thus, he may not get back to you immediately. You can be sure, however, that in the meantime the recruiter has been discreetly checking you out—probably with former employers, former subordinates of yours, and through your personal references. If you are dealing with an executive recruiter of professional calibre, you need not worry that he will jeopardize your present position. He will take every precaution to ensure against damaging you in any way.

"If you are one of the final candidates to be presented to the company for whom the executive search is being conducted, you can figure there are probably four or five other candidates in the picture.

"The company will now be identified to you. At this point, it behooves you to find out all you can about the company so that when you walk in for an interview, you are in a strong position. Take as much time as you can to get and digest all the facts about the company. Do your homework.

"If time does not permit this—if you are interviewed the day after you discover the name of the company, for example—explain at the beginning of the interview that you have not had time to prepare yourself."

Kiernan remembers one outstanding example of preparation for an interview of this kind. George A. Daniels was a candidate for a position of financial officer (he is now secretary-treasurer) in River Brand Rice Mills, Inc., of Houston, Texas. Daniels was working in Ohio at the time, but he came to New York and spent two days in the library of the New York Stock Exchange studying the River Brand Rice Company. Then he met with the board chairman of the company at the Union League Club in New York. George Daniels was far and away the outstanding candidate for the job because no one had done this kind of preparation. He walked away with the job.

"If you have done your homework on the company," says Kiernan, "you don't have to do any 'fact dropping' or take any other overt action to show that you are prepared. It will be evident in the way you handle yourself.

You may use only a small fraction of the information about the company you have acquired, but in so doing you will prove that you have carefully prepared yourself.

"At the interview, handle yourself with confidence and dignity, but don't play hard to get. Remember, the company's recruiter has come to you— you're not the one who is looking for a job. But on the other hand, bear in mind that both of you are there to investigate a possible mutual benefit.

"If you are one of the final candidates for a key job, anticipate several interviews. During these interviews, don't be afraid to ask questions. Don't be afraid to admit you don't know something. Don't minimize yourself, but on the other hand, don't make yourself out to be more than you really are. Don't hesitate to state your commitment to your present company even if it means you cannot be totally flexible in your availability for interviews or to start a new position. If you indicate you are willing to walk out on your present company even if it might damage them, the new employers might wonder whether you would do the same thing to them.

"By all means, don't knock your present company or the people in it. And don't be afraid to protect the confidence of your present employer. If a question comes up in an interview that infringes on classified or confidential information, simply point out that this is something you can't discuss, and explain why. If there is persistent probing in this direction, it should be a red flag to you that the company might be after you more for what you know than what you are."

Robert A. Huttemeyer offers two cautions to prevent collapse of developed plans, to the embarrassment of all involved:

"The executive should discuss the possibilities provided by the job offer at home early in the game. Any problems a wife or other family member foresees should be ironed out before negotiations go too far.

"A description of the job being filled should be used as a tool for self-evaluation. Questions to be answered by this process: 'Am I convinced that I can perform as required? Am I sure that I'm not getting in over my head? Am I considering the job for sound career reasons, and not just being tempted by a few more dollars?' "

Twelve Vital Do's and Don't's in Final Negotiations

Kiernan then goes on to suggest these specifics:

1. "Don't talk too much—or too little. Act interested. Dress conservatively.

2. "Don't start talking money too soon. If the company is interested in you, they will pay what it takes to get you.

3. "Don't indicate that you think small by asking questions about vacation policies, moving cost policies, and so on.

4. "Don't put too many conditions into the deal, and don't ask for a contract.

5. "Ask to have the specifications of the job—in terms of responsibility and authority—spelled out in detail verbally.

6. "If you are offered the job, don't hesitate to ask for a couple of days to think it over. If they have offered you the job, they are not going to change their minds in that amount of time.

7. "But don't say, 'I'd like to talk this over with my wife.' Even if you do value your wife's judgment highly, don't imply to the company she makes your decisions for you, or even influences them.

8. "If you have been offered the job, it makes sense to ask to meet some of the people you will be working with. Sometimes this isn't practical, but there is no harm in asking.

9. "Incidentally, one of the best ways to do your homework on a company prior to an interview is to talk to people who were formerly with the company. You can often obtain a deep look inside the company in this way, provided you are able to weigh the information you get from the point of view of why it is that this man is no longer with the company himself.

10. "If you decide to take the position, ask for a letter of agreement, reviewing all the things you have discussed and specifying the responsibilities of the job. This can help to avoid any possible misunderstanding.

11. "At this point, if what you prefer in terms of compensation, etc., does not match up exactly with the package the company offers, it does no harm to ask for changes.

12. "Once you have accepted the job and agreed to a starting date, stick to your commitment at all costs. Your primary loyalty should now be to the new company, and you should make whatever compromises are necessary elsewhere to satisfy this commitment. If you fail to live up to your initial promises, even in the face of extenuating circumstances, you may get off on the wrong foot and perhaps even damage your professional reputation."

8

The Ads—Exposure in the Square

This advertisement recently ran in the London evening newspapers:

Chauffeur required. Good knowledge London and excellent references essential. Must have mechanical experience. Preferably single, aged 28-40. Write the private secretary to H.R.H. Princess Margaret, Kensington Palace, W.8.

Londoners couldn't recall seeing the royal family advertise before. But a spokesman at the palace confirmed that the Princess had authorized the ad. "How else can you get staff?" he asked.

The same attitude toward space advertising as a means of finding personnel exists in our own country. Ads have always been one of the major ways of recruiting executives and unearthing executive openings. At the same time, there are many misconceptions as to their real effectiveness.

In this chapter some of the most common misbeliefs are set straight as we examine the steps leading up to the "executive wanted" ad and find out how companies can get better results from space advertising. Leading recruiters also give specific do's and don't's for the executive who desires to advertise his talents via the space ad.

Light under the Bushel

"Space advertising is a stepchild in the executive-recruiting field," comments the personnel vice-president of a Midwest engineering firm. "It has neither the glamor of the executive-search operation, nor the service features of the employment agencies." Nevertheless, it still gets a healthy slice of the total sum spent in the executive job market.

Figures developed in surveys often are misleading on this score. When a

82

study shows that, "X per cent of companies use newspaper and magazine advertising to locate executive talent, Y per cent use employment agencies, and Z per cent use search firms," an *overlap* is often camouflaged. The employment agencies and the search firms often resort to space ads for finding executives, though the fact is sometimes slurred over. And almost every other type of firm involved in the executive job market uses space advertising: For example, the job counselors use space advertising to sell their services, as do the resume writers, executive registries, and so on.

What Your Money Buys When You're Advertising for an Executive

Space advertising, sometimes called "the town crier" approach, can produce unique results for the company looking for an executive. Many companies use ad agencies that specialize in personnel advertising to increase effectiveness.

Typical of the executive recruiting ad is the following, from *The Wall Street Journal*:

> MANAGER OF COST ACCOUNTING. Excellent opportunity for experienced person to direct cost accounting function for rapidly growing manufacturer of housewares with sales of $30 million. Metal fabrication experience desirable. Please send resume including salary requirements. All replies treated confidentially.

Within three days after the ad appeared, the company received 123 replies, at a cost of $108 for two insertions. This case illustrates the two big strengths of space advertising: The direct expenditure is comparatively low; the response is almost immediate, coming usually within forty-eight to ninety-six hours.

Each newspaper and magazine has different rates, based on circulation. Specifically, rates range from $3.30 a line in the *Los Angeles Times*—which carries the greatest amount of classified advertising in the country—to 10 or 15 cents a line in a small-town low-circulation newspaper.

In addition to per-line costs, most media have a space minimum. Personnel ads are usually run in classified sections, which have a two- or three-line minimum. But the standard minimum for a display ad is column width, and 1 inch (fourteen lines) deep.

The display ad is often run in large metropolitan newspapers, such as *The New York Times*, that have a business section as well, and is known in the trade as "business-section advertising."

Occasionally, someone may try an offbeat insertion. For example, one executive recently ran an ad in the sports section. But one reaction was discouraging: "If he's that much of a sports addict, I don't want to hire him."

If You're Looking for a Position

Job seekers' luck with space advertising can't be stated in a single sweeping conclusion; results vary all over the lot. Many individuals use them successfully. For example, one personnel executive, happily ensconced in the top personnel spot in a large engineering firm, has landed four jobs in ten years by means of ads. A plant manager of a Buffalo food-processing firm got his job by a single insertion in Sunday's *The New York Times*.

Balancing these success stories, however, is at least an equal number of negative experiences, such as that of a sales executive with international experience and a command of six languages, who has handled top-level government contracts, seeking a connection at a modest "asking price" of $20,000. His repeated ads find no solid takers.

In the words of one personnel man, wise in the "ad game": "The job seeker who advertises is shooting crap for the cost of the ad." Says Michael Horne, copy director of Edward Weiss Advertising, an agency specializing in personnel advertising, "For the executive job seeker, space advertising is a long shot."

Limitations of Space Advertising

Companies and individuals alike should be aware that space advertising has built-in limitations, including the following:

1. *It's a shotgun approach.* Not even the best newspapers in the executive ad field, such as *The New York Times* and *The Wall Street Journal*, can guarantee that the "best" man or the "best" job opportunity will turn up through an ad. This is so despite tremendous readership. But advertisers assume that the laws of chance will operate and turn up enough good prospects to provide an acceptable choice.

2. *Large percentage of useless replies.* Any net cast out into the broad public pond is bound to come up with all sorts of strange objects—and space advertising is no exception. Out of hundreds of replies to a "man wanted" insertion only 4 or 5 per cent may meet specifications. This requires the advertiser to do considerable screening to separate the good from the useless replies. Executives running job-wanted ads have often had the same experience; they get numerous replies that have nothing to do with job offers.

An interesting sidelight: Just as an engagement announcement brings an avalanche of letters from catering services, travel bureaus, etc., down on the heads of a soon-to-be bride and groom, so does the job seeker frequently get inundated by solicitations from agencies, counselors, resume-writing services, and agencies after he places an ad. At worst, however, this is only a nuisance.

3. *Respondents are just job-shopping.* The experienced recruiter is no

longer surprised when a qualified applicant who answered his ad fails to show up. The statement of one such ad answerer explains the mystery: "I think it's a good idea to know how much you're worth on the open market. From time to time I send out a few resumes to find out. You couldn't really say I'm seeking a new position. . . ."

4. *The blind ad is hazardous.* "Send complete resumes to Box #746. . . ." For various reasons, companies often recruit via space ads without revealing who they are. But the use of a box number instead of a company name sometimes presents problems. There's generally a lower rate of response. And some ad answerers have found themselves in the embarrassing position of replying to ads run by their own companies. Companies *not* using blind ads have similarly found themselves tipping their hand that they were recruiting before they were prepared to pass along this intelligence to their staffs.

5. *Misuse of the ad medium.* Abuse or misuse of the ads doesn't happen often, but when it does, there may be unpleasant results. For example: Company A decides to test the loyalty of a key executive. It runs an ad that it feels will attract the man. If he answers, he reveals himself as "looking"—and kills his chances for promotion because he's not sufficiently "with" the team.

Then, from job seekers, come these specific complaints:

6. *Job descriptions differ from what's actually wanted.* One bewildered job seeker reported: "I answered an ad, got an interview, and found that the job the interviewer was talking about bore only a slight resemblance to the one described in the newspaper."

True enough, this type of executive mind-changing or failure to communicate clearly can occur in other connections. But the executive's complaint underlines the need on the part of both the recruiting agency or company and the job hunter to make the ad as clear and unambiguous as possible. Failure to accurately describe a job or qualifications in either an ad or in response to one is almost certain to lead to frustration and time waste for all concerned.

7. *Biased—or inept—screening.* "Can't understand why my reply to an ad didn't at least gain me an interview," one unemployed executive says. "My qualifications were right on target." Unfortunately, the answer may be unsatisfactory screening of the replies received.

Too often, a batch of replies is turned over to a secretary or a subordinate who may lack the intelligence or experience to judge and evaluate the responses an ad brings in. Or, when an ad brings in a mountainous response, fatigue or boredom on the part of the "screener" may mean that after one or two promising candidates are found, the balance of the responses get short shrift—both an unfair and inefficient practice.

8. *Form-letter turndowns.* This point is no reflection on the effectiveness of space advertising, but does rub some job hunters the wrong way.

"I spent a whole day answering a very attractive ad," reports one executive. "I went to some trouble to research the company, identify the name of the official at the receiving end, and to send him a personal letter. All I got back was a formal note thanking me for my interest, and the no-promise promise that if there were another opening suited to my qualifications, I'd be notified." Of course, there are many instances where even this formality is lacking, much to the annoyance of the ad answerer. Unfortunately, these irritations seem to be in the cards when you're dealing with the ads.

The Leading Newspapers for Space Ads

Naturally, the newspapers in large metropolitan centers tend to be best for executive personnel advertising. Heading the list are *The New York Times*, especially the Sunday edition; *The Wall Street Journal*, which is regionally distributed so that an ad may be pinpointed in any one of four geographic areas; and the *Los Angeles Times*, carrying perhaps the largest volume of personnel ads of all.

In addition, specialists who place ads in newspapers think highly of the pulling power of these newspapers: *Atlanta Journal Constitution; Boston Globe; Chicago Tribune; Cincinnati Inquirer; Dallas News; Kansas City Star; Miami Herald; Minneapolis Star Tribune; Philadelphia Inquirer; Seattle Times; San Francisco Chronicle; Washington Post.* However, the list is by no means complete. Many other newspapers, dailies and weeklies both, have produced results. The key to effectiveness is the readership of the publication and its "prestige" status in the community.

A recent study of the *Wall Street Journal* readership shows why it rates high. Its readers consist of an impressive array of high-echelon executives in a wide range of industries. Other top papers serve this type of audience, too. Here is a breakdown of the *Wall Street Journal* audience, according to industry, as revealed by the survey:

Industry and commerce	Per cent
Manufacturing	27.74
Mining	0.86
Construction	2.80
Public utilities	1.06
Transportation and communication	2.28
Agriculture, forestry, and fisheries	2.24
Wholesalers	8.47
Retailers	7.72
Service	7.35
Insurance	2.71
Real estate	2.88

Finance

Banks and savings banks	3.14
Investment bankers and dealers, stock and commodity brokers	3.99
Financial, miscellaneous	1.19

Other   25.57

A breakdown by title and position revealed this pattern:

Chairmen	0.62
Presidents	11.35
Owners	8.55
Partners	4.37
Directors and trustees	1.71
Vice-presidents	6.19
Secretaries and secretary-treasurers	1.44
Treasurers	1.14
Comptrollers	0.61
Officers and assistant officers	2.67
General managers	1.33
Department managers and assistants	10.95
Superintendents, supervisors, foremen, and assistants	2.65
Editors	0.15
Engineers	4.64
Chemists	0.29
Purchasing agents and buyers	0.50
Cashiers and assistant cashiers	0.28
Agents, brokers, salesmen	4.84
Other	35.72

Typical Results from Newspaper Ads

The pattern of response to executive space advertising is fairly well established. It can be expected, for example, that an ad placed by a company looking for an executive will draw about fifty times as many responses as an equivalent "position-wanted" ad.

It is also known that responses tend to follow a probability-curve dispersion. For example, if an ad is placed on Monday, chances are the answers will trickle in during the ensuing week like this:

Monday	1
Tuesday	4
Wednesday	12
Thursday	6
Friday	4
Saturday	2
Monday	2
Tuesday	1

The third day after an ad is placed is almost always the peak day of return. When it comes to the total number of responses, however, figures vary widely, depending on the nature of the ad.

Quantities of replies vary all the way from a rare zero to hundreds. Quality, too, varies. In general, the more specific the ad, the smaller the number of replies, but the smaller number generally represents a much higher percentage of useful prospects. Booz, Allen & Hamilton reports that typically it gets 2 to 4 per cent *usable* replies out of the total response when it runs ads for executives. And usually, the higher the title of the executive wanted, the greater the range of persons answering the ad. Seemingly, everyone from the shipping clerk on up cherishes a secret dream that he could run a company, given the chance. But when a job such as market research director or chief chemist is advertised, few reply except those with research or chemical backgrounds.

How to Use Newspaper Advertising

People who are experienced with this type of recruiting generally recommend three insertions in a week's span. Four insertions sometimes will give the maximum response, but over four the law of diminishing returns sets in. This rule holds for individual and company alike.

Flippancy, cuteness, poetry fall flat in executive advertising. Factual ads generally pull best. But an eye-catching headline or opening phrase *is* desirable, to gain attention. It's appropriateness to the job advertised that's the key.

Here's one successful exception to the "don't try to be slick" rule. John K. Smith, national classified advertising manager of *The Wall Street Journal,* remembers that one of the best-pulling ads in his experience was headlined " 'Atlanta's best salesman.' The clever sales executive took 6 separate inches of space, each starting with the same catchy headline and covering a specific point in his experience to outline his achievements: 'Boosted company sales $2 million in six months', 'Opened six new major accounts for the company within a year's time,' and so on. Interested employers practically broke the doors down to get at this executive. It was solely through his ad that he suggested he had a lot on the ball." Notice, however, that it was a sales position—a profession in which flamboyance is often an asset.

"Start with a salient or key point," suggests one expert to men seeking an executive spot, "and leave out details such as marital status, number of children, and so on. They're important after contact has been established, but they only clutter up an ad that has, as its simple basic purpose, the bringing together of a company and a man."

Where to Find Ideas for Ads

Newspaper personnel can offer some help in preparing ad copy. Clearly they can't write the ads, but often they can suggest improvements in proposed copy, and their advice should by all means be sought. A frequent suggestion, either to the job-seeking executive or to the personnel man, is "Go through our files of past ads and check off those that approximately tell your story."

Also, if the ad placer spots an ad that interests him, he can find out how well or poorly it pulled. Frequently this information can be very helpful, if only to suggest an effective word or phrase. For example, the word "transferable" in a position-wanted ad will often draw an unusually high number of replies because companies frequently are unable to find men willing to relocate.

Secondary Uses of Newspaper Ads

Newspaper ads are sometimes run for other reasons than directly to get a job or find an executive. Three of the most common of these "indirect" purposes are:

Reprint. Frequently an executive will run an ad in a newspaper that tells his story. He then has the ad reprinted and sends it to a list of prospects with a covering letter which says, in effect, "Did you see my ad in today's _____?"

Testing the state of the market. Sometimes an employer will advertise an executive vacancy at the same time he counts on using other avenues of recruitment. In this case, the ad is merely run as a backup. There is no effort to screen the answers, but the resumes that come in are gone through on the chance that one or two red-hot prospects might just possibly have been turned up. And, of course, if this is done in advance of using the other media, it can be the least expensive means of recruitment.

Institutional advertising. Occasionally companies use positions-available advertising to help "build their image." This type of ad becomes a verification of the growth and expanding requirements of the organization.

Recommendations for the Job Seeker

"Three recommendations I'd make to an executive looking for a job," says Michael Horne of the Ed Weiss Agency, who has had years of experience in designing and executing personnel advertising for hundreds of companies and individuals:

"1. If there is a trade or professional journal that is appropriate for the kind of job you're seeking, give it preference over newspapers. The difference is in the kind of readership these so-called 'vertical media' get. An executive—that is, a potential employer—is likely to read the business journal through from cover to cover. When he reads his newspaper, he's apt to be much more cursory, and do less 'miscellaneous' reading—of non-news items.

"2. If you're going to run an ad, *make it a big one.* True, that means a bigger blow to your pocketbook. But a small ad just belittles the image of executive impressiveness you're trying to project.

"3. Sell yourself the same way you'd sell a product. Tell the potential employer what you have to offer *him,* and get your strong points in early. Make it clear, also, that you'll back your statements with facts contained in your resume."

How to Answer an Ad

If all employers were alike, there might be one "right" or "best" way for an executive job seeker to answer an ad. But they are not, and an approach that might meet with approval by one individual screening responses for his company may call forth disdain from another.

One aspect of the operation that is fairly standard, however, is the processing of the replies. An understanding of this procedure can be helpful to the job seeker, if not an iron-clad guide. Here is the way it is handled in one West-coast utility company:

Regardless of the department for which the executive is to be hired, the personnel office places the ad. All replies sent in are channeled to one or more personnel employees. Each reply is then screened and placed into one of three groups:

Group A. Letters and resumes from applicants considered good possibilities for the job.

Group B. The "doubtfuls." The applicant may lack one of the requirements, but still may be promising.

Group C. Complete rejections. For one reason or another, the applicants are unacceptable.

At this point, there are two possibilities: The responsible executive—often the superior of the man to be hired—may be sent the entire batch of applications in group A and perhaps some of the "possibles" in group B. Or he may tell the personnel department screeners, "I only want to see three (or five, or ten) of the best-qualified applicants."

Whichever method is used, eventually the selected candidates will be asked to report for interviews. From that point on, the hiring procedure follows the logical course.

Should You Play It Straight?

One of the questions an executive may have to decide in answering an ad is this: "Should I stick to the bare facts requested in the ad or should I try to frame a more imaginative reply to indicate my originality and creativity, and to get attention?"

Most seasoned personnel people counsel, "Stick to the facts, provide exactly what the ad asks for." By this advice they would bar not only extraneous details in the written reply, but also some of the so-called "creative" approaches:

The phone call: "I saw your ad for a marketing executive, and my qualifications are so outstanding that I felt a direct contact would be better than a reply in writing." Usually, this departure from requested procedure irritates. Personnel people also veto the *lengthy telegram*, and, even more strongly, the *personal appearance* (where the job seeker has learned the identity and location of the company advertising).

Despite the heavy weight of authority against the offbeat approach, the job seeker who takes the bull by the horns and violates some one of the don't's mentioned above occasionally is successful in gaining his audience, and even a job. But such outcomes are relatively rare and depend on the unpredictability of the human being—a sudden weakening of resolve in the face of a pleasant smile or very attractive appearance.

When You Play It Straight

In the vast majority of cases, the best way of responding to an ad is to follow the line it suggests. If a resume is asked for, submit it; if a detailed biographical sketch is asked for, be sure it's forthcoming. Here are the steps that represent a straight down-the-line approach:

1. *Read the ad carefully.* "I've found," reports one executive who has done a considerable amount of recruiting, "that as many as 25 per cent of the responses would never have been sent in if the individual had taken the trouble to figure out exactly what we were looking for as described in our ad."

Another personnel executive provides this example: "We specified that we wanted a production man to handle our printing. You'd be surprised at the number of letters we got from executives with experience in metal fabricating, the assembly of electronic units, and other manufacturing operations."

2. *Don't waste your time just "sending out mail."* In describing a recent hiring session, the vice-president of one engineering firm remarked on the great number of replies he'd received from individuals who clearly lacked

major qualifications outlined in the ad. "These people seemed to take the attitude, 'I'll send in my resume just on the off chance that it will get me an interview.'" As the vice-president said, this rarely happens unless the job opening requires such unusual experience that the lack of some qualifications can be ignored.

Another type of wasted effort is represented by the overconfident job seeker who blithely overlooks key features of the job—such as salary level, willingness to relocate, etc.—assuming that the employer will retailor his requirements once he meets the dynamo. This seldom happens, and there's no point in starting a process that won't be completed.

3. *Submit fresh, updated material only.* "It's important to remember," says one experienced screener, "that our initial impression of a man comes entirely from the material he sends us. A dog-eared resume or an old one that has been updated by handwritten additions is bound to make an unfavorable impression." (Read Chapter 14 for full details in the developing of an effective resume.)

"Covering letters are generally advisable," most screeners agree. However, they should be short, and written on a letterhead or stationery that adds a dimension of courtesy and stature to the resume or other material submitted. In this day and age, handwritten material is generally ruled out. Similarly, informal personal stationery might be fine for friends, but is likely to cause a poor reaction in the upper-level business context.

4. *Make your replies specific and concise—but highlight key points.* Any important factual material not covered in the resume should be added briefly either in the covering letter or on a separate sheet. For example, one company advertised for an office manager who had had experience abroad. A highly qualified executive lost out because the facts of his foreign experience were buried in one line in his resume, which evaded the eye of a screener who was trying to make time through a big pile of reports.

For a job that's particularly desirable, it pays to write a resume that will prominently highlight the particular points of interest specified in the ad.

"I Don't Fill the Bill, but . . ."

Executive applicants often ask the question, "What if I feel I can do a job but lack one or more of the qualifications stipulated?" There are two ways of handling this situation:

A. You may admit at the outset that you lack some of the qualifications in question, but then quickly point out your offsetting advantages. For example, one applicant got himself an interview by writing as follows:

"While I have only ten years in the plastics field instead of the fifteen you ask for, my experience has been extensive. For example, my responsibilities encompassed not only the production of sheets, rods, and tubes but also molding powder and films. Also the nature of my responsibilities gave me particularly broad contacts. . . ."

B. The second implication is touchy in the extreme, for, as one executive bluntly puts it, "It comes down to the question, 'Should I lie?' "

Take the case of a man whose background and experience are directly in line with what is wanted. However, he has had only two years of college instead of the degree the ad asked for.

Obviously, no one is going to answer the question "Should I lie?" in the affirmative, even though individuals who have slurred over a gap in their qualifications have been hired and performed satisfactorily in their jobs.

The Score on the Misrepresenters

One management consultant was asked to investigate the qualifications of a group of engineers hired by a large company, without a reference check. To everyone's astonishment, a whopping 10 per cent of the relatively large number checked were found to have lied about their education. For example, some professed to have advanced degrees when they actually had only a B.A. But in all cases, the individuals were performing satisfactorily— even though the education qualifications had been specified by the company as an essential requirement to do the job.

Perhaps just as frequent, however, are the instances of applicants who have misrepresented their qualifications, had the misrepresentation found out either in the course of the interview or the reference checks, and then been ruled out forthwith as much for the fraud as for the lack of the quality misrepresented.

Many experts in the field say that reference checking, or rather "investigation of a man's record," in which no holds are barred, is becoming more frequent, particularly for key and top jobs. The company that has spent several thousand dollars for recruiting a key executive is going to spend an additional $200 to $500 for an intensive investigation to make sure there are no "dark spots" in the man's record.

5. *Weave the "sell" into the factual material.* "There is a type of resume developed by the professional resume writers that I throw out automatically," says the personnel executive of a Chicago office-equipment manufacturing company. "This is the one that is all sunshine and roses; it's all *sell* and very little *tell.*"

On the other hand, a response to an ad that simply says, "For five years I was head of the X division; for three years I was head of the Y division" may be stating facts, but it's not very revealing. Instead, the letter writer might state that in the course of his five years' stint as head of the A division—

- Production methods were improved (in some measurable way);
- Output was improved (in some measurable way);
- Profitability was increased (in some measurable way).

Stated this way, the information is not only more helpful but also more favorable. Ideas that the ad answerer originated, achievements scored, gains accomplished should be included in a factual way along with the responsibilities held. Although measurable accomplishments are more easily shown for certain types of jobs than others—sales, for example—nevertheless, no matter what the job category, any unusual contributions or developments due to the applicant's efforts are properly included. (Again, see Chapter 14 on resumes.)

How to Write an Effective "Executive-wanted" Ad

Of the two ads below, one pulled 55 responses and provided a successful applicant. The other pulled 358 responses but only 3 were qualified applicants.

PRODUCTION MANAGER

FOR SAN FRANCISCO BAY AREA

Opportunity for an aggressive man with an electrical engineering degree who has had complete responsibility for the operation of a printed-circuit facility for at least 5 years. The man should have the ability to make quotations, meet cost considerations and assume responsibility for quality control program. Previous short-run production experience essential. Attractive salary and fringe benefits. Send resume and salary requirements.

Notice how clear and specific the copy is. The requirements of the job are outlined in sufficient detail to screen out those who aren't close to the target.

OPPORTUNITY IN MANAGEMENT

We are seeking a college graduate who is interested in having a future in the management of a large organization which is leading its industry. He is presently employed in an executive position and is satisfied but is curious about the management potential that exists. The opportunity is most suitable to a man with a proven record. Please submit resume including education, work history and past earnings.

Notice how general and unclear the statement of qualifications is. Almost any job seeker might fit himself into this foggy set of requirements.

The company whose ad is well written saves both time and money, for the effective ad brings in a good sampling of qualified applicants. The poorly written ad, on the other hand, is not only a money waster but a trouble causer. It can involve hours of useless screening, for example, or tie up a company switchboard with applicants phoning in, bringing all other business to a dead halt. The recommendations below spell out some of the guidelines for designing an effective ad.

1. *Select the appropriate medium,* i.e., the newspaper or magazine most likely to be read by the kind of people you are looking for.

Newspaper-wise personnel experts say that in the executive area, four newspapers are topflight: *The New York Times, The Wall Street Journal,* the *Chicago Tribune,* and the *Los Angeles Times.* However, every locality has at least one newspaper that may be used effectively. In addition, almost every executive function boasts one or more professional journals.

2. *Key the ad to the dignity of the job you're seeking to fill.* Executive-wanted ads for advertising executives generally differ in tone and approach from those run for financial executives, for example. Understandably there will be a different acceptance of the bright and original phrase in the advertising world than in banking circles.

Newspaper people who are familiar with life inside the classified sections also suggest that smart-alecky or cute ads be avoided, particularly when seeking executive talent. There are two reasons for this injunction. Any unnatural attempt to be "lively" may give applicants an unbusinesslike idea of the kind of organization behind the ad. Second, offbeat ads are likely to attract offbeat people who don't fit the job specifications.

However, as one executive who uses newspaper ads points out: "We're all selling ourselves, and the big outfit often has an advantage. This means the smaller the firm, the harder the sell."

3. *Walk a tightrope between the specific and the general.* If your ad spells out job qualifications to the nth detail, you may screen out many people you'd want to consider. On the other hand, if you're too general, you'll get a large percentage of responses from people who really don't satisfy your needs.

One experienced recruiter declares that the degree of specificity depends on the availability of people in the job category. If he's looking for a hard-to-get executive, he'll loosen up the qualifications. But if there's a glutted market, he'll raise the qualifications a few notches to skim off the applicants from the top.

4. *State the advantages of your job.* In a competitive market it's always important to stress the special attractions of the job or your company, such as "air-conditioned offices," "central location," "executive dining room," "profit-sharing plan." Special bonuses may give you a desirable edge.

However, there is always the exception that proves the rule. Here's an ad that was run in the classified section of *The New York Times,* by the Connecticut Mutual Life Insurance Co. It has absolutely no company "sell"—and yet it pulled what the company says were "excellent results." Note the freshness of the approach and the writing:

WE NEED A MAN

He is bright and educated. He thinks of himself as a salesman. He is a dedicated problem solver. He is fed up with 'orderly ascensions.' His successes validate his confident manner. He resists being passively molded. He has the capacity for extreme outputs of energy. He is involved. He is a controlled thinker—not an effusive outpourer of garbage. He has an unusual ability to put things in plain English. He does not need the group approach. He is capable of being very honest with himself—All in all, a very superior type—and something of his own kind of guy. Salary plus commission commensurate with ability and background.

5. *Consider when and how often to run your ads.* According to one newspaper ad manager, "Wednesdays are best for secretarial ads, Sundays for executives." Actually the "best" days of the week may vary from area to area or even from one newspaper to another. There is no mystery about this; the person in charge of the classified section can usually give you a helpful steer, but you'll have to pin him down.

Also, as mentioned before, three insertions of an ad generally bring the optimum return. Above that, returns start to diminish in proportion to cost. Keep in mind, however, that responses to executive-wanted ads are *numerically* high. Many companies have found a single insertion brings them the person they eventually hire, especially for the not-hard-to-fill job.

6. *Should you use a blind ad?* There are arguments pro and con on the advisability of identifying a firm name in an ad. But more companies seem to favor the "open" ad, that is, one giving the company name. For one thing, response to an open ad is invariably greater. And, in general, the more you tell about the company, the greater the response will be. Some of the big "name" companies, such as IBM, GE, and GM, have so successfully projected a public image that just giving the company name is sufficient to acquaint the reader with the company picture.

"Use the firm name for high-level jobs, but not for the lower-level ones," advises one veteran personnel officer. His reason: For the higher-level jobs there will be only a few applicants, less likelihood of having a crowd of job seekers turn up at your reception desk the day the ad is placed.

Says another frequent user of space advertising: "I've heard people say, 'We use a box number to save ourselves trouble.' I say if you're looking for a good executive, it pays to take the trouble. You'll certainly get a better response, for many executives simply refuse to answer a blind ad."

7. *Phone screening?* Some companies give the company phone number in the ad because this makes phone screening possible. By asking three or four "knockout" questions a personnel clerk can quickly winnow out unqualified people. The knockout factor may be a specific point relating to experience, education, willingness to relocate, and so on.

If you're afraid that this might jam your trunklines, you have an alternative. In most areas you can have a temporary phone number set up for $10 to $20 as a minimum monthly charge.

8. *Should you mention salary?* One company sometimes tries to solve the salary problem by mentioning a range. Trouble is that every applicant eyes the top figure and justifiably feels cheated if he is offered anything less.

"If I'm hiring a mail boy," states one recruiting executive, "I always state the salary because I know we won't deviate, no matter what experience is involved. In fact, for any job in the lower echelons I'm pretty set on what I'm going to pay.

"At the higher levels, however, I try to leave the salary open. Obviously, a highly qualified man with considerable promise is worth more than a man who just about qualifies but doesn't seem to have much more on the ball than the job calls for."

Some idea of salary levels should generally be given, however, so as to avoid the trouble of screening applicants who ultimately find the salary level unsatisfactory.

The X Factor

Even the most "expert experts" confess that some ad factors are unpredictable:

"I ran the identical ad for an engineering executive on three consecutive Sundays. I got ten responses the first time, ninety-seven the next, and thirty-two the next."

There are all kinds of explanations for an ad's pulling power, or lack of it: The weather on the day the ad runs, the position of the ad on the page, its relation to other ads for similar jobs appearing in the same paper. But in any specific case, it's difficult to pin down *the* reason.

When the Best Costs Less

Obviously, the better-written an ad, the less it costs in the long run. A good ad will smoke out the person you're seeking after one or two insertions. Indirect cost is also lower. The higher the percentage of qualified people who answer the ad, the less time wasted by the initial interviewers.

Should You Use an Advertising Agency?

A number of advertising agencies specialize in personnel and recruitment advertising. In New York City, they include, for example, the Ed Weiss Agency, Deutsch & Shea, Equity Advertising, Diener and Dorskind. One of the biggest firms in this specialized area is located in Philadelphia: the B. K. Davis Agency. Companies utilize these specialists for their considerable know-how on market and media.

Actually, *any* advertising agency can place ads for you and advise on the visual aspects of the advertisement. If you have a good idea as to which newspaper or journal is being read by the people you're looking for, and in which geographical area you're likely to find your man, it will probably pay you to use a small ad agency to do the job, since it won't cost you any more.

The reason is that the agency works on a commission, payable by the advertising medium. You're charged only for the cost of the space, and the agency collects 15 per cent commission for its services—from the medium.

There is one exception to this rule. Some newspapers charge what's called a "locality rate"—a low rate for local companies that isn't commissionable. In this case, the agency would expect to collect a fee—about 15 per cent—from the advertiser.

Dealing through an agency has another advantage; the agency can sometimes save money by contracting for bulk and frequency rates—not generally known to those outside the trade. And an agency can place ads anywhere in the country. For example, an ad that is to be run in fifteen newspapers can be handled by an experienced agency as a matter of routine.

Making Your Ad Dollars Pay Off

Sherman Boxer of the Equity Advertising Agency says his company has 2,500 clients, 70 of which are among the country's so-called "blue-chip" corporations. Boxer's approach to effective space ads, as summed up in the following do's and don't's, is particularly worth noting.

Emphasize and highlight what you're after. "One of the nation's largest electronics companies ran a full-page ad in a well-known Sunday newspaper. It was an expensive flop," says Boxer. "What caused the failure? The ad's sparse recruitment 'sell' copy was buried at the bottom of a page full of type and failed to make clear the nature of the managers being sought."

Build your copy around the factors that motivate executives to change jobs. In telling your job story, relate it to factors that traditionally attract executives: advancement opportunities, salary, location, the prestige of the company or industry.

Don't run a stale ad. Personnel advertising, as other perishable commodities, gets stale when it has been around too long. Says Boxer: "After an ad has run for three insertions, our research department finds a noticeable drop in response, particularly in scarce-talent categories." The best procedure is to alternate different ads, making sure that none of them have been repeated more than three times in the same medium.

Stay clear of gimmincks. Gimmicky headlines, copy, and artwork are questionable in recruitment advertising. Rather than attract executives, these approaches may have the opposite effect. Worst of all, these devices can have an adverse effect on your company's corporate image. However, where the offbeat idea doesn't insult the intelligence, it has been known to score high in appeal.

Communicate with executives in their own language. Executives of particular functional categories tend to use a vernacular all their own. The most effective recruitment ads use this language. But beware: If the copywriter can't handle the special language, it's best for him to avoid it. Using the wrong word in the wrong place can ruin an entire ad. And while still in the language department, avoid clichés such as "challenge," "stimulating opportunity," "unusual position." If you want your ads read, keep their use to a minimum.

Make answering the ads easy. Whatever it is that you want from executive respondents, spell it out simply and clearly. This applies not only to the material you want submitted, such as resumes, but also to the simple matter of the return address. The easier to answer, the more replies your ad will draw.

9

Referral—the Great Glad Hand

"I'm sorry we have no opening for you," says Harry King, president of the East-West Import Company, "you certainly have a lot on the ball. But come to think of it, Ben Larrabee over at Russet Oil has been looking for a marketing man. Ben's their executive vice-president and a friend of mine. I'll be glad to phone and ask him to set up an appointment with you. . . . "

A referral has just been made. Unimportant? Far from it. Seldom mentioned in the personnel textbooks, referrals probably account for as many of the outstandingly successful executive placements as any of the formal methods. And they cost nothing—to the job seeker, or the company.

Referrals can also start at the other end of the hiring process. For example, Lester Bailey is having lunch with Henry West of the law firm of Baruch, Leland, Tomplin and West. Says Bailey: "Hank, we're hunting for a really bright young guy to put in the No. 2 spot of our real estate department. Eventually he'll be head. If you happen to know of someone who's ready to make a change. . . . "

The referrals discussed in this chapter are those that spring from *informal* sources. Technically speaking, formal sources—employment agencies, the so-called "executive registers," job guidance counselors—also make referrals since they recommend clients to specific employers. But the pages immediately ahead focus on those job leads that come about seemingly by chance or, at least, through individuals or organizations not ordinarily in the business of job prospecting. The possibility of the informal referral not only opens up a whole new set of opportunities for the job seeker, but also requires new approaches on his part.

For the company, too, the informal referral can be an excellent means of recruiting—and a method too often neglected precisely because the
100

"rules of the game" are not clearly defined. We hope to rectify this gap here.

A Greatly Underrated Method

Referrals may be the least expensive and the quickest way for job hunter to meet talent seeker. From a company's viewpoint, referrals may prove an excellent way to get recruits. For example, from time to time General Electric has asked its technical and professional personnel to recommend friends and acquaintances for jobs, with very good results. "The quality of the people we get by this means," says a GE spokesman, "is gratifyingly high." Yet, as a recruitment method, referral is perhaps the most slighted. There are several explanations for this "low estate." First, referrals depend largely on chance. Second, they involve personal relationships that sometimes bend under the burden of a touchy favor. Third, they are uncommercial; no large profits are involved; therefore, no one pushes the method.

The key question for both company and job seeker is, "How can the referral be made more effective?" In part, the answer lies in a better understanding of just how the procedure works. Accordingly, this analysis starts with a consideration of the advantages and disadvantages, as well as the various mechanisms involved in the referral process.

Advantages to the Job Seeker

One of the main attractions of the referral route is that it costs literally nothing. (Token gifts in appreciation of the helping hand that led to a job don't really count.)

Another benefit: The interviewer is likely to be more relaxed and friendly than in the usual job interview because of his shared acquaintance with "the middleman." The job seeker, on his part, usually benefits psychologically from the "referral atmosphere." The relaxed manner of the interviewer is contagious, and he'll find it easier to sell himself before a friendly audience.

There are two unique advantages to coming into an interview under the aegis of a friend or business contact. (1) The job seeker avoids the three traditional hurdles: that guardian angel of an executive's privacy, his secretary; diversion to a lower-echelon executive; diversion to a personnel-department interviewer, who seldom plays a part in executive hiring. (2) In many cases the middleman's relation to the interviewer may actually influence the latter to favor the job seeker over other candidates for the job. This is apt to happen if the middleman is a big customer of the employing company, if he's a top executive in a hiring operation taking place down the line in his company, or if he's "owed a favor" by the prospective employer.

Finally, the referral interview can boast a further advantage. If the interviewer has no job opening at the time, and he has a sense of obligation, he is likely to be willing to suggest other executives or companies that the interviewee might contact. This, of course, makes him a middleman in his own right, and continues the referral chain.

Disadvantages to the Job Seeker

No path is rose-strewn its entire length, and the referral route is no exception. Here are some of the potential disadvantages.

• *The referral is a chancy method.* Since you don't know in advance when, from whom, or to whom you'll be referred, you cannot prepare for a standardized process. For example, the middleman may fail to properly assess the job seeker's qualifications or career interests and send him on a wild-goose chase. Or, if the job seeker tries to make referrals a major part of his job-finding program, he may be unable to find any middleman capable of suggesting worthwhile calls.

• *Time can be wasted.* This happens for a number of reasons. For example, Job Seeker X is recommended to top executive Y. But Mr. Y is away on a business trip, and won't return for three weeks. X may defer other calls until he sees Y because it's an important referral.

A more direct loss of time may come about precisely because of the good relations between the middleman and the interviewing executive. "I'll be glad to see you," says a plant manager, when contacted by a job seeker under the sponsorship of the manager's brother. This very willingness to see a job seeker may result in interviews even though there is no opening, no need for the seeker's particular skills, and so on.

• *Risk that news will leak out to the present employer.* In certain cases, the referral route becomes perilous because the job seeker must let it be known that he is on the prowl for a job. If he is presently employed, and is looking for a job in a tightly-knit industry where everybody knows everybody else's business, following up on a referral may let the cat out of the bag.

• *You're on the receiving end of a "favor."* Some individuals are made uncomfortable by the fact that referrals depend on the kindness of others and on the seeker's ability to accept "favors" from strangers. Actually, however, although such sensibilities are understandable, they are not really appropriate. In the first place, most people get pleasure from being able to lend someone a helping hand. They will often remember back to a time when they were job hunting, and identify favorably with the man they are interviewing.

Second, sentiment aside, many executives feel that it's good business to refer job hunters to possible employers. It keeps the business ball rolling. And, when a capable man is placed, the middleman not only knows he's done a good turn, both to the seeker and the employer, but that the "bread cast upon the waters" may return to him at some later date.

Advantages to the Employer

The obvious advantage to the company in the market for executive talent is that referrals involve no expense. But absence of cost isn't the only reason for using referrals as a recruiting method. Others may be equally attractive.

• *Goodwill of employees.* Few men, regardless of their job level, can help being flattered when asked by the boss to refer friends and acquaintances for possible employment. It gives them a chance to do a favor. Some shrewd executives have even used this request to hold the confidence of an executive who might feel threatened by the new hire.

• *Free PR from an authoritative source.* When a company employee plays the role of middleman, he inevitably talks up the company to his friends, dwells on its attractive features. Even if weak points are mentioned, the predominating picture must be favorable, or the middleman wouldn't expect his candidates to follow through on his recommendations.

• *Minimum of prescreening.* If you give employees or business friends a clear idea of the kind of man you're looking for, you're unlikely to get any large percentage of unqualified people to waste your time.

• *Chance to pay off a "debt."* This needn't be as crass as it sounds. Businessmen occasionally owe a return favor for services rendered. Asking a colleague or a business friend to send along a prospect for a job can be a pleasant way to even up the balance.

Pitfalls for Company

Some companies shy away from referrals because they've been burned. Unfavorable experiences may result from situations such as these.

• *The job seeker isn't hired.* Companies run some risk that the feelings of the middleman will be hurt if the man he recommends doesn't get the job. He may take it as a reflection on his judgment or his astuteness in "knowing how to pick a man." But this possibility can be generally avoided if the interviewing executive makes it clear to the person presenting a job candidate that the chances of hiring are uncertain: "I'd be glad to see anyone you think I should talk to," says one veteran executive, "but as you know, our needs are so specific and unique that we cannot make any promises about taking on your man. However, why don't you have him call me for an appointment. . . . "

• *The executive recruit doesn't work out.* "We hired the good friend of our company president," reports the personnel vice-president of a California chemical company, "and we all had reason to regret it. For reasons beyond anyone's control, the man failed in the job, badly. Then we were stuck, because we didn't feel as free to replace him as a man we had picked up by impersonal means."

Of course, in similar situations, there can be a kickback if the man doesn't work out and is fired. "One of my customers has held it against me because I had to fire a protégé of his who just wasn't up to the job we'd given him. Pretty small-minded of him, I must say." And unrealistic as well. No matter how well-recommended a man is, failure at the job is always a possibility.

• *Time wasted in "courtesy" interviews.* Occasionally top executives come to feel they're sitting ducks for relatives, friends, and business contacts seeking jobs for their friends. "I'd have to be the United States government," says one company president wryly, "to be able to place all the people I'm asked to see." Despite his cynicism and his awareness of the time wasted, he continues to see job prospectors who are referred to him. He does just enough screening to avoid the completely unqualified prospects.

Several executives who don't feel troubled by courtesy interviews, however, report that they manage to keep interviews short without hurting any feelings by showing a friendly interest, yet staying close to the purpose of the meeting. Says one, "You can discuss a man's background and career goals, express interest in what he's done, and, at the same time, let him know you have no opening: 'Unfortunately, because of the nature of our business, your particular experience just has no application here. I'm sorry, because I've certainly been impressed by. . . .' "

How Job Seekers Can Rate the Potential of a Referral

Any executive job seeker who secures and uses referrals learns early that referrals *per se* don't all have equal value. One may be extremely worthwhile; another may be a complete waste of time:

REFERRAL 1. "My boy," says J. P. Jones, "you go see Jerry Rice at Acme Leverage. He'll give you a job. . . . " The "boy" in this case can be pretty sure he'll be offered a job, because old J. P. happens to be a major stockholder in Acme Leverage.

REFERRAL 2. "It's a big company," a friend tells the job hunter, "and I imagine they could use you. Why not go up there?" Value, zero.

There are two factors that determine the value of a referral to a job seeker: (1) the degree of job availability, (2) the ability of the middleman to influence a hiring decision.

How a Company Can Develop Good Referral Sources

The trick to developing unsolicited referrals is to recognize the types of middlemen who are most likely to be in contact with the types of employees you want.

Needless to say, this depends on the nature of the job you're trying to fill, and the kind of business you're in. Here are the most common referral sources and what to keep in mind with respect to each:

Banks, etc. Companies seeking financial or accounting executives often turn to banks. As noted in *The Fringe Operators* section, page 65, some banks serve almost as professional searchers in referring individuals to clients. Banks are a good source because they must be aware of their own interests; hence, they will only make referrals that they feel will be favorable to job seeker and company alike. The problem for the employer is to describe accurately the job he is trying to fill, and the man he needs to fill it.

Law firms, accounting firms, and, in some cases, *insurance companies,* also will refer qualified people to customers or clients who are seeking executive personnel.

Employees. Generally, it's not advisable to ask employees to recommend people for jobs at higher levels than their own. There are two reasons for this. First, the employee may simply fail to understand the requirements of the job. For example: "There is an unemployed executive who lives in my apartment building," says a mail boy, trying to be helpful, to the head of the personnel department. "Shall I have him get in touch with you?" Despite the good intentions of the mail boy, it's unlikely his executive neighbor is likely to have the background that's being looked for—but to him, an executive is an executive.

Second, the applicant who walks into an interview bearing an introduction from someone down the line is at a certain disadvantage. He feels a burden, either real or psychological, to raise himself in the estimation of the interviewer. While this hurdle can be readily enough cleared if the man has the desired qualifications, it may be rough on him at the start.

When you broach the subject of referral to a company staff member, make sure that there is no reason why he shouldn't be made privy to the hunt.

Professional contacts. If you're looking for an executive in a specific field, your best source of referrals is likely to be friends and acquaintances in the same profession. Almost every executive function has its own professional organizations. Also, these people have friends from their professional schooldays.

People "in the trade." Many companies are part of a fairly well-defined business area—textiles, advertising, the theatre, mining, chemicals, oil.

These enclaves in the total business picture tend to have a unity that puts many people in a position to "know what's going on." Another characteristic of an industry unit is the "grapevine," fed by salesmen, trade journals, professional and management organizations, and so on.

People in the trade know what's going on. They know that the X company is hiring. They know that Philip R———, who bought for Y company for five years, is "looking." They know which companies are growing, merging, going bankrupt, reorganizing, and so on. These individuals in the know can be excellent middlemen, for either end of the recruiting scale.

Friends, club and social contacts. Of all the referral sources, social and community contacts are in some ways the best. Nevertheless, it's generally the most difficult to capitalize on. Since your relationships with these individuals exist outside the business framework, unbusinesslike attitudes and values may intrude. And, as one top executive in a real estate firm reported, "Everyone in my community who has an unemployed relative seems to think I can give him a job. When it develops that I usually can't, the word goes out that I'm a stinker."

Nevertheless, even this source can yield riches if properly mined. The following section explains how to go about it.

How a Company Can Develop "Talent Scouts"

Naturally, you will vary your approach, depending on the individual or organization you're using as a source of referrals. You would approach your banker in a different manner than you would a personal friend. For that matter, you would probably expect different sources to refer different types of people. This is the first rule:

1. *The source should be appropriate for the type of man you're seeking.* Just as you can't expect a company employee from the lower echelons to recommend a top executive, don't look to your law firm for an engineering executive or to your accountants as a source for a good sales manager.

In most cases, the appropriateness of the source vis-à-vis the type of executive you're looking for is fairly clear-cut. A personal friend who is a production man is obviously a good source for a referral if you're looking for a production executive. A fellow member of your golf club might be able to recommend a management engineer if he is one himself. An old hunting and fishing buddy of yours might be able to recommend a bright young graduate of the Harvard Business School if he himself is a Harvard alumnus.

2. *Make your approach tentative.* It's very important that you commit yourself to nothing in advance. Otherwise, your middleman may mistakenly believe that anyone he cares to recommend will automatically get the job.

One executive keeps himself out of trouble by making a very offhand pitch: "Jim, we may be in the market for an office manager in the next few months. If you happen to know anyone who you think would fit in, I'd be glad to see him along with some of the other candidates I've already been interviewing."

3. *Make sure the middleman understands what you're looking for.* Granting the middleman's ability to understand (the importance of this was shown earlier), it is up to you to get across to him the qualifications you're looking for. Important to remember: If you were using an executive-search specialist, you might have to spend a couple of hours describing your needs. The nonprofessional "searcher" requires at least an equally complete and careful briefing.

4. *Once you have set the middleman in motion, you are more or less obligated to see anyone he recommends.* This is a matter both of logic and courtesy.

For one thing, you're under some obligation to follow through on the action you started. But secondly, if the man who is referred to you is all wrong for the job, you should find out the reason. Does it reflect uncertainty on your part about what the job needs? Lack of confidence in the candidate's qualifications? Your inability to communicate what's wanted to a second person? Or is it poor understanding on the middleman's part that resulted in the misfit?

5. *Follow-through.* Most top executives, as a routine courtesy, send thank-you letters both to the middlemen and the applicants they have sent along. This is not only good public relations but also a means of keeping your middlemen for further service, should you need them again.

The remainder of this chapter will be devoted to the means by which the executive job hunter can develop referrals as an effective part of his job-finding program.

How the Job Seeker Can Develop Job Spotters

When the executive is seeking a job (rather than a new employee), referrals, too, can frequently succeed when other methods of job finding fail. Certainly, it's an approach that should be included in *every* job-seeking program, regardless of what other methods are tried.

Referrals can come from a great variety of sources:

Colleagues and other executives in your present (or former) company.
Friends and relatives with business connections.
Business acquaintances, especially those "in the trade."
Other job seekers, met in the course of the hunt.
Suppliers, service companies that do business with the types of companies considered potential employers.

Executives you interview for a job who, for one reason or another, fail to make a job offer. (These tend to be particularly good sources of referrals, since they know the field at which you're aiming.)

In addition to these expected sources, the job hunter who remains alert to his surroundings and the people he meets can often secure perfectly good referrals from virtual strangers.

However, to use the referral path effectively, you've got to develop and follow a systematic approach. Here are the most important factors to take into account:

1. *Expect the snowball phenomenon.* "Everyone is so eager to help," remarked one executive with surprise, after his first week of serious job hunting. Yet this sums up a fairly general experience. People do like to help, and they will sometimes go to extreme lengths to give the job seeker a boost.

The snowball phenomenon is so called because one contact can lead to several referrals, and each of these in turn may lead to still others.

Many job seekers have discovered that all they need to get the snowball rolling for them is to start a job hunt. Out of the process of job seeking itself come the helping hands.

2. *Learn to spot the potential middlemen.* Regardless of good intentions, not everyone can bird-dog a job opportunity for you. But you can easily develop the ability to spot the people who are likely to be helpful out of the many you'll meet in your job-hunting travels.

Here is a partial list of some of the situations that produce worthwhile middlemen:

• *Chance contacts in your job-hunting rounds.* You may visit an employment agency that tells you, "Sorry, we don't do any placing in your field." No reason for you not to ask whether they have any ideas as to how you can go about uncovering job leads.

Almost anyone you contact may be asked whether he "has any ideas" for leads, whether he can "suggest anyone to see." Surprisingly often, executives report, "I got a referral from another job hunter. He'd heard about a job opening that was in my field, not his, and passed it along."

• *Tapping those who know "business influentials."* If you "know someone who knows someone," or still better, if you know someone yourself who is highly placed in business, it's usually worth trying to follow up on the contact. As has been pointed out, banks, accounting and law firms sometimes do recruiting as a sideline. In one sense, *every* company and every top executive does informal recruiting. If asked, a top-echelon executive might very well be able to furnish half a dozen leads. The referrals won't always mean jobs, but they'll get the job seeker that much closer to a job payoff.

Your social contacts, your professional contacts—your doctor, lawyer, banker, clergyman—may be the "someone" who knows a business influential.

Your friends, relatives, lodge brothers, fellow club members, all may have contacts that are worth noting down, and scheduling for follow-up as part of your job-finding program.

• *Job interviews that don't pan out.* As long as there is any chance of a job interview's producing an offer, you should forget about the referral possibility. But in the course of your job hunting you're likely to have half a dozen or so interviews that may not lead to a job. Once you're sure that there's no likelihood of your being hired, you can simply shift gears with the man you're talking to. Where you approached him originally as a possible employer, now you want to convert him into a middleman.

Various approaches can bring this transformation about:

"Mr. Smith, I guess it's pretty obvious that your needs here at the Acme Company are outside my experience. Do you perhaps know of other companies that might be interested in a man of my background and capabilities?"

"Mr. Jones, it appears that your type of operation isn't the kind to which I can make an effective contribution, despite my experience. Are there any other companies in this field that you could recommend to me?"

3. *Get the man personally interested in you.* This may seem like a vacuous recommendation, but the fact is, referrals depend on spontaneous goodwill, and you want to be sure to elicit positive feelings. If you've ever been a middleman yourself, you will remember that it was the other man's friendliness, forthrightness, and ability to gain your interest that stimulated your desire to help him.

These are the same qualities that will make a booster out of the man you're talking to.

4. *Be forthright and clear about the kind of position you're after.* Avoid putting yourself in an embarrassing position—and eliminating a good middleman—by letting him make false assumptions about the type of job or salary level you're interested in. You want to avoid communications that end in dead ends such as this: "Yes, Mr. White, I am looking for a treasurer's job, but the firm you described couldn't possibly pay at the salary level I'm asking. . . ."

5. *Give him enough information so he can help you.* Give your potential middleman your job resume and a brief description of the kind of position you're seeking. You don't have to go into details, but at the very least designate possible job titles, size of company, the field of business in which you're interested, salary level.

In addition, give him the chance to ask you any specific questions he might have. He may have some contacts in mind. But before referring you, he might want to know whether you'd be willing to move or to leave one line of business for another, whether you'd take a position as "second in command," etc.

6. *Ask for contacts.* As every salesman knows, you don't get the order unless you ask for it. If the potential middleman doesn't volunteer the names of companies or executives right away, this doesn't mean he doesn't know of any. The one thing you must do to elicit referrals is to make a direct request. This needn't be done in an aggressive or unpleasant manner. Nor do you have to give the impression you're putting the man on the spot. The trick is to be direct and yet give him a chance to say "no" gracefully. For example: "Mr. Black, you undoubtedly have contacts in the machine-tool field since you do business with machine-tool manufacturers. Are there any executives in those companies that you think I might call on?"

There's another trick to getting referrals. Always ask the executive whether he can think of "two or three companies" that might be interested in your qualifications, *not* "Can you give me the name of another company?" One veteran job hunter says the difference in response is amazing. Asked for several names casually, an executive may rattle off five or six. Asked for "one" good referral, the same man will scratch his head and say he's sorry but he just hasn't heard of any openings recently.

And no matter how many referrals you get, if said in the proper tone, you may put in, "Any other possibilities you'd like to add to the list?"

7. *May I use your name?* Executive after executive stressed the willingness of a middleman to pick up the phone and call a friend or a business contact for a referral interview. The more on your side a potential middleman feels, the greater the lengths he will go to help you.

Despite this willingness, it's always desirable where the individual has not clarified this point to ask, "In talking to Mr. White, may I use your name?"

Usually the answer is "yes." But the middleman may, for reasons of his own, prefer that his name not be used and then, of course, you have no choice but to respect his wishes.

In this case, follow-up on his referral requires a little more circumspection than when you're free to use a name. In practical terms, it means falling back on such openings as "I have been led to believe" or "A mutual acquaintance whose name I'm not at liberty to divulge."

8. *Get the name of the right man to see.* This is crucial for the worthwhile referral. Being told by a well-meaning middleman that there may be an opening at the Y company because it has just opened a new subsidiary is not a referral. The bona fide referral is to a person, not to a company; it's to a specific executive, not a branch or a department.

One special caution, urged by many job seekers who have been burned: "Make sure your entree into a company isn't *at a lower level than the job you're seeking.* If you're looking for a job as production manager, for example, and a middleman says, "I know Jim Haynes over there, he's head of Engineering . . . ," find out somehow where Jim Haynes is on the organization chart—at, above, or below the production manager job. Otherwise, you may spoil your chances in the company irremediably.

Some people say it's all right to come in at the same level as the one you're aiming for: "If you're looking for a job at division level," says one personnel executive, "it's all right to have your entree into the company be through another division head." Perhaps—but there's no doubt that the higher the level of your referral, the stronger your position will be.

9. *Thank the middleman for his efforts.* And let him know the outcome of your call. The only caution here is to avoid overdoing it. You want to express your appreciation without being saccharine, and you want to let him know the outcome without excessive demands on his time.

If the interview has fallen through, a brief note, with a restatement of your gratitude, is appropriate.

In the happy event that the referral has led to a job, a letter of thanks is usually adequate. Some executives would also think that a material token of thanks might very well be in order.

But it's the sincerity of your gratitude that is important. Many a successful job hunter has made a permanent friend and ally of the middleman who has helped him find a position. And, of course, it works both ways.

10

Direct Mail—
Let the Mailman Do Your Legwork

There is no "one best way" to find a job, or to recruit an executive, says Jack Pierson of The Personnel Laboratory, Stamford, Connecticut. The most effective approach is to work "in parallel" rather than "in series." In other words, you carry on several different approaches at the same time, instead of trying one and exhausting it, turning to the next, then to the next, and so on.

In the various "parallel" combinations, one of the most-used approaches is direct mail. It has a particular virtue for the job seeker—it doesn't conflict with other job-hunting activities. The executive can carry out the mail campaign evenings and weekends.

Direct mail also has a special advantage when a company is recruiting. Once a procedure is set up, the talent hunt can be turned over to a secretary, with the responsible executives coming into the picture at key points —to select mailing lists, write the letters, assess the returns, etc.

Do Executives Read Direct Mail?

Some job hunters may hesitate to start a direct-mail campaign because they've heard that "top executives don't read mail" or that their correspondence is so finely screened by superefficient secretaries that only official business gets through.

"This is just not true," contends Al Buchanan, former president of New York's Mail Order Club, member of the board of governors of the Direct Mail Advertising Association, and executive in charge of an outstandingly successful selling-by-mail operation, "There is an amazing acceptance of mail by recipients in even the highest echelons."

Research studies bear him out, indicating that about 58 per cent of

112

people who receive mail will read it, regardless of the subject matter. Although this figure is partly offset by some 10 per cent who strenuously object to receiving any kind of mail, even communications from friends, it is clear that there exists a comfortable balance of potentially interested readership. Of course, the more skillful the letter, the better the response.

The most effective approach is a sharpshooter letter, aimed at a small and specific target group. A resume or other material may be enclosed. But it is the pertinence of the letter, and its direct appeal to the reader, that brings the desired result. The executive interested in changing jobs would like the postman to ring twice: once at the prospective employer's door, once at his own. Such a result can be achieved by a procedure modeled along the lines spelled out below.

The Essentials of a Direct-Mail Campaign

Any job-hunting executive will almost certainly get results if he follows the six ground rules below. But it should be noted that although the rules are simple, their application requires time, effort, and thought. Moreover, *all* are important. This is no occasion for shortcuts.

1. *Understand the purpose of your letter.* The communication you send has one purpose, and one purpose only—to get you a job interview. It's not supposed to get you a job. Essentially it's what magazine writers call a "query letter"—one written to sound out or to create interest.

The importance of this point is that it acts as a guide to what you say and how you say it. For example, the wise direct-mail campaigner won't include a torrent of material about himself that is sure to douse any flicker of interest that he may have generated. First and foremost, you want to arouse interest—to a level sufficient to get you an interview.

2. *Develop your mailing list carefully.* Remember, what you're after is the establishment of a personal contact with the responsible executive in a company where you'd like to work. Accordingly, you should resist the temptation to scatter your shots. If you're looking for an R & D job in the plastics industry, don't send a letter to every plastics company in the phone book, or to every president of every plastics company. Here's an example of an effective approach.

A printing-production executive decided he wanted to work in a large company as liaison man between the company and its suppliers of printing. He spent hours talking to his friends in the printing field until he finally sifted out the names of six large companies who were major purchasers of printing. Out of his six letters, he got four interviews—and eventually a job with one of the companies.

Most job seekers will start out with mailing lists made up from their own or their friends' knowledge of the trade or industry. These may become exhausted before results are achieved. At this point selected industry lists may be bought commercially. For example, two firms that sell mailing lists to the public are Dunhill International List Company, 444 Park Avenue South, New York City, 10016, and W. S. Ponton, 44 Honeck Street, Englewood, New Jersey. Both these companies have catalogues showing thousands of different list classifications, and will send you one or more catalogues, free on request. There are many "list" companies. Ask your friends who may be familiar with them to make recommendations, or check the yellow pages of the phone directory.

While the commercial lists are not likely to be as satisfactory as those compiled from personal knowledge (they are not completely accurate, for one thing), they may be worth the price if you are willing to undertake a shotgun approach, and if you have an idea as to the category of company you want to reach. A major objection to the bought list is that it doesn't tell you anything about the individual companies. The importance of this point is explained below.

3. *Get the "low-down" on the company.* The companies that belong on your lists should be selected on the basis of the kind of job you're after. Then, just as in selling a product, you should know something—at least the essential points—about the company that you're "calling on." (See page 180 on the job interview for details of how to get a line on a prospect company.)

Suffice it to say here, only when you know enough about a company's operations can you decide whether or not it may be able to use your services.

4. *Be sure it's addressed to "Mr. Rightman."* To a considerable degree, the "pull" of a letter depends on its getting to the desk of the appropriate man in the prospective company. This "Rightman" often is the company president. But he may also be the chairman of the board, head of a particular function—engineering, production, marketing, and so on.

Exactly who Rightman is depends on the company and the nature of the job being sought. Most executives have sufficient organizational know-how to understand that a letter, as an executive candidate himself, can readily be referred down the line, once contact has been made. Movement upward is less likely to take place. In other words, when in doubt, aim the communication *higher up* the ladder, rather than lower.

There's a simple way to learn the name of the man you should be addressing. Telephone the company, and ask the name of the man in charge of the function in which you're interested. Such inquiries are routine, and generally everybody from the switchboard girl to Mr. Rightman's secretary will be glad to oblige you. Where telephoning is prohibitive because of distance, write and ask the personnel department for the information.

Another possibility: Refer to directories. For example, Dun & Bradstreet's *Million Dollar Directory* gives the names of all company officers, including those responsible for specialized functions in firms with a net worth of 1 million dollars or more. Also, most industries have their own special trade directories which show the names of managers. The standard reference book for locating these volumes—on the shelf in most libraries that have a business section—is *Klein's Guide to American Directories.*

5. *Write your letter.* If you're good with words, you'll naturally write the letter yourself. But if you have any doubts about your letter-writing ability, don't hesitate to call on friends or colleagues for help. A combined effort may produce the exact result you want. And don't confine the possibilities to your own circles. Many executives have found that it pays to utilize the services of a professional writer, such as an advertising copywriter, newspaper reporter, magazine editor, or even a customer-relations person who does correspondence.

One warning: No matter how skillful the writer whose services you employ, you should do the final editing to make sure the letter has the right *tone.* For example, if you're an engineering executive, technical language might appear in your letter. An outside writer, unfamiliar with those terms, may sound a false note. It's up to you to see that the "feel" of the letter, as well as the grammar, clarity, development, and so on, is completely acceptable.

6. *Be systematic.* Of course, you should be methodical in all your job-hunting plans and actions. But a mail campaign, in particular, requires records to help you keep track of what you've done, what needs doing, and what should be followed up.

An adequate record-keeping system should include all of the following steps:

- Make written list of prospects.
- Keep carbons of all letters sent, and make a note on each carbon of any enclosures.
- Decide how many letters to send off in each mailing. Don't make your mailings *too small.* Some job seekers unconsciously do this to prolong the usefulness of a short list. But equally important, don't make them *too big.* One man sent out two hundred query letters, then got bogged down for weeks in the details of reading, sorting, and answering the responses that asked for more information, suggested meetings, and so on. On the average, twenty letters at a time is about right, at weekly intervals.
- Chart date of sending and date replies are received. Although your carbons will show the date a mailing went off, you may want to keep a record on a chart, so you can see at a glance whether you're getting replies to your letters.
- In cases where a company's reply requires another letter from you,

set up a filing system with all communications between you and the firms that are showing an interest, in individual company folders.

Setting the Right Tone

Despite the six ground rules above, there is no "one best way" to write the job-hunting letter itself. This is because the effectiveness of a mailing piece depends largely on the nature of the persons at the receiving end. And in such a campaign, you're often sending letters out "blind," addressing yourself to an unknown reader or readers. This creates some problems.

For example, should your letter be short or long? It may just happen that you are dealing with a man who likes as much detail as possible before taking action. He may interpret brevity as a lack of substance, and toss the short letter into the wastebasket.

But the reverse is also possible. A factual letter, replete with personal details, may fall into the hands of an executive who prefers his communications to be of the bare-bones variety. Accordingly, he'll mutter, "Haven't the time," and wastebasket the carefully detailed missive.

Obviously, the best you can do is to work along in a direction in which the odds favor you. If your background has many interesting or unique facets, you'll take a chance on a longer rather than a shorter letter. But most executives will do best to follow a middle course, making the letter neither short nor long, neither too detailed nor too skeletal. The guidelines below can help you.

1. *Visualize the man you're addressing.* See him in his milieu. It's a fairly safe bet, for example, that your letter will be received with a pile of other miscellaneous mail. The prospect will probably be under the pressure of a typical executive work load. Chances are, too, that there will be at least one secretary standing between your letter and the executive. Once you "see" these details, some of the reasons for the kind of letter you will write become clearer.

2. *Start off on the right foot.* The stationery you use, the quality of the typing, the format of the letter should enhance your image as a qualified executive. Further, in your very first sentence you should try to catch your man's attention. This *doesn't* mean that you use a slick advertising ploy—"Now at last, Mr. Executive, your problems are over!" or "Found! A production genius who can double your profits in a year's time."

More-appropriate attention-getting beginnings are possible:

"Mr. X, yours is one of five companies to which I am sending this letter. I have carefully selected these five firms because. . . ."

If the letter is a follow-up of a referral by a middleman, use the name at the outset: "Mr. X, Elmer Q. Smith suggested that I write you. . . ."

3. *Make it personal, direct, and dignified.* Breeziness and informality

may be acceptable for an advertising copywriter, but it won't do for the average executive. The same qualities that are valued in the executive personality are virtues in a letter. Your ability to get to the point, to express yourself clearly, to be personal without being offensive—these are all desirable elements.

4. *Have a second person read the letter.* No matter how good a letter writer you are, you'll probably want to get some outside reactions and suggestions. But use your judgment in evaluating the comments of friends and family. For example, a wife, however well meaning, may simply be unaware of executive attitudes, values, practices. A comment that "it sounds fine," or, "do you want to be that aggressive," or, "aren't you being a little too polite" may be way off the beam. At any rate, she's your wife, and you'll have to judge.

On the other hand, a business friend or an executive in the same echelon as the man you're addressing can be of great help. In addition to the reactions he'll volunteer, you'll want to ask questions such as these:

"What sort of picture emerges from the letter? Does it reflect my best characteristics? Is it appropriate for the job I'm seeking?" For example, a marketing executive and an engineering executive should produce two letters with entirely different tone.

"Have I been provocative enough, and aroused sufficient interest to make someone anxious to see me?" You don't want to promise anything you can't deliver, but you certainly should be able to generate some "buy" interest—or at least a "will see" impulse—by highlighting your strong points.

"Have I angled the letter to a single sharp point?" (The elements of a good letter will be presented shortly.)

"Have I left in any negative points, fuzzy spots, misleading statements?" Of course, you don't want to misrepresent. But if there are any points in your background that you suspect may be an obstacle to your being hired, leave it to the job interview to take care of them. Inserted in your letter, they will quench interest at once.

Developing Hot Leads

The alert job seeker need not rely entirely on industry lists and other standard sources for leads. Trade papers and business pages of newspapers can give you timely prospects. For example, one topflight sales promotion manager says that he twice secured jobs by writing to firms who were advertising for salesmen, on the principle that if they wanted to develop their sales force, they probably had a need for his talents, too.

Another executive points out that newly promoted executives are often good targets. They can be reached when they are in a mood or mind to reorganize and employ new people. (One executive even spotted a vacancy by reading the obituary columns!) The crucial point in developing such leads is to distinguish between those that are and aren't appropriate. Not likely to be well received is a query letter that says:

"Dear Mr. Smith, I see by the papers that you've just been made president of your company. On the chance that you're in the market for capable executive talent, let me tell you my outstanding qualifications," etc., etc.

By contrast, a letter angled to a specific activity indicates by its contents that the applicant knows the score. This approach, for example, won the writer an interview:

> Dear Mr. Jones:
> Congratulations on your recent appointment to head up a new information retrieval operation in your company. My background in the information retrieval field, as sketched out in the enclosed resume, may be of interest to you. May I stop in to see you one day next week, to explore employment possibilities. . . .

"I Recommend My Friend Mr. X"

The previous chapter on referrals suggests that occasionally a middleman, instead of simply giving the job seeker a name, or making a phone call, may be willing to write a letter of recommendation.

A letter of this type generally gets a favorable response if there is any job possibility at all. The recipient is likely to feel, "If Bill has gone to the trouble of writing me, he must feel this guy is worth my time."

If the job hunter is lucky, he will find an influential middleman, perhaps his ex-employer, who volunteers to do a mass mailing for him. That is, he'll mail out ten or twenty letters to his professional and business contacts, telling of the availability and qualifications of the job seeker. He may even include the job seeker's resume. Sometimes, he may ask an agency that does personnel space advertising, or that specializes in direct mail, to undertake this type of job-finding assignment.

Such an approach can be highly effective. Not only is it a help to the separated executive; it also has advantages for the company. Helping a man get a job is always impressive to the rest of the staff. It's one of the critical situations in which a business organization can demonstrate its interest in the welfare of its people—even those who are no longer on the payroll.

Direct mail is a particularly effective means of job-finding when undertaken by a company on behalf of a soon-to-be-separated employee. The "personal touch" represented by a letter is appropriate. The fact that the company can use a selected list of prospects gives the effort additional impact.

For the executive leaving a company, this suggestion may be made: If your employer is willing to cooperate, you may ask that such a campaign be undertaken on your behalf. Assist the effort by offering a list of companies you feel would be promising targets for a letter—in addition to those your employer might suggest.

Successful Campaigns—Two Experiences

Any serious use of direct mail for job hunting should be organized as carefully as any other consistent and planned effort. Reports one St. Paul company president: "I know of a young man aged thirty-three who was unable to find a job suitable to his talents and salary expectations. A friend worked up a letter and circulated it among presidents of national corporations in groups of ten, so that all inquiries could be followed up promptly. At the end of six weeks, a job was secured with an outstanding national firm."

Another case history, reported by an executive of a building-materials firm in Boston: "A purchasing agent in Boston, receiving a substantial salary and employed by a multimillion-dollar building concern, decided to move to Florida, partly for health reasons. He contacted all major builders in the state of Florida through a series of mailings. Within a month, he received four favorable replies, one of which led to the purchasing job he wanted."

Mechanics of Production

In using the mail, the physical appearance of "the package" isn't everything, but it's *almost* everything. Poorly typed letters, sleazy stationery, badly assembled material are the equivalent of turning up unkempt and bleary-eyed for an interview. If the job hunter has any doubts about his ability to produce an attractive mailing on his own, he'd do well to call for professional help.

Any city of 25,000 population or more usually will have a "letter shop" listed in the yellow pages of the local phone book. Such services will address envelopes, produce a facsimile letter (preferably with a hand-typed address and greeting), reproduce a resume, and do the mailing.

Six Ways to Increase the Effectiveness of Your Letter

People who have had experience in writing query letters to prospective employers say that the job-hunting executive tends to be puzzled by a number of questions. Here are the six most commonly asked questions and some useful answers:

Q. "Should I enclose a resume with my query letter?"

A. Generally, yes. The reason is that the executive you have addressed may want to pass your query along to a colleague. If you provide a resume, the two men will then have something specific to talk about—your qualifications. Also, if he should want to mention you to someone outside the company, he might hesitate to pass along your letter since it has been directed to him personally. But the resume doesn't have the personal quality and makes the referral possible.

Q. "What can I do if I don't receive an answer?"

A. If you're particularly interested in a company, write a follow-up letter. Or, if possible, phone and explain that you are calling to find out whether a letter you sent had arrived. (If a secretary asks why you're calling, you can use the same approach with her.) At this point, there are several possibilities—

• The executive may have discarded your letter, in which case you may be told, "I'm sorry but we aren't interested."

• A negative decision may have been made, but the answer may be, "You'll be hearing from us in a few days," at which time you will simply receive a courtesy reply that tells you there's nothing doing.

• You may be told, "You'll be hearing from us shortly," and there will be some indication of hesitation. At this point you might ask if there's any further information or material you could send along. This provides an added chance to keep the contact open.

• The executive may not have taken action on your letter. In this case, use your phone call to attempt to set up the interview then and there.

Q. "What do I do if I get the typical courtesy turndown? Does that close the matter?"

A. Yes, unless there is some special reason for believing that the company is still a good possibility. *But*—if you feel that an oversight at the other end is possible, that negligent handling of your letter accounts for the lack of interest, send a second letter. State your case, making the point that you selected the company carefully. Give your reasons for the selection (the particular appropriateness of your background and experience, for example). And ask for an interview.

Q. "Is there a best day of the week to mail?"

A. Some experts say it doesn't make any difference what day you send off your letter. Others say, avoid a mailing that arrives Monday (a big mail day, ordinarily) or Friday (when there's usually a rush to wind up the business of the week). Accordingly, a Monday mailing might be best, since your letter will arrive in the middle of the week.

Q. "Are there any special means by which a letter can be got past the secretarial screen?"

    If the letter is written as the result of a referral, be sure to mention the name of the middleman. This adds a personal element likely to persuade the secretary to pass along the letter. However, executive secretaries, the experienced ones, can't easily be circumvented. If the boss has issued an order, "Send any job applicant letters to Mr. White in Personnel," that's where the letter will go, no matter what. However, this is likely to be the case in a small percentage of the cases. Only if a letter is obviously misdirected, or the work of a crank, is it likely to be kept away from the executive.

    Q. "As a follow-up on a referral, is a letter better than a phone call?"

    A. Yes. It's a more formal approach, more in keeping with executive status and dignity. However, a phone call may be used if a time factor exists: "Mr. Jones, our mutual friend Bob Green suggested that I phone you when I visited your city. I'm here just for the day, and I wonder whether I might see you for a few minutes. . . ." If no special reasons favor the phone call, the letter is more desirable, since it gives the prospective employer the opportunity to fit your interview into his schedule at his convenience. Finally, when you include background data with or in your letter, and an interview is forthcoming, the odds are much greater that there's a job possibility. An interview following a brief phone exchange sometimes quickly ends with, "Oh, I'm sorry. If you'd explained your background over the phone, I would have told you at once that we have no opening right now for a man with your qualifications."

Two Letters that "Pulled"

    Below you will find copies of two letters that succeeded in getting job interviews for their writers. One interview ended in a job, the other in a number of helpful referrals. But the important point is that each achieved its fundamental objective—a face-to-face meeting with a prospective employer.

Mr. Harold Humes, Chairman of the Board
Humes Construction Company
Philadelphia, Pa.

Dear Mr. Humes:

    After six years of successful operation as Controller of the Lightstone Building Corporation, I am seeking a new affiliation for the purpose of career advancement. As the enclosed resume shows, my experience has been particularly strong in the financial areas in which your firm is active. The nature of your company's operations is, of course, widely known in the trade, and the opportunity to work with as enterprising a firm as yours is extremely attractive to me.

    I would appreciate the opportunity to meet with you, so that I could go into some detail as to exactly how I might apply my experience and skills to the benefit of your firm.

Sincerely,

David Tallman

Mr. Samuel J. Scott, President
Acme Metal Stamping Company
116 Maltese Drive
Cincinnati, Ohio

Dear Mr. Scott:

Mr. Val James of this city suggested that I write you about an upcoming vacancy in your Purchasing Department.

As the enclosed resume shows, I have won considerable recognition as a purchasing executive in your field. While head of the Purchasing Department of a Los Angeles metal stamping and decorating firm, I developed some highly successful techniques for value analysis and inventory control that can create unique profit-making opportunities for the company that applies them.

While presently employed, I am interested in changing my affiliation. I would be glad to come to Cincinnati to discuss the possibilities. As a preliminary, I would be glad to furnish any additional information you may want.

Sincerely,

Peter Helm

Five Elements That Make an Effective Combination

The points of particular interest in the two examples above are these:

1. *Brevity.* Note the shortness of the letters. They were correctly designed as an introduction to the enclosed resumes, as attention getters, as a means of creating a personal bridge.

2. *Interest hook.* Each letter includes a single pertinent highlight of the resume. To pique the interest of the reader, each writer has included an outstanding selling point.

3. *Appropriateness.* In each case, the writer shows, both implicitly and explicitly, that he has some knowledge of the objectives of the company which he is prospecting. He in effect tells the reader, "I'm especially interested in your company."

4. *Purpose.* Both letters make it clear that all the writer is seeking is an *interview.* Neither letter seeks to commit the recipient to anything more than a half-hour's preliminary talk. This is an important point. Too many executives misuse the covering letter, treating it as a vehicle for a strong "sell." Actually, any attempt to hook a prospective employer, to get him emotionally committed, is almost sure to backfire. The basic purpose of the direct-mail approach is to *win an interview,* not a job.

5. *Tone.* The letters are forthright without being pushy, dignified without being stilted. Especially note the manner in which the writer says in effect, "Mr. Prospective Employer, I'm sure you'll want to see me since you have nothing to lose, and the possibility of considerable gain." It's this assumption that the recipient of the letter will want the interview for his own benefit, as well as the writer's, that gives each of the above communications a quiet and attractive assurance not likely to be gainsaid.

Some executives, who feel uncomfortable using the "I" form report that the third-person usage works better for them. If this is your preference, the letter is constructed no differently in substance, but the form goes like this: "The writer has had considerable experience, and an outstanding record of achievement in your line of business as production manager. He has developed highly effective straight-line procedures . . . ," etc.

However, it should be stated that such rhetorical indirection is annoying to some. This is a case where you must take your chances.

Mail Recruiting for the Company

For a number of reasons, companies seldom take the direct-mail route to find executives. Although they often circularize a community to recruit lower-echelon employees, the feeling is that a highly paid, uniquely experienced executive is not likely to be uncovered by blanket mailings.

One deterrent is the impersonality of the "To whom it may concern" approach, which may be considered inappropriate by some firms. Another obstacle is the lack of appropriate mailing lists. However, where the executive being sought has a technical background—medical, engineering, scientific, for example—a mail search is often feasible. Mailing lists of such professionals are available, and, being specialized, they ensure against a deluge of unqualified or crackpot correspondence. However, when the executive being sought fits no general category—for example, a production executive in a highly specialized field—ordinary approaches by mail offer little hope of success.

Direct mail is frequently used by second parties to executive recruitment—executive-search firms, employment agencies, and so on. Typical of the approach is the following letter sent out by an executive-search firm to key figures in the advertising field—a list of these being available from some of the commercial list companies:

Dear Mr. Michaels:

We are a management consulting firm, representing a client with an opportunity that we consider particularly noteworthy. We are taking the liberty of describing our client's needs via the attached job description. We respect your position in your company and in your industry and feel that you may know of one or more people with backgrounds appropriate to the enclosed specifications.

Any suggestions you make regarding individuals who might be interested will be held in complete confidence unless you indicate otherwise. If this opportunity is of interest to you personally, we naturally should like to know about it. We appreciate any suggestions you wish to make.

Sincerely,

Below is reproduced the specification that accompanied the letter.

The company	A large regional bank
Location	Southwest
Position	Reports to the president, and is responsible for:

1. Initiation, development, and administration of the advertising budget for the main office and all the branches. This includes:
   * understanding of management's long-range goals and objectives
   * close liaison with all bank officers
   * supervision of the activities of the advertising agency
2. Merchandising of the advertising throughout the bank and all its branches. This will require:
   * close liaison with staff-customer relations
   * intimate working relationship with all branches of the bank
3. Administration of the advertising department and co-ordination of all collateral material produced internally by the advertising agency.

Required background Experience as an account executive in an advertising agency or as an advertising manager with a corporation. An intimate knowledge of banking is not mandatory, but some knowledge of finance would be helpful. Experience in dealing directly with the public; e.g., department-store merchandising would be desirable. A sense of the importance of customer relations is desirable. Should be able to identify himself with community activities.

Future opportunities Excellent, vice-president of marketing is approaching retirement age.

Compensation Up to $20,000 depending on experience and past earnings. Pension, profit sharing, club membership, insurance. Fringe benefits are exceptionally good.

Despite general practice, there is no reason why direct mail may not be used by a company in search of executive talent, provided appropriate lists of prospects are available. Two approaches are possible:

1. The company sends out a brief letter stating that it is in the market

for an executive with such-and-such qualifications and inviting the recipient to send in a resume if he feels he qualifies.

2. The company sends out a detailed description of the job to be filled, and the qualifications of the man wanted, with a letter asking whether the recipient of the letter knows of a man qualified and available. The prospective applicant—either the recipient of the letter or a colleague—is asked to send in a resume, or to phone "our Mr. Smith for an appointment."

The advantages of the mail route for recruiting is its comparatively low cost. Its obvious disadvantage is that lists tend to be limited.

11

The Registries, and Some Offbeat Approaches

Besides the common paths of recruitment, there are a number of less-familiar methods that have helped executives develop new job opportunities, and companies find fresh executive talent. They are less frequently used for a number of reasons: They may produce results only in special circumstances; they may require considerable initiative or imagination; they may not be available in certain geographical areas, or face obstacles in some professional or industrial categories; some are new and relatively little known.

For the executive who wants to try a unique tack, however, the ideas in this chapter may spark the approach that leads to a new job. Similarly, for the employer seeking somewhat unusual talent, or interested in minimizing recruiting costs, the methods described here may suggest approaches that can inexpensively locate the right man. At any rate, they may be worthwhile for complementing other methods.

The Registry Services

A new type of service organization has been appearing in the executive job-finding field, the so-called "registry services." They operate essentially as clearing houses for executive positions. The executive job hunter pays a fee to have his resume kept on file. As the registry gets calls for executives from companies, executive-search firms, consultants, etc., it matches these requisitions against the resumes on hand.

Typical of such an operation is the Executive Register, with offices in New York City and New Canaan, Connecticut. William F. Breitmayer, president of the firm, explains his operation as follows:

"Our objective," states Breitmayer, "is to fill a communications gap in the executive-search field by providing a center in which available positions and the executives qualified to fill them can be brought together effectively and at relatively low cost.

"Unlike some other recruiting services, we can produce almost instant results because we have on tap a constant inventory of executives qualified for all types of positions in all kinds of industries. We handle only positions paying from $15,000 to $80,000 and we operate abroad as well as in the United States and Canada."

Executive Register charges the job hunter $75 for a six-month listing. This charge includes developing a resume, classifying and incorporating his file into the system. Renewal fee is $10 for an additional six months. Companies looking for men pay $300 for each position they want to fill. Companies that are active recruiters, as large ones often are, may be charged an annual fee that varies with the number of searchers.

Breitmayer's firm does a preliminary screening on the applicants and suggests a one-page resume according to a standard format. When an executive is placed with a recruiting company, no additional fee is charged either executive or employer.

Some interesting statistics emerge from Executive Register experience: Seventy per cent of all the executives on file, says Breitmayer, are currently employed. They are, he suggests, "reasonably happy, but curious." In other words, they consider the Executive Register facility a means of keeping tabs on the job market for their particular area of interest. They can do this at a comparatively low cost, and with a minimum of inconvenience and risk of exposure. Resumes are never sent out without the registrant's approval.

The registry offers a good means of keeping up to date, since the job market is increasingly characterized by rapid turnover and obsolescence.

Breitmayer points out that not all would-be registrants are accepted. Backgrounds and resumes are screened. Such factors as low pay level (below $15,000 annually), inadequate experience or background lead to a rejection of about 15 per cent of those who apply. On the other hand, 80 per cent of all registrants receive at least one referral in a six-month period; 58 per cent receive more than five referrals.

As for the company that subscribes to Executive Register, Breitmayer says that each job specification submitted brings in initially an average of fifteen qualified candidates. Depending on the nature of the position, a request may turn up from two to fifty candidates. In addition, a company may expect a continuing flow of about two new candidates a week, if the initial group fails to yield a successful applicant.

To maintain confidentialness Executive Register registrants are notified by mail when a job opening turns up for which they qualify. The executive then sends back a release form that starts his resume on the way to the prospecting company. A registrant usually tells ER whether there are any companies he *doesn't* want contacted, such as his customers, certain competitors, and so on. (Naturally, his own company is on the proscribed list.)

Some Possible Flaws

Along with their advantages, the registry services have some potential drawbacks, not in *theory* but in the practical *operation*. Before paying a fee, companies and job hunters alike should satisfy themselves on the following questions:

1. *How extensive are the personnel files?* Where a registry bases its services entirely on the registrants who come forward to be listed for a fee, there's danger that the inventory may be too limited. One of the first questions to ask, therefore, is to what extent the service utilizes newspaper advertising and other appeals to locate candidates.

2. *How carefully are the files maintained?* In addition to the simple mechanics of filing, the effectiveness of a registry service depends on:

• The care with which the registrants are screened—so that unqualified people are not used to pad out the files.

• The intelligence with which the files are set up in terms of categories, subcategories, and so on. One registry, for example, notes that it uses the Royal McBee Keydex system for cross references and utilizes the government Standard Industrial Classification codes with both company and individual for matching purposes.

• The skill with which talent requirements of prospecting companies are interpreted and matched against available personnel.

One of the points stressed by the registries is the confidentialness of the service. This is obviously a major selling point. It is suggested that a would-be registrant to whom this is a major factor reassure himself on this score by asking what means the services use to ensure that the files are "peek-proof." and so on.

World Executives Inc.

Operating out of a central headquarters in Chicago, World Executives Inc. claims to have "the largest executive manpower pool in the world." It serves both the job seeker and the talent-scouting company, and claims to have representatives in over one hundred foreign countries, besides every major metropolitan and industrial area in the United States.

World Executives charges its registrants an "initial deposit" of $390. This covers out-of-pocket expenses incurred in preparing special material and developing contacts for the job seeker. The fee is refunded when a registrant accepts a position obtained through World Executives. (It is forfeited, however, if the registrant finds a job on his own "and leaves the fold.") The hiring company pays a "finder's fee" when it hires a World Executive registrant. This is usually 10 per cent of the starting base annual salary, though it could run as high as 15 or 20 per cent on a particularly difficult search order.

World Executives bases its claim to rapid service on a Western Union Telex system that speeds individual profiles to prospective employers. Forty-eight hours later, a representative follows up the profile with a direct telephone call that seeks to set up an interview.

Career-Ways

The Career-Ways system, centered in Princeton, New Jersey, bases its services on an "electronic library" of executive talent. Executives pay $24 a year to be kept "on file" in the computer. Corporate members pay $450 for each plant or location that uses the service. This fee gives the member the privilege of "challenging" the electronic library as often as it wishes when trying to fill a job opening.

Candidates selected are notified by a computer print-out, and given details of the position they've been matched against. They, in turn, give Career-Ways permission to inform the client of their identity (all names are kept confidential up to this point, codes being used for identity). If a position is filled, no additional charges are made to either party.

Career-Ways notes that the annual income of its registrants ranges from $8,000 to $80,000, and that a broad variety of skills and disciplines is represented. The organization also says that 90 per cent of its members are currently employed and, as such, not available through normal recruitment channels.

Berman and Company

The Berman Executive Register is one division of a Detroit firm that also offers services in the fields of market research; clinical, industrial and personal psychology; and personnel. The register is open to executives in all types of business and industry earning $10,000 or more annually. (Berman, as most such services, reserves the right to reject applicants if their objectives are not "realistically aligned with their qualifications.")

The job seeker pays an initial charge of $100 to register for a year. Thereafter, he can maintain his listing for $25 a year. Berman performs the following services:

• Professional analysis of an executive's background and preparation of all required materials—resume, and so on

• Continuous exposure of his qualifications to job specifications of companies looking for executives

• Updating of his portfolio as changes occur in his job status or objectives
• Periodic reports on job market conditions

Unlike some other registery services, companies looking for people to fill executive positions may consult the Berman register without charge. Only if they hire one of the registrants do they pay—5 per cent of the first year's base annual salary.

Sales Manpower Foundation

SMF is a non-profit division of the Sales Executive Club of New York. Essentially, it is a "registry" type of service, free to the job seeker. For a fee of $250 a year, a subscribing company is offered recruiting services in the sales and marketing field. Current classified files contain over 2,000 candidates ranging from sales trainees to marketing vice-presidents. The subscribing company may have free access to the files or may submit job descriptions and ask SMF to forward the resumes of individuals meeting the requirements.

In addition, SMF sends out a printed job-opening list twice a month to qualified applicants all over the country. The list, which contains current job openings in subscribing companies also goes to local sales executive clubs, chambers of commerce, employment committee members, and so on.

As new resumes are received—and SMF states they come in at the rate of about 500 a month—they are screened and checked against job openings on hand. Those that qualify are brought to the attention of the prospecting firms.

A typical issue of the job-opening list describes about fifty sales-manager positions. Here are two listings from a recent mailing:

> OFFICE EQUIPMENT MANUFACTURER: Seeking Training Director. College, advanced degree preferred but not essential. Must have a broad successful background in skill training and particularly management development. This man must have a keen insight into staff and line problems and the ability to improve, through training, individual performance, existing abilities and develop management potential. Starting salary $15,000 to $17,000.

> MARKETING MANAGER: TOILETRIES: Create original marketing strategy product development, advertising program. Must have an outstanding record. Salary $22,000 to $25,000.

Any sales executive looking for a new affiliation should find Sales Manpower Foundation's services particularly helpful. Under the direction of Henry K. Astwood, SMF provides the job hunter with concrete help in achieving his objective. A booklet entitled "What to Do When You Lose a Job" gives him down-to-earth advice. Astwood himself frequently helps job seekers merchandise themselves, develop resumes, and so on—and often, provides specific leads to companies that are actively recruiting. There is no charge to the executive for any of these services.

Other professional associations provide services similar to Sales Manpower Foundation. The absence of a fee, inside knowledge of the trade, and usually a genuine interest in being helpful, all recommend this type of organization to the job seeker if there is one available in his area or in his profession.

Other possibilities: colleges, technical schools, even some religious service organizations offer employment services of the same general type of SMF. Usually free, they are worth a try.

Similarly, employers are likely to find such services worthwhile because of the absence of a fee, or comparatively low fee, and the professional level at which they operate.

The Odd and Offbeat

There is almost no limit to the *uncommon* methods that have been developed by ingenious individuals to trigger a favorable man-meets-job chain of events. These offbeat approaches are mentioned here to emphasize the fact that there need be no hard-and-fast procedure for job finding or talent recruiting.

• *Card in the window.* The president of a food-importing firm used the same method for recruiting an assistant that he had used to find laborers when he was a foreman in a food-processing company. He had a sign painter make up a few large display cards that described his manpower needs. He placed one in the hallway of his office building, tacked another on the company door. But it was one he had taped to his automobile window that finally brought in the winning candidate.

His reason for taking this approach was logical. "I was looking for an unstuffed-shirt type of fellow, one who would be enterprising enough to follow up on that kind of lead. I'm happy to say I got what I wanted."

• *Resumes from thin air.* One young job seeker who wanted to attract the attention of top agency people in a West-coast city, made up several hundred resumes on 4- by 5-inch cards, and had an aviator friend of his drop them over the business district during lunch hour. This method developed one unexpected cost. He was fined $25 for littering, and had to pay $50 for the cost of cleaning up the flying cards. But the idea got him an interview, and a job.

• *An arranged "chance meeting."* The editor of a nationally distributed trade journal was after a job as an account executive with a well-known advertising agency. When he learned that the president of the agency was staying at a California resort, he made a reservation at the same hotel and developed a nodding acquaintance with the agency head. He checked out of the hotel the same time as the agency executive, and by arranged "coincidence" was seated alongside his target on the homeward-bound plane. The two men became quite friendly over food and drinks. But the editor, playing his cards carefully, uttered no word about his job interest. After the plane landed, the two men shook hands and parted.

A week later, the editor sent the agency head a note saying that he was thinking of changing jobs, asking for a half hour's time to discuss the possibilities in the agency business. The president suspected the background of the appeal, but he was sufficiently impressed by the editor's venturesomeness to see him. The story ends happily—the editor was hired.

The Limiting Factors

While there may be no theoretical limits to methods of unearthing jobs or applicants, there are several practical ones.

From the job seeker's viewpoint, it must be remembered that the method is identified with the man. The job hunter who walks up and down the business district with a sandwich sign advertising his qualifications may be ingenious, but a prospective employer might interpret his action as showing poor taste, excessive enterprise, and an overly strong tendency toward the offbeat.

The nature or context of the job is another key. Unusual methods may not be in keeping with the executive dignity required in most jobs, although they are obviously effective in others. Certainly an advertising executive has a wider latitude in his job-seeking methods than a bank executive, because cleverness and flamboyance are likely to be considered desirable attributes in the former case, though not in the latter one.

The talent-prospecting employer, too, must take care in using offbeat recruiting methods. An engineering company seeking hard-to-get candidates for key jobs distributed free bottles of liquor to "influentials" who were attending a professional conference. Inside each package was a sheet describing the jobs that were available.

Response was disappointingly meager. The image the firm inadvertently projected by using this technique was unattractive to professional people. In other words, there must be some measure of appropriateness between the recruiting methods used and the character of the company. What is suitable for company A may be decidedly inadvisable for company B.

Another factor that must be considered by employer and job seeker both is that recruiting methods have short-range and long-range effects. The shock approach may get you a man, but at the expense of your company's overall reputation, as in the case of the engineering firm mentioned above.

12

Counseling — The Helping Hand,
Free and for a Fee

"Shall I consider looking for a new position?"
"How do I find a job?"
"What kind of job shall I look for?"
Some executives know exactly where they want to go and how to get there. But the average career-minded executive faces somewhat the same problems and decisions as a man about to build a house. He may have a general idea of what he wants, but to transform his wishes into reality he needs help—everything from the services of an architect to a landscape gardener, with additional specialists in between.

Even before a decision to change jobs arises, a man may need someone to listen while he talks out his aspirations and problems. Self-doubt may arise, or career crises may strike: "Joe Smith got the promotion I've been working for"; or "I've just been offered a job completely out of my specialty. Should I take it?" In such situations, regardless of his abilities or accomplishments, a man looks for guidance. This chapter describes some of the methods, organizations, and individuals available to help the executive resolve some of his job and career problems.

This chapter can also be of considerable help to any employer who must let key men go. A small but growing number of companies today are utilizing the services of job counselors to ease the impact of terminations on executives. They send them to counseling firms for help and advice in making the transition to a new job. The cost is considered well worth paying, in terms of the effect on other employees and on the communities in which these companies operate.

Help Is Just a Person Away

In one sense, almost everybody is in the career-counseling business. A man's wife, his colleagues, friends, relatives, business contacts—all stand ready to toss out advice or to make a pitch for one or another course of action. Such assistance may be invaluable, useless, or downright dangerous. Often, it's the executive's inability to tell which that steers him to the professional guidance counselor.

The executive's needs, whether he's unemployed or merely has doubts about his professional future, are threefold:

• *He may need information.* "Where shall I look? Should I go to the agencies? Do I really need a resume?"

• *He may need guidance.* "Which of these two possibilities shall I choose? Shall I take this lower-paying job? Shall I consider a job outside the country?"

• *He may need reassurance.* Important to have is the feeling that he's not alone, that *someone* cares about his fate.

The Range of Choices

When an executive decides to seek professional advice, he faces a large variety of job-finding helps. No system of classification is likely to be completely acceptable because many of the services overlap in one or more degrees. However, one way to get an idea of what's available in the counseling field is to look at the three methods commonly used in career guidance:

• *Psychological.* By testing, depth interviewing, and so on, counselors with psychological orientation evaluate a man's capabilities, assess his problems, and try to help him solve his career difficulties by improving his self-understanding, and thereby the relationship between his abilities and his aims.

• *Practical.* By supplying information and know-how on anything from writing a resume to types of firms to contact, services attempt to expedite the job-finding process.

• *Motivational.* Organizations that operate by this means essentially attempt to hasten the job hunt by reinforcing an individual's self-confidence. The idea is that this will increase his capabilities in all steps of job finding.

Few companies operate *exclusively* in only one area. Many combine some elements of all three types of assistance.

There is another set of categories into which counseling services may be put:

1. *The resume writers.* These organizations see the essential problem in job finding as that of developing an effective resume. Certainly this assist can help sharpen an essential tool. The *Manhattan Yellow Pages* lists over sixty firms under the heading, "Job Resume Service."

Fees run from $15 up, depending on the amount of time required, or the number of pages the resume requires. Average fee, including reproduced copies, $60.

2. *Contact suppliers.* Next comes a group of organizations that supply the job-hunter with lists of prospective employers. For example, two organizations that offer this service are Dunhill International List Company and Dun & Bradstreet, publishers of *Million Dollar Directory.* Firms of this type must be contacted and queried for the varieties of lists—particular industries, executives, and so on—in which the job hunter is interested. Most of the list companies will supply catalogues of their lists free of charge.

Other firms do a combination job. That is, they will prepare a resume for the job hunter and also do a mailing to an appropriate list of prospective employers. Firms that offer this service are World Executive, Nesinc, St. Clair and Welch.

Fees charged for a resume, plus mailing to selected lists, may range from $200 to $1,000 depending on the salary sought, size of the mailing, and so on.

3. *Psychological testers.* Of particular interest to the executive who wants to find out more about himself before he takes another step in his career are the psychological testing services. Firms such as Klein Institute, The Personnel Laboratory, BFS Psychological Associates, Psychological Corporation, give tests, discuss the results with the executive, and make recommendations for further job-hunting moves. Some detractors of this type of service say it "only confirms what the man already knows." Others insist that an individual can achieve better self understanding only through the psychological discipline. Fees may run from $100 up, depending on the number of counseling hours.

4. *The skill improvers.* Universities, correspondence and technical schools aim to improve an executive's administrative abilities, human relations, and leadership skills. Every area has its colleges or other training and development institutions.

5. *The motivation boosters.* Some organizations seek to help the executive by boosting his morale and motivation. They feel that most people have what it takes, but must be helped to mobilize their personal resources.

6. *Free services.* Services offered by church groups, professional organizations, civic clubs, and so on can be of welcome help. By and large, these organizations assist the individual by providing encouragement, and getting him to mobilize his own job-finding capabilities. Some job-market guidance may also be given. For the executive who has a basic career problem, such minimum help is no solution, but for many others, it may provide effective help at no expense.

Where Career Counselors Get into the Picture

The executive should remember that "counselors" are in business not only to help the *unemployed* executive, but also to assist the *employed* man advance in his personal career objectives. Sometimes the quickest, if not the only, move toward career improvement is by switching employers. Because the uncertainty and risks of job hopping are often a deterrent, the services of a good career counsel can be of real help.

The question often arises as to whether counselors are worth the money. They're often referred to as "blood-suckers" for the simple reason that their clients may be unemployed, and counseling fees, sometimes running to hundreds of dollars, may have to come from shrinking personal resources.

The defense offered by the "blood sucker" is quite matter-of-fact: "True, our fees may have to come out of a man's dwindling reserves. On the other hand, if we help him get a job, what's the complaint?"

Statements of this kind dodge the issue, which is: "Can you, *do* you, actually help the executive in his job search?" To this question, there are three answers: Yes; perhaps; no. And there is evidence that supports each view.

Many investigators have given much thought to this question. Attempts to pin down counseling firms generally are met by evasion. No one is eager to reveal his competitive situation by answering the question, "What percentage of your clients have actually found jobs through your efforts?" The fact is, it would be difficult to answer the question in any event: A client lands a job. Was it because of counseling reinforcement, or would he have got it anyhow?

On the other hand, every organization in the field can show letters from "satisfied clients." But whether these letters represent 1, 10, or 100 per cent cannot be ascertained.

A conversation with one executive job seeker was both frustrating and revealing. After speaking bitterly about the "blood suckers" he admitted, ". . . And yet, if I had my job hunting to do all over again, the first thing I'd do is register with outfit X" (one of the costliest of the counseling services).

What the question boils down to, both for the individual and the company seeking help for its executive DPs is this: "Is the money you spend bringing you a reasonable return in terms of improved prospects or job-finding capability?"

The answer must be sought in how well the service seems to fit individual needs, its record of success (as substantiated in part by past clients), and reasonableness of fees.

The Psychological Counselors—Pro and Con

Many people are biased against psychology and its applications in the business world. Some are more frightened by Freud than they are persuaded. And all the bitterness against what is considered a pseudoscientific interest in "sex and bathroom habits" results in a discarding of anything even vaguely tied to "psychology." Such people view testing as an invasion of privacy, and rightly or wrongly will refuse to submit to, or use, psychological tests.

There's a counterbalance—some people tend to overuse psychology. They depend *too heavily* on test results. They will "buy" the suggestions of psychological counselors wholesale, without submitting the ideas to any sort of realistic evaluation, based on their own experience and self-knowledge.

Many industrial psychologists will privately confess that the profession has a need to clean its own house. They admit there's a touch of truth to the idea that some industrial practitioners spend their mornings making promises that can't be kept and their afternoons depositing checks they haven't earned.

However, the record of successful, high-standard performance by established psychological services is certainly strong enough to recommend them in appropriate cases. To help you decide the pros and cons in the matter of psychological counseling and guidance, here are some of the findings in cases reported by psychologists operating in the testing and counseling field.

Some Common Career Problems

Executives considering a career move often have problems ranging all over the lot, from the simple to the complicated, from the practical to the emotional. Some of the help seekers can be readily given what they seek. Others may not find what they want this side of Heaven.

King Whitney, Jr., head of The Personnel Laboratory, provides a list of types of problems individuals bring to professional counselors:

• *An unresolved career conflict.* "My father wants me to become a doctor," says a young careerist, "but I have no real interest in the medical profession." Another version: "I want to start my own business, but my friends (or parent, brother, colleague) tell me I should stay with my present company."

Whitney points out that often what the help seeker wants is unrealistic. He may shy away from advice that makes good sense, in favor of immature or poorly considered personal aspirations. But it can also work the other way, particularly when the would-be adviser is an overly ambitious wife, or parent, or simply a friend who is uninformed.

A person in this situation can often be helped to resolve his dilemma. Since the usual path to solution lies in establishing the realities of the situation—(1) what the man can do, (2) what he wants to do, (3) what's available—a business-wise psychological counselor can supply effective aid.

And so can other business-oriented advisers who can lead the executive through the steps of self-questioning and self-analysis that lead to insight and self-understanding.

• *The "much-tested man."* Here is a special version of the "career-conflicted" executive. Just as doctors are familiar with the hypochondriac who continually makes the rounds of medical offices for reassurance, so the testing services see men who have been tested many times, but who are still looking for the magic word that will immediately resolve all their career problems. "And why shouldn't it come from a psychologist," thinks the man who equates psychology with the mumbo jumbo of witchcraft.

"It's not unusual," says one experienced counselor, "for such individuals to be suffering from a conflict between limited ability and a vague wish for superior accomplishment. This person can often be helped by a psychology-oriented or even a practical counselor who gets him to face up to the contradiction between what he *can do* and what he *wants to do,* and thereby proceed on a more realistic basis."

• *An extreme emotional problem.* Occasionally, an individual who can't be helped by ordinary means will turn up for counseling. The man may be suffering from extreme anxiety, depression, or from some personal problem that puts him under extreme tension and interferes with his ability to perform. In such cases, the experienced counselor recognizes that the problem is not one in the vocational area.

Or, as one counselor puts it when talking to a troubled client, "Yes, you do seem to have a job problem, but you're not in a position to solve it now." Such individuals have two possible sources for help:

1. *Psychotherapy.* This may mean anything from counseling sessions with a trained psychologist to an extended course of treatment by a psychiatrist.

2. *Readjustment in the anxiety-causing situation.* For example, an executive with a problem of failing performance came to a psychological-guidance organization. Interviews uncovered the fact that severe marital problems were affecting his job performance. With professional help, he and his wife realized that a divorce was the best practical solution. Once this difficult decision had been made, the executive had a much clearer state of mind, and his job situation rapidly improved.

Professional counselors point out, however, that in some cases, an unhappy home life actually *sparks* a man's career. He throws himself into his work as a partial escape from a distasteful home situation. This motivation, as undesirable as it might be in general, nevertheless can have the effect of raising levels of achievement.

• *The "seal-of-approval" seeker.* Reports psychologist Wes Shaw of Richardson, Bellows & Henry, management consulting firm: "An individual will come in for conseling because he wants to use our findings to show his present or prospective employer how high his IQ is, or how many desirable aptitudes he possesses."

More often, an individual will submit to testing to try to find out once and for all, "what my aptitudes actually are." Psychologists are not opposed to this type of information seeking, but they point out there's a practical limitation to their assistance. Says one practitioner: "It seldom helps an executive of fifty-five or sixty, for example, to learn that he has musical aptitudes, or that he has latent promise as a language expert."

• *The "job hater."* From time to time the counselor's door is darkened by an executive who feels he's in the wrong job. His complaint may range all the way from "I hate to go to work in the morning," to "I'm not getting much satisfaction from what I'm doing." Or he may simply register disinterest: "It's just a job."

The satisfaction-starved executive obviously faces a problem because he's blocked from superior performance. There are several possible explanations for this state of affairs.

A. UNDERPLACEMENT. He may be in a job that doesn't sufficiently challenge his capabilities.

B. HE'S IN THE WRONG TYPE OF JOB FOR HIS INTERESTS. This particular problem takes many forms. One type is the man who is essentially aesthetic-minded. Since his major preoccupations in living are artistic, he feels repelled by the commercialism of ordinary business operations.

C. A SITUATION FACTOR IS DRAGGING HIM DOWN. An unsympathetic boss, colleagues who are hostile, a disparity between the community and the man's essential style of living, all can make an individual feel like a misfit in his job.

When a man is out of tune with the job environment, he can seldom resolve his problem without making a full-scale examination of what he wants not just from his job, but from life in general.

It's a big order. But people who have successfully performed this type of self-examination, either with the help of a psychologist or psychiatrist, or by their own concentrated self-examination, have discovered surprisingly simple conflicts at the heart of their difficulty. Immature idealism is often the villain. One executive discovered that a childhood fantasy about being a "great scientist" caused him to be dissatisfied with *any* degree of practical accomplishment. When his ambitions were brought into line with his capabilities, he went about his work with better grace.

• *"Why haven't I got further in my career?"* From time to time, a relatively successful executive will have the feeling that he's spinning his wheels. He may see desired promotions given to colleagues. Expected increments in his earnings may not be forthcoming. Such feelings may be fed by the man's conviction that he has capabilities that are not being recognized.

A man in this situation often develops one of two attitudes:

A. He rationalizes and decides that there's some "kind of plot" afoot to hold him back. He may attribute his failure to a self-seeking superior, office politics, and so on.

B. He may feel that an unsuspected weakness in his make-up is holding him back.

Both these ideas may crystallize into one, due to the success of a counselor in helping the executive get to the bottom of his problem. For example, one top executive discovered that he *was* being passed over in favor of colleagues when promotion plums were being handed around. The reason eventually became clear: Although he was highly skillful in the technical aspects of his job, he was weak in his dealings with people, both subordinates and superiors.

• *"I want to look before I leap."* An executive may suddenly find himself confronted by the prospect of a career change. For example, he is fired and must set about looking for another position, or he is offered an advancement in his own company, or he receives a job offer from another firm.

A common reaction to this situation is, "I don't want to make any moves until I know what I'm capable of." In the case where a man has been fired as a result of poor performance, the feeling may be more specific: "I don't want to make the same mistake twice."

One executive related: "My company offered me a chance to go to Florida to head up a new division. It was a tough job. Before taking the gamble, I wanted to try to stack the cards a little more heavily in my favor by discovering just what I had on the ball."

This man went to a psychological counselor to get an appraisal of his capabilities and aptitudes for the specific responsibility offered him. The psychological tests indicated that his chances for success were good, and helped him decide to make the move.

• *The man with the avocational problem.* Psychological counselors also feel they can be of considerable help to the man who is about to retire and is afraid to "turn into a vegetable." This problem crops up with men in the Armed Services who retire after twenty years of service at ages forty-two to fifty. In cases such as this, the psychological counselors feel that their ability to help a man examine his capabilities can minimize problems and clear obstacles to sound career planning.

There is, unfortunately, no simple way of deciding what type of problem is best treated by a particular type of service. Problems in the vocational area have no easy access point.

In the next chapter, you will find a variety of counseling services described in some detail. Methods differ, and undoubtedly effectiveness varies from firm to firm and case to case. And, of course, costs run a wide range from a few dollars up into the high hundreds. The descriptions will give you some basis for evaluation. However, before describing how the counselors work, here is a case history that illustrates how a *company* made good use of a counseling service for a group of its separated executives.

How Employers Can Benefit: Jobs for Forty-two out of Forty-four Displaced Executives

Here's an example of how a company can benefit from an outside guidance service. Actual corporate identity is masked, in accord with the firm's expressed preference.

Late in 1962, the XYZ company faced a difficult personnel situation. After a period of reorganization in which the roster dropped from 4,800 to 2,000 in two years, the company faced the problem of separating a number of executives whose jobs had simply been wiped out.

A "career guidance" program was developed, in the hope that it would provide at least a partial answer. Forty-four men enrolled. Their characteristics were roughly as follows:

Average salary $10,560; range, $8,000 to $15,000
Average age 46; range, 37 to 56
Average length of service 23 years; range, 8 to 36 years

Clearly, those in the higher age and income brackets represented a tough job-finding situation.

Using a combination of group and individual counseling and following a planned program (developed and administered by Bernard Haldane, whose approach is described more completely on page 146), the men were exposed to a variety of assists over a two-week period. In addition to the prescribed program, the counseling staff furnished continuing guidance.

Within ninety days, 80 per cent of the original group had found new jobs. And significantly, the average starting salary was only about 10 per cent lower than the salaries the men had been earning after their long tenure with XYZ.

• Why Companies Buy Career Guidance

The XYZ experience should be of particular interest to organizations that, as a result of reorganization and/or automation and other technological advance, face the problem of executive layoffs.

Top officials make no secret of XYZ's satisfaction with the success of the group-counseling experiment. For XYZ, as for many other organizations, the separated executive represents an especially sensitive problem, having roots in economic, ethical, and social considerations. The emotional ties that exist between the executive who is leaving and his ex-colleagues magnify the problem, and make a solution all the more eagerly sought.

As long as a company is concerned with only one or two executive separations, ordinary procedures are adequate. Traditionally, companies have found jobs for displaced executives by direct referrals to other companies —customers, suppliers, even competitors. But when larger numbers are involved, ordinary methods may not suffice.

An XYZ official points up some of the special difficulties confronting the forty-four-man group:

Many of the men thought their experience was so unique to the XYZ type of business that no other industry could use it. Yet, one man with highly specialized experience in refrigeration and the movement of liquids in an oil-refinery context found a job at twice his previous salary with a chemical company.

Another problem was the relatively advanced age of some group members. Says the official, "The counseling seemed particularly effective with older people. I saw some fellows with heads drooping to the floor come bouncing back after a week, ready to do battle with the world." This result is explained by the fact that the counseling approach used is largely motivational.

It is part of XYZ's policy to ease, as far as is practical, the financial blow of involuntary separations. Early retirement is made possible in some cases at age sixty. The cost of such a policy is, of course, high, and the official says, "The fees we paid for counseling ranged from $250 to $500, at a group rate, and were low compared to other severance costs."

Executives who are familiar with such figures say that average separation cost for an upper-echelon executive is from one to two years' salary. In other words, it might run from $20,000 to $40,000 for a $20,000-a-year man.

It's Not All for "Charity"

Business firms' interest in helping executives find new careers stems from several factors other than the desire to be humane:

• *The morale effect* on the executives and other employees remaining on the company's payroll.

• *The public relations effect.* Compare, for example, the image of the "heartless corporation" that emerges if a company remains passive, with the favorable one when management shows it is taking every possible action for the benefit of its displaced personnel.

• *Top management's peace of mind.* It may seem to be stating the obvious, but the fact is, many a top man has lost sleep worrying over the fate of a valued friend and colleague who was being let go after years of service. The XYZ experience suggests that job or career counseling may be a key to easing future executive shifts.

The next chapter describes the operating approaches and methods of a number of different counseling organizations.

13

How the Counselors Work

There's counseling, and there's counseling. Examination of the different kinds of counseling help offered by representative companies in the field shows a range of approaches, techniques, and costs.

Keep in mind that the use of a counseling method or the service of a particular company for descriptive purposes or by way of example here does not represent an endorsement. Although the majority of the service firms are headquartered in New York City or vicinity, similar types of service or reasonably close facsimiles are likely to be available in all large metropolitan centers.

Counseling by a Psychological Service

Psychological-service organizations, seeking to help executives further their career goals, generally rely on testing and depth interviews for information on the individual's aptitudes, interests, intelligence, and personality. Channeling this information back to the client, the counseling psychologist can often help the executive by increasing his self-understanding. Here is a case history that reinforces this kind of claim:

Mr. H. turned up in the office of a West-coast psychological testing service with the following story: At the age of forty-five he had been the executive vice-president of a publishing firm and, as he thought, in line for the presidency. But in the appointment of the top man, he had been passed over.

Mr. H. then changed companies and got another close-to-the-top job in another publishing company, this one in Boston. The same thing happened: Although he felt he was in line for the presidency, another man got the job.

His question to the psychologist-interviewer was this: "There must be some reason for my not getting the presidency in both of these cases. Although I've thought about it a great deal, I haven't been able to figure out the answer. Can you help me?"

Mr. H. was interviewed and tested and eventually with the help of the counselor, he came to understand and accept the fact that it was his inability to deal constructively with people, particularly subordinates, that was the basis for his career block. He was the kind of person who was more interested in ideas than people. His aggressiveness in attaining objectives tended to make him inconsiderate of people who were not as single-minded or goal-driven as he was. He tended to chop heads rather than to work cooperatively with subordinates who needed training or development.

With the new insight he gained, Mr. H. became more willing to accept a one-rung-below-the-top role, while trying to improve his work relationships.

A Typical Pattern

A psychological-service firm typically proceeds in its counseling through four basic steps:

1. *Establishing rapport.* The first session with the executive client is devoted to a general discussion of the executive's business background, his career ambitions, and the problems as he sees them.

2. *Testing.* There is a considerable variation in the types of tests different psychological-service firms use. For example, some use projective techniques—such as the Rorschach (inkblot) and the Thematic Apperception Test. Others use less sophisticated, formal tests and rely more heavily on interviewing. In any case, a trained psychologist works with the executive client until he gets a clear picture of the man's capabilities and problems.

3. *Feedback.* The psychologist proceeds with the actual counseling procedure, the object of which is to help the client gain better insight into himself and his past. The number of counseling sessions varies depending on the nature of the problem. Some firms feel they can do an adequate job in a single session; others may undertake several guidance periods.

4. *Wrap-up session.* The client is given a written report, restating the test results, recapitulating the facts and ideas that have been developed in the counseling session, and suggesting possible conclusions or directions that the client may want to pursue. If the psychologist feels the client's problems are of a more severe kind than can be helped by ordinary counseling, psychotherapy may be recommended. However, "Most of the executives that come to us," says the head of a Los Angeles psychological-counseling service, "can be helped without recourse to psychotherapy or psychiatric treatment. "

Psychologists who practice in the guidance area feel that they can frequently help clients make basic readjustments that may evade other counseling methods. King Whitney, Jr., of The Personnel Laboratory, offers this case in point:

A successful salesman in the insurance field developed emotional problems when he was given management responsibility. He had always had difficulty in taking direction from superiors. As manager, he found that he also had difficulty in giving direct orders to subordinates.

Interestingly enough, as a salesman this man had had little difficulty in his organizational relationships, and had in fact thrived on the competitiveness of his job. But once put in a management position, his problem with the handling of authority became critical.

Psychological counseling helped this man to understand the nature of his emotional problem, and he was able to function effectively as a sales executive. However, his approach to supervising subordinates was different from the usual pattern—direct supervision, giving of orders, and so on. He led his group largely by example, since he remained active as a salesman. Understanding his own weak points, he was able to function in this somewhat unorthodox fashion.

Sums up Whitney: "The right job, or carrying our responsibilities in a particular way, can relieve a considerable amount of emotional difficulty. For example, selling can help a man get rid of a lot of his aggressions, alleviate pressures, and relieve symptoms of emotional conflict."

Psychologists point out other examples of the natural linkage between a particular psychological make-up and an individual's suitability for particular executive jobs.

Says one professional counselor, "I recently worked with a man who had a compelling need to 'see the whole picture.' He liked to feel in control of things, but he was simply not able to deal effectively with people on a face-to-face basis. However, he could work very well through figures. This man found himself a job as a treasurer, and it proved to be the ideal position."

Fees for psychological counseling tend to range from $100 to $350. A typical charge is $150, which includes either four or five sessions. Some firms charge additional fees for specialized tests such as the Rorschach.

Additional Approaches

Following are descriptions of services offered by other organizations in the counseling field. They were chosen not because they are necessarily the best, but because they illustrate the different kinds of assistance available to the job hunter or career-puzzled executives.

The Haldane Approach

"We don't do anything for a man that he couldn't do for himself," explains Saul G. Gruner, president of Executive Job Counselors, "but we show him how to do it faster, avoid many pitfalls, and end up with a better job than he could get by his own unaided efforts."

Executive Job Counselors is a New York firm operating under a license from Bernard Haldane Associates. The Haldane technique EJC uses is described in detail below, for two reasons: It is the approach the XYZ Company used successfully to find new careers for its terminated executives. (See page 141). Second, the method offers several unique features, such as success factors analysis, and the emphasis on referrals, that a job hunter may profitably apply on his own. Here is a typical case history taken from EJC files.

The Case of W. R., Sales Manager

At the age of forty-five, W. R. had been a top salesman for a furniture company for eight years. After "another" argument with his boss, he quit and joined a competing firm. Five months later, his new employer went bankrupt, and W. R. found himself looking for a job again.

W. R.'s job search wasn't helped by the fact that his previous employer, irked by his abrupt resignation, refused to give him a favorable reference. After a number of weeks of fruitless searching, he finally turned to Executive Job Counselors for help.

Here, in greatly condensed form, is a summary of the program which ultimately led W. R. to his proper niche in the business world:

STEP 1: *Analysis of the present situation.* First thing EJC did was to assign a counselor to work with W. R. throughout his job-seeking program. W. R. did a lot of talking, and the counselor a lot of listening. The upshot was that W. R. realized that had he planned his career properly, he wouldn't have left a good job to join a company destined to collapse. Further, in his discouragement, he was planning to move out of his industry when this was exactly the wrong direction to take.

STEP 2: *Success-factor analysis.* Several sessions were spent reviewing W. R.'s personal and work history in terms of specific achievements. His interests, avocations, and skills were examined closely. From this emerged a picture of his *strengths*, the factors that had contributed to past successes —he had considerable management ability—as well as the weak points that blocked his progress.

STEP 3: *Development of job description.* A study of W. R.'s success factors showed that his proper objective should be a sales-management job, with opportunities to assist the general manager in operating a specialty division handling styling, pricing, product line, etc. The study also highlighted areas where W. R. needed further self-development.

STEP 4: *Development of functional resume.* In contrast to a chronological listing of previous jobs, a "functional resume" was developed for W. R. called a "report of values." This showed the responsibilities and jobs he could assume, along with examples of previous successes. It showed the prospective employer the kind of position W. R. might be able to fill successfully. The counselor had W. R. prepare most of the resume himself because it was felt that it would help him stand on his own. In job interviews especially, when a resume is rehashed, the applicant who has devised his own resume is in a stronger position.

STEP 5: *The job campaign.* This crucial phase consisted of a series of interwoven activities. W. R. developed contacts by writing to key people in his industry. The letters did not ask for a job, nor did W. R., in the ensuing interviews. He asked for information and advice, and, because people referred him to other executives, he kept building a list of companies to interview.

During odd hours, he utilized the other, more-common job resources—employment agencies, newspaper ads, even executive-search firms. The counselor recommended that he spend most of his time on the contact-development part of the program, however, and it was from this that he ultimately obtained his job.

W. R. also took an interim job upon the advice of his counselor. This step, called a "stop-loss job" by EJC, is worth consideration by every unemployed job seeker. Although this job cut into searching and interviewing time, W. R. needed the income, and it proved a wise move. Also he learned the seriousness of his poor reference and, with the counselor's aid, worked out a way to overcome the difficulty, by a forthright explanation of the reasons behind it.

Meanwhile, one of the most important contributions of the counselor was to sustain W. R.'s enthusiasm and morale when he tended to let down in his job-hunting effort. Several counseling sessions were also devoted to teaching him how to be a more effective interviewee.

Within two months, W. R. received a job offer, leading to Step 6.

STEP 6: *Salary negotiations.* Discussion with the counselor covered more than the question of what annual or monthly salary W. R. should request. It covered general commitments on the company's part as to how fast W. R. could advance and how he would be compensated in future years. And most important of all, it emphasized the basic relationship which W. R. would initially have with others in the firm; how his superiors and peers would be made to think of him, how he thought of himself.

STEP 7: *Plan for future progress.* Counseling didn't end with getting the job. W. R. also received help in planning his future progress. The counselor instructed him in keeping a diary of his accomplishments, showed him how to review his own progress, how and when to discuss it with his superiors. W. R. was also taught how to keep track of the influence of other key personnel in the organization, and to plug into the real power lines when necessary. At the end of the counseling program, W. R. was ready to accept and live up to the responsibility of doing *two* jobs well: the job for his company and the job required to build and develop his career, with continuing improvement in communications techniques and human relations.

Fees for this type of service vary with the individual and the nature of the problem. Age, education, background, and salary level are also key factors, to the extent that they influence the counseling time needed. The lower limit is $650, and it may go as high as $1,500 for the more difficult case.

Center for Career Planning, Inc.

The Center for Career Planning, Bridgeport, Connecticut, offers a service consisting of two phases: an *observational step* in which a staff consisting of a clinical psychologist and professional personnel people interview and evaluate the client, and *a series of guidance sessions*. Here's the way the procedure develops:

1. *Psychological evaluation.* A clinical psychologist spends a minimum of an hour with a client, conducting a depth interview which seeks to assess such factors as his emotional stability, home situation, career potential, self-sufficiency.

2. *Group interview.* Three staff members with experience in the personnel field conduct an observation session in which the executive's background, aspirations, and problems are discussed. The client is told in advance that this meeting will be purely exploratory. This phase lasts two hours, usually in two separate sessions.

3. *Staff meeting.* Information and views are exchanged between the psychologist who has conducted the depth interview and the staff that has participated in the group interview. Out of this meeting develop general directions for the last phase.

4. *Individual counseling.* "The counseling takes about four or five hours, usually one hour a week," says Sherman Hoyt, President of CCP. "Our aim is to help the client get to know himself so that he can make intelligent decisions about his future moves."

Hoyt gives an example of a successful outcome of the CCP approach: "A highly effective executive, a sales engineer, had been promoted into an administrative job. His new responsibilities, along with a boss with whom he didn't hit it off well, precipitated a job crisis. This man came to us resolved to leave his 'blankety-blank' company. As a result of our working with him, he came to see that he had a very promising future with his present company, provided certain adjustments of responsibility could be made. The company president was happy to work out a new job arrangement, and the end result was extremely satisfying both to our client and to his company."

Hoyt points out that it was the evaluation of the staff psychologist, coupled with the organizational know-how of the group interviewers that made such clear-cut guidance possible.

CCP charges a flat fee of $500 for its services. If clients return for help, additional counseling is billed at the rate of $35 per hour.

Hoyt has several interesting observations to make about career counseling: "A man's wife is often our toughest competitor," he remarks wryly. "She may take the stand: 'Why pay all that money for advice when I need a new winter coat? I can tell you all you have to know about yourself, and for nothing.'"

Another observation of Hoyt's highlights a difficulty that guidance specialists run across. Many a job hunter asserts that he needs guidance, indeed seeks it. But when it comes down to brass tacks, it develops that he's *not* interested in self-evaluation, self-understanding, insight, or anything like it. What he wants is a *job*. Granted, the attitude is practical enough, but it tends to interfere with the achievement of permanent improvement in the client's career or outlook.

Another counselor sums it up: "As most people, the job hunter is often scared to death to learn the truth about himself."

A Springfield, Missouri, Service

Manford F. Ettinger of Springfield, Missouri, says of his executive-job-counseling service: "In most instances, our assistance is confined to planning, counseling, and helping prepare resumes or other documents. 'Editorial assistance' would be a more descriptive term, since I encourage my clients to write their own resumes, letters, etc. We also help clients in the actual job search, including personal representation in the early stages."

Ettinger also prepares clients for employment interviews and suggests postinterview procedures; makes recommendations on salary strategy, psychological testing, and related areas.

In addition to helping with the preparation of resumes, Ettinger offers guidance with particular job-career problems. The service helps assess job-search plans and makes suggestions for the improvement of job-scouting documents. For executives whose companies are undergoing reorganization, Ettinger will make suggestions to help the client work out his own situation.

Ettinger bills his clients at $24 an hour for individual attention, and requires an advance retainer of $48.

For resume revisions, costs range from $12 to $24 a page, depending on the amount of work involved. Where the written material is extensive, the service gives a quotation for the material submitted.

Forty Plus Club of New York

For almost three decades, an idea has been kept alive by a group of dedicated businessmen. In 1939 a group got together to ponder the situation of the unemployed executive likely to be handicapped by age. Result was the Forty Plus Club. Since then, with thousands of successful placements to its credit, Forty Plus has continued to make itself available to "male executives who are unemployed American citizens, who are over forty years of age and in good health." Here's how the organization operates:

The applicant visits the club's office at 15 Park Row. He is interviewed by one of the group's membership committee (all are nonpaid participants, usually in executive categories). If he meets the simple admission requirements and he decides he wants to join, his references are checked.

Then, assuming all is in order, he appears before an admissions committee and is elected to membership. At this point, the executive makes an initial contribution of $50, with the understanding that he'll continue to contribute $1 weekly as long as his membership continues. When the member secures employment, Forty Plus suggests a parting donation, "such as may be justified in your own opinion." In addition to the contribution, members are required to devote 2½ days each week to one or another aspect of Forty Plus's operations.

Forty Plus maintains a crew of thirty to forty men in the field. They contact companies and try to locate and develop job openings for members. Through its experienced participants, the group offers a variety of services:

• *Individual job counseling.* Experienced executives discuss the job seeker's situation with him, seek to help him resolve any difficulties. These counselors provide the objectivity of an outsider who, nevertheless, has been "through the mill" himself.

• *Help in preparing a resume.* Here again, guidance proceeds from first-hand experience. Objective is to help the job seeker resolve any problems he may have in writing up or organizing his experience in a factual resume.

• *Guidance in developing a campaign.* The member is urged to develop a broad and systematic campaign, aimed at exploring the most promising areas for his particular background.

• *Availability for openings developed by the field group.* As job openings are developed by the Forty Plus field force, they are referred to eadquarters to be matched against the resumes of members. Those that ualify are sent to the prospective employer.

• Resumes are publicized in the Club's monthly *Executive Manpower Directory*. Listings are broken down under five headings: Accounting & Finance, Advertising & Public Relations, Engineering & Manufacturing, General Management (including planning, management, marketing, production), Sales & Marketing, and Sales, Technical. FPC's *Directory* goes ut to a list of 7,000 companies.

A particularly useful aspect of FPC's service to members: It provides a New York City business address from which an executive may conduct his job-search campaign; free telephone answering service; use of typewriters, current business newspapers, and industrial directories.

The modest fees and the non-profit nature of the Forty Plus Club, as well as its good record of placement, recommend it to any over-forty job seeker who feels the need for experienced assistance in his job hunt.

Since the days in which it was founded, the club has developed into an efficient and purposeful organization based on the idea that people who help each other are better able to help themselves. The job seeker achieves two important gains: *objectivity* (he can see his own position in that of his fellow Forty Plusers), *encouragement* (the very existence of the FPC tells him that despite his age, he has a chance for a job, since many others in the same boat have succeeded).

As for the *company* seeking executive manpower, Forty Plus offers an obligation-free and fee-free service that might pay off handsomely for the price of a phone call or letter of inquiry.

Today, FPC's average member is fifty-two years old and has earned $16,000 a year. Ages range from forty to seventy-four, and most recent salaries range from $9,600 to $50,000. Employers list about three thousand job openings a year with the organization.

Man-Marketing Clinic

The Sales Manpower Foundation sponsors the Man-Marketing Clinic, which for the past thirty-one years has counseled thousands of men and women in their search for better positions. The clinic is free and does not limit its service to sales people. Anyone from sales clerk to company president can attend, and he may go to as many sessions as he needs to perfect his job resume and develop a successful job campaign. Many business leaders contribute generously of their time and counsel, to act as working staff of the clinic.

The clinic meets one evening a week in the New York Life Insurance Annex Building on the north side of 27th Street, between Madison and Fourth Avenues, New York City.

Meetings are open to all those who feel they can benefit from the guidance of experienced men who know the problems and solutions in volved in job seeking. Any preliminary questions one may have can b cleared up by a call to the office of Sales Manpower Foundation listed in the Manhattan phone directory.

Resume-writing Services

For the job seeker who finds it hard to present himself objectively, th outside resume-writing service may provide an answer. Needless to say, resume should sound as if it were the distinctive product of the applicant Yet such services flourish precisely because many individuals do not know how to "write like themselves."

The procedure is simple. The service spends an hour or so with th job seeker, eliciting from him facts about himself, his previous jobs accomplishments, abilities, and other relevant information. He and th resume writer agree on the points that should be stressed, those that shoul be played down or explained. (Help on the latter point may be especiall welcome if a man has had a long period of unemployment, frequent jol shifts, or some other hard-to-explain factor in his job history.)

After the resume is drafted, the client can make any changes he find necessary before it is reproduced. Charges are fairly modest. Resum Planning Service in New York City, for example, charges from $35 up t write a resume. For duplication, charge is $9 for fifty copies, $10 for on hundred (of a two-page resume). This firm will also prepare a lette of transmittal for another $5.

Executive Career Development, Inc.

Executive Career Development, Inc., headquartered in Chicago, offer a rather unique service. Listed as a private employment agency in th state of Illinois, its president, James J. Smidl, suggests that it operate essentially as a counseling service.

The details: "We carefully screen the people who contact us," state Smidl, "and pursue matters with about 10 per cent. We're interested onl in the man who has a reasonably good record of success behind him. Suct a record can be measured in many ways, one of which is earnings. But many intangibles affect our judgment, too. Our business is built on a reputatior for seeking out exceptional men and placing them in outstanding com panies.

"In all cases, clients come to our offices in Chicago. We spend five to eight hours in the initial interview just to find out whether he's a man we want to represent, and whether we can serve *his* needs.

"Such a conference does not involve psychological or personality testing," emphasizes Smidl. "Whether a man likes to eat Wheaties or run through the living room naked is of no concern to us. Our meeting is a realistic appraisal of the man in depth. Our aim is to determine *what* it is he *wants* to do and *why* he wants to do it. *Can* he do the things he *says* he wants to do? *Should* he do these things?

"We provide objective judgment and analysis of the man's aspirations and qualifications. We may even help shape his thoughts, but the conclusions reached are his own. By the time our conference is ended, we have pinned down his career objective—the maximum result we both agree can be obtained.

"Next step: We carefully instruct our client in the preparation of material facts we will need, including an explanation of his attitudes, opinions, philosophies, personal family life, or whatever seems appropriate. Now we are fitted to present his case to selected companies and speak with intelligence on his behalf.

"Next, we contact top executives in selected companies in a variety of ways: telephone, telegram, personal handwritten notes, letters, printed biographies, personal visits. We also make contacts through our lawyers, management-consulting firms, banks, and similar sources. We talk directly with chief operating executives, board chairmen, principal stockholders, occasionally with personnel people.

"We also carry on a continuous research program, searching for mergers, acquisitions, new companies, personnel changes—anything and everything that may mean a possible opportunity for a client. In short, we search the entire range of logical—and sometimes illogical—possibilities that exist. It's the exploration of many avenues that finally spells success in finding the right job for our man.

"When a promising opportunity is uncovered, we open negotiations. This in itself is valuable to our clients. We introduce him under favorable circumstances, establish a bargaining position for him, and give him any guidance he may need at this critical period. Occasionally we restrain him from taking a job, because we don't believe it is in his best interest.

"One feature of Executive Career Development's service is the circulation of a specially prepared, four-page brochure, detailing a client's personality, background, and qualifications, often with a photograph, printed in three colors on fine quality stock."

The company operates nationally, and, to an increasing extent, internationally. Smidl notes he's served clients from India, Mexico, Chile, Canada, Switzerland, Korea, among other countries.

Fees are in keeping with the broad range of services provided. In most cases a retainer of $600 is charged, payable by the client after he has accepted a position. (There is no charge for the initial day-long conference.) Executive Career Development requires an exclusive position in each case, generally for 120 days, sometimes for a year. There is also a contingent fee, paid when a man is hired, usually by the employing company. This fee is based upon first year's salary, graduating upward 1 per cent on $1,000 to from 10 to 20 per cent on a $20,000 or higher salary.

The firm stands behind its placements for two years. That is, if the client leaves his new employer voluntarily within two years after he is accepted, ECD will undertake to find a satisfactory replacement without charge to the company. The same guarantee applies to the client. If the position turns out to be other than represented and he's performed "honorably," ECD will undertake a further job search for him at no further cost.

The next type of guidance is several times removed from the approaches just described. It's connected with no scientific discipline, is based on no recognized procedural rules, yet can be extremely helpful.

The "Control Committee"

There are few job seekers who, at one time or another during a job hunt, haven't wished they had a sounding board to test out ideas, suggest new approaches, and provide objective answers to the question, "How am I doing?" Wives may not fit the bill. As one executive said, "My wife considers the address of a company a major indicator. If it's in a 'good' section of town, she's all for my taking the job; otherwise, thumbs down."

Yet, most men have more resources at their command than they realize. A seldom-used yet very effective way to get a sounding board, is to organize a group of friends and interested business contacts who are willing to meet once a week, biweekly, or at whatever times will be most helpful. The purpose: to listen to an account of how the search is going and make helpful suggestions. A thumbnail agenda for such a conference might include the following:

1. *Detailed recounting of moves made during the past period*—ads answered, people seen, possibilities developed.

2. *Discussion*, between the "board" and the job seeker, to develop full details and nuances of what's been happening.

3. *Evaluation session* to pin down dead ends; poor use of time, energy, and money; and promising developments.

4. A *discussion of "next week's program,"* detailing the next steps in the job hunt: people to see, firms to contact, ideas to apply.

The value of such a "board of directors" obviously depends on the capabilities of its people. There is little doubt that the know-how of two or three experienced business people teamed up to reinforce the job seeker's own efforts can be extremely fruitful.

Usually, the more varied the group, the better. Prime qualifications for a "panel member" would be: knowledge of the job hunter's abilities; knowledge of the field in which he seeks his job; knowledge of business and, especially, employment practices.

Preventive Career Guidance

A growing number of companies today are turning to psychological-service firms to assist executives having job troubles. They find that a man developing emotional difficulties in connection with his job, or one whose effectiveness seems to be constricted, can often be straightened out by timely counseling.

Says Sherman Hoyt, president of the Center for Career Planning: "I very much favor the idea of guidance *in advance* of career crises. From time to time I come across an executive with a severe job problem, and I'm sure that if he could have received professional guidance while he was in his earlier years—let's say in his early thirties—he'd have been able to avoid later difficulties."

Hoyt goes a step further, and suggests career analysis and guidance for the seemingly *successful* executive, one whose future seems relatively without career pitfalls. For the company, as well as for the individual executive, this concept of *preventive* guidance has in its favor the same logic that recommends a physical checkup, or a periodic dental examination, before gums start to bleed or cavities develop.

14

Resumes—How to Read
and Write Them

"The employment world floats on a sea of resumes," observes one employment-agency official wryly.

"Resumes are a necessary evil," adds another. "Few job seekers are hired without one."

Resumes are seldom an unmitigated blessing, either to the writer or the reader. Too often, the weaknesses of the medium are taken as flaws in the source: A capable executive sends out a group of letters, baited with his resume. Week after week goes by, and he doesn't even get a nibble. The cause is not lack of qualifications, but his failure to make the bait sufficiently attractive.

Outside Help?

One resorted-to remedy, of course, is for the job seeker to take his problem to a professional resume-writing service. This may be a worthwhile investment. On the other hand, there is some evidence that many resume screeners—particularly experienced personnel managers—reject the "factory-made" resume because it is just that—a production-line job that often has too much "sell" and not enough "tell." At any rate, even if an executive does use help in constructing a resume, he must be its final editor, since he is the one who will have to back up the resume, in case a job interview is forthcoming.

For the prospective employer, too, resumes are often a headache. Instead of helping him evaluate applicants quickly and accurately, they are often confusing, time-wasting, and downright misleading. Result: The executive who is hiring shuffles through dozens of resumes, selects the few that look interesting, and limits his interviews to these. He may, in the process, pass over the best-qualified men.

This chapter is designed to help both the applicant and the employer solve some of the mysteries of this troublesome yet vitally necessary tool. The ABC's of resumes will be given short shrift, since the average executive has had considerable experience with them. But the DEF's are missed by many, including the executive who handled thousands of resumes as an employer but who develops a severe case of writer's cramp when he must put himself down on paper.

The Two Problems of Writing a Resume

When the average executive sits down at his desk to prepare a resume, he immediately confronts two difficulties:

1. *The writing problem.* Writing anything, from a play to a business letter, is an art, a specialized skill. Not everyone has it. Yet, the general assumption is that the job seeker possesses the inherent skill to write a good resume. How wrong this assumption can be is known by anyone who has ever had to screen resumes. "Fully half of the resumes I see," says one veteran personnel director, "are so badly put together that they automatically disqualify the applicant from an interview." This holds true despite the highest qualifications.

2. *The emotional problem.* Said the philosopher George Santayana, "Nothing requires a rarer intellectual heroism than willingness to see one's equation written out." The fact is that many of us, normally self-confident and courageous, quail at the task of putting ourselves down on paper. The strain on the ego and the painfulness of self-exposure often prove a real handicap to satisfactory performance.

Fortunately, both these problems, as well as the routine ones, can be overcome. The road to victory is no simple garden path. But a few basic ideas can provide a serviceable roadmap for reaching the final objective —an eye-catching resume that does justice to what the writer is, and what he can accomplish for a prospective employer.

Why Not Plagiarize?

The easiest way to write a resume is to pick a model from any of a dozen sources—a pamphlet on "How to Write a Resume," a sample that got a colleague a job, or one sent the job seeker when *he* was hiring. This approach is a benign form of plagiarism at worst, and it may produce results. But the job seeker who produces a resume without understanding how it works runs a great risk of copying the wrong things and building trouble into an interview, should he get one.

The paragraphs that follow are designed to help you write a resume that not only packs a punch but that fairly represents *you*. By following the suggested guides, you *can* proceed with confidence to adapt other resumes to your own purposes. The appendix includes several resumes that you may want to consider as models. But it is suggested that you turn to the samples only after you've familiarized yourself with the basic principles of what a good resume should do.

Guides for Resume Writers

Since this chapter presumes to cover the DEF's of resume writing, such strictures as "Don't send out finger-marked copies"; "Don't send out carbons," will get only brief treatment. (This doesn't mean they should be ignored.) The secret of a good resume lies in a number of principles:

1. *"The resume is not the man, but must seem to be."* Every quality considered desirable in the executive applicant should be reflected in his resume. For example, dignity is an asset for an executive. Accordingly a resume pitted with raffish humor or offensive informality will quickly meet the wastebasket. If clear thinking and decisiveness are required in the job, a resume that rambles, equivocates, and confuses will be discarded—regardless of the virtues of the man it represents.

This doesn't rule out originality. Unusual devices can still be related to the position being sought. One executive, applying for a job as marketing manager for a paper company, had his resume typed on a special grade of tinted bond. And, no accident, it was manufactured by the company in question. He correctly figured that the tinted paper would attract attention, followed by the recognition that it was the company's own product. It was an ingratiating approach, and it worked. Out of fifty-three applications, his was one of four that moved to the interview stage.

2. *Choose the rifle over the shotgun.* As between the "one universal resume," and the one slanted to a particular job or employer—the weight of logic and experience favors the latter. Said one executive in surprise over an ex-colleague's job-hunting approach, "Why, Jim has nine different versions of his resume!" Nine may be just the right number, if Jim has capabilities that qualify him for nine varying job prospects.

It helps to think of a resume as being a precision tool, shaped and sharpened to perform a specific job. Job hunters who make up a "universal resume" and send it out in wholesale batches seldom land the job of their choice. There's a good reason. Competition is tough, and a "universal" resume will inevitably seem vague when stacked up against one that has been tailored to the particular job opportunity.

3. *Keep the screener's attitude in mind.* The resume reader is likely to be as impersonal as a ticket taker at a movie. If the resume seems to "have

the ticket," it's put into the O.K. group. If not, the discard is immediate. Most screeners have a negative bias. That is, they look for reasons to rule out an application, since it is by the process of elimination that screening progresses at the early stages.

Says one veteran: "Whenever I come across a resume sent in by X [naming a firm that specializes in writing resumes for its clients], I toss it right into the wastebasket. It's overwritten, I'd never be able to figure out the man's real qualifications."

In the final stages of hiring, there is, of course, a greater willingness to spend time with the selected final candidates. But most recruiters feel that to be painstaking at the early resume screenings simply represents an inordinate waste of time.

This attitude clearly puts the burden on the job seeker, to develop the best "ticket" he knows how. An especially helpful idea is suggested by Maxwell Harper, head of the Harper Employment Agency: "One thing I always tell an executive who is looking for a new affiliation: 'Remember that what you are doing is *selling your services.*' With this thought in mind, he won't confine himself to telling a prospective employer what he has done for other companies, but will suggest to the prospective employer what he can do for him."

4. *Know the effect you're after.* A resume doesn't get a man a job. When it's successful, it gets him a job interview. This fact is of major importance in resume design. It means several things.

• The resume should seek to arouse interest, rather than to completely satisfy it.

• It shouldn't try to answer all possible questions, or to contain a person's entire work history in full detail.

• It should contain nothing that can't be substantiated in a face-to-face meeting with a prospective employer. (If successful, it will provide the foundation for the subsequent job interview.)

• It should highlight those facts that especially recommend the applicant to the prospective employer.

The later sections of this chapter devoted to telling the company executive how to read a resume can be especially helpful to the resume writer. He'll gain new understanding of just how the screening process works, and thereby will better understand how to avoid its knockout tactics.

5. *Avoid "resume-ese."* One executive who sees more resumes between breakfast and dinner than the average manager sees in his entire professional career has this to say: "My pet peeve is the man who hides behind the third person, grammatically speaking. I'm sick of these no-character no-sell resumes that use phrases such as 'Was responsible for,' and 'Had intensive experience in.'" He concludes by saying, "I like 'I.'" Others

are indifferent on this particular point, but agree that they abhor abbreviations, obscure trade terms.

The resume, as every other type of writing, has its clichés. They can be avoided quite easily by taking a straightforward, unpretentious approach that sticks to facts and states them with clarity. And, whether writing your resume or adapting one of the samples in the appendix, don't try to be "literary." Your best writing style is your own. But remember, clarity and brevity are the twin supports of an effective resume.

6. *Decide whether your career history is best presented by job or by function.* The particular job you're aiming for will determine the most effective method of organization. In general there are two types of resumes:

a. BY JOB. In this form, you start with your most recent job and go backwards in time, naming your various employers, the types of firms, and the work you performed for each.

A chronological listing of jobs is particularly effective when you've had an impressive series of positions to your credit. Of course, if the jobs were short tenure and suggest job hopping, the method becomes less desirable.

b. BY FUNCTION. You start with the function of greatest interest to the prospective employer and follow up with others in the order of their pertinence. The functional approach is particularly useful in occupations of a somewhat technical nature—such as marketing, public relations, engineering, and so on, where the work is varied or there are frequent changes of assignment.

The functional method also is best for the executive who has held his last job for a considerable length of time. Here the chronology of jobs is of less interest than the description of the various responsibilities the job seeker had in his last job affiliation.

In some instances it may be best to combine the two approaches. Here, the applicant indicates a chronology of jobs held, but also indicates briefly the functional responsibilities held in connection with each job assignment.

7. *Slanting the resume.* To the professional writer, "slanting" simply means that one aspect of what is being described is given more emphasis than others. Accordingly, in writing a resume, the slanting comes about when you do the following:

• Point up *qualifications* of most appeal to a prospective employer.
• Emphasize those *responsibilities* that are of major interest to the prospective employer.
• In describing *accomplishment*, highlight those of greatest interest to the employer. For example, if what he is seeking is a man to take over complete charge of an operation, you emphasize that part of your experience that demonstrates your past performance of this kind—ability to assume complete responsibility, and so on.

Emphasis also has a visual aspect. You can highlight important information by the use of headings, capital letters, underlining. All such devices help the resume reader to quickly find the key elements of your qualifications.

8. *Does your resume look good?* "We've had resumes come in here for top jobs," says a veteran personnel executive, "that were dog-eared, smeary carbon copies, updated in purple or green ink, changes pasted over with paper patches. I won't say this kind of thing kills the applicant's chances, but it certainly increases the odds against him."

In addition to being neat, un-dog-eared, and definitely not a carbon copy, your resume should suggest compactness. You achieve this effect by putting your principal qualifications down on a single page. Backup pages—one, two, or three—are usually adequate to expand on the brief statements covered on page one.

When you are sharp-shooting for a single important job, it's a good idea to submit a freshly typed resume. However, if your job campaign calls for many copies, you can have them reproduced by some clean, inexpensive method—such as mimeograph or some offset method. Somewhat more costly is reproduction by a multityping process, in which each copy looks like an original typed job. In all cases, there should be an individual covering letter. The gist of this letter should be that you're applying to the company because you feel your qualifications are uniquely appropriate. To back up your statement, call the attention of the reader to one or more points of your resume.

9. *Weigh the offbeat versus conventional.* While it's easy enough to rule out the really *gauche* appeal—the Hollywood-type adjectives that assure the reader that the applicant has "terrific qualifications"—the real problem is somewhat more subtle: You want to attract attention without offending.

To some extent, what causes a positive (or a negative) reaction will vary from industry to industry, job function to function, executive recruiter to recruiter. What is considered "imaginative" in the advertising or entertainment world might seem "pushy" in banking circles. One man's meat, etc.

Yet balance should be struck between being completely conventional—therefore undistinguished by originality—and being "far out." The best approach, in general, seems to be one that departs *slightly* from the conventional:

• An executive indicates in his covering letter: "I know your ad asked for 'full biographical details.' Instead of a conventional form, I'm taking the liberty of sending you a profile of me that appeared in a recent issue of *The Wall Street Journal.*"

• A textile executive whose professional advance had been marked by rapidly rising earnings, typed the salaries for his various jobs in red, and stated in an opening summary: "The steady increases in earnings highlighted below in red are a direct indication, I feel, of the growing contribution I have made to past employers."

As far as appearance is concerned, unconventionality may be achieved by the color and type of paper, color of ink, method of printing, layout, and so on. One of the more handsome resumes to land on a recruiter's desk was printed in black and gold on grey paper, with a very wide column for headings at the left, and boxed copy in a rather narrow column to the right. (Usually, the shorter the line, the easier to read.)

This resume "looked expensive," and it was. Two things made it highly acceptable. It was done in excellent taste. The effect of the black and gold ink was rich-looking, not garish. Second, the executive who had devised it was looking for a job in publishing. Implicit in his resume was the message, "I know how to create a quality printing job." On the other hand, had he been aiming for a treasurer's job the offbeat resume might have ruled him out.

In short, originality, when tempered by good taste, will nearly always attract favorable attention. Otherwise, it can be dangerous.

10. *Understand the value of brevity.* The streamlined resume invariably has the edge over its padded opposite number. First, the screener is likely to be under time pressure and will want to skim the resume. The more fat he has to get through before getting to the meat, the greater his impatience.

Second, a resume that goes on at needless length makes a weaker rather than a stronger case. Much can be said in a few words, as this statement taken from one resume shows:

"For seven years I headed up maintenance for the ———— company. For this three-building plant, overall maintenance costs were cut 15 per cent during my tenure, in the face of expanding operations and generally rising costs."

Obviously, the engineer could have gone on at length to give the background of his cost-cutting feat. But in so doing, he might have lessened the impact of a major point. The details can always be filled in during an interview. In part, that's what it's for.

"One type of resume I always discard," reports one screener, "is the one that paints a bright picture of a man's potential, and provides little information about what he's already done."

The lesson suggested here is this: If a man can "talk himself into a job," the place to do it is in the job interview, not through a resume. Rosy writing matches up poorly against resumes that tell a straightforward story of accomplishment.

One professional writer gives his advice in a terse phrase: "Avoid adjectives like the plague."

11. *Give your resume a "cold stare."* This is a final step, giving the finished effort objective scrutiny. Here are the kinds of things to look for:

• Is all the "get-in-touch" data down in black and white, and on the first page where it can be quickly spotted? Your name, address, and telephone number should be blocked together.

• "Sometimes it's hard to tell what they're applying for," says a personnel official of a large food company. He's referring to the failure of some resumes to show plainly the type of job the applicant is seeking, especially on unsolicited resumes.

• If you have used the "Personal," or "Personal Data" heading, have you included everything that's appropriate, and omitted the unnecessary? Usually, age, marital situation, number of children and their ages, physical condition are all that's required. If you're proud of your height and weight, add those. One executive needlessly included an item, "Travel Experience," under "Personal Data." Did this represent business experience or pleasure travel? Under the "Personal" heading, it was clearly out of place. And watch your wording. One widower, giving his family status, wrote, "Single, three children."

• Are you sure you haven't given too much space to data that are relatively unimportant? Lumping jobs together may make sense. One executive indicated in a single paragraph that early in his career he had "held three jobs selling apparel items to department stores." In this case, merging made sense, since the job he was after was in an entirely different field—office manager for a toy company.

To further help you solve the writing problem mentioned at the start of the chapter, refer to one or more of the resumes contained in the appendix, starting on page 261. These resumes have been selected as well-written examples of their kind. In adjusting your own information to one or the other form, phrase your material as concisely and clearly as possible.

What about Career Handicaps?

A frequent question resume writers ask is, "What shall I do about a negative element in my work history?" They may be referring to anything from a job from which they've been fired to an overly long period of unemployment.

The only general answer possible for this question is this: Remember that the resume is designed not to get you a job but an interview. Since questions on this touchy area may arise in the course of an interview, it is inadvisable to misrepresent such facts. However, there's no reason why they cannot be minimized as much as possible in the resume. For the handling of such matters in the interview, Chapter 15 on the job interview will make specific recommendations.

The balance of this chapter is directed primarily to the employer. But it can provide extremely helpful information to the job seeker as well.

How to Read a Resume

"I've seen hundreds of dollars wasted," says the top executive of a Chicago corn-products company, "simply because resumes from job applicants were screened by the wrong people."

It does happen from time to time: A company spends money on newspaper ads to seek out applicants for a job opening. Then, when the resumes start rolling in, they're dumped on the desk of an inexperienced personnel assistant along with vague instruction to "pick out the good ones." Even with more than minimal instruction, the average untrained person isn't likely to be able to "pick out the good ones." The ability to read and evaluate a resume requires considerable know-how.

Five Tips for the Resume Reader

Whether you do the screening yourself or assign the job to a subordinate, it's important that the job be done systematically. Otherwise, even though you wind up with a man for the job, you may well have failed to get the *best possible* man, or the best man represented by a resume. The following steps will help:

1. *Write out the job specifications,* so that the resume reader knows what he's looking for. This means you must give more than the job title. It means even more than knowing the statement of the qualifications —as they may have appeared in a newspaper ad, for example. The screener must know enough so he can detect a variety of knockout factors:

   • What qualifications would be *insufficient* for the job?
   • What elements would mean that an applicant was *overqualified* for the job?
   • What types of *related experience* would especially recommend an applicant?
   • What specific qualifications of education or experience are particularly desirable? For example, the ad may say, "college degree." You may feel that a particular college or group of colleges would give you a better-qualified man. The screener should have this information.

2. *Use a clear-cut set of categories.* A simple three-category system may be set up:

   PILE 1: *"The O.K.s."* Applicants who definitely qualify for the job.
   PILE 2: *"The Doubtfuls."* Those who are generally qualified but have

something in their work experience that raises a question as to suitability.

PILE 3: *"The N.G.s."* Those who definitely do not qualify.

You may use a system of three categories, or set up four or more. It all depends on the nature of the job and the number of resumes you get. Obviously a two-category system also is possible, in which applicants either qualify or do not. This method saves time as a preliminary step when you have many qualified applicants.

Especially if you use a two-category screen, you want to make sure that resumes that raise questions are *not* automatically assigned to the "N.G." pile. One executive, checking on his assistant's screening, went through the rejects and found an outstanding applicant: "How come you ruled this one out?" "Salary," said the screener. "He asked for $2,000 more than we're offering."

A question such as this should be settled at a later stage in screening. The screener should be reminded, "When in doubt, leave it *in*." Subsequent screenings can handle questionable cases. Once a resume goes into the reject pile, it's finished. To a large extent the latitude you adopt depends on the number of resumes you get. The more qualified resumes, the tighter you make your screen.

One recruiter uses two stages in his preliminary sorting. He first goes through all resumes quickly, assigning them to categories after a few seconds of skimming. Then he goes back to each pile, gives each resume fuller consideration, and adjusts any misjudgment of his first impression.

"It's important to give all resumes approximately the same type of screening treatment," states one veteran screener. "This tends to minimize personal biases—as to style of resumes, for example."

If possible, subsequent screenings should be performed by executives who will be in on the final hiring decision. It's not unusual for an executive who is to make the final decision to ask for "the best five or six resumes." But if these five or six are to be distilled from a group of twenty or thirty, it's unwise to leave it to a subordinate to select the "better-qualified" out of a group of qualified applicants.

A "Special" Category? "I tell my screeners to set up a separate category for "specials," reports a personnel executive who does recruiting for a major auto-parts manufacturer. "I've found it a good time-saver."

What he has in mind are resumes that may be off the track, but nevertheless deserve attention. For example:

• Men who are not exactly qualified for the immediate job opening may be excellent possibilities for other positions in the company.

• Applicants asking for too high a salary may have unique and highly desirable qualifications that would justify changing the job specification.

• Says one West-coast recruiter: "We set aside promising resumes from people who live a great distance away. If the job is difficult to fill, or they're more promising than the locals, we may be willing to see them, and pay their travel expenses."

•   Executives outside the preferred age range—below or above—may get special consideration if their other qualifications are impressive. "We hired a bright youngster, even though we were looking for an older man, because he had so much on the ball." Provision for a "special category" gives the screener the opportunity to consider the otherwise "unqualified" man.

3. *Read between the lines.* The experienced screener develops a feel, a "sixth sense" for resumes. There's no mystery about this ability. It consists of developing a keen eye for elements such as these:

•   *Peculiar emphasis.* An expert explains, "An executive with twenty years of working experience who gives inordinate space to his Ivy League college background and his college honors is likely to have little to boast about in his professional career."

•   "I take *job titles* with a grain of salt," says a Chicago employment-agency manager. He discounts a job title in favor of the functions the man actually performed in the company. In many companies, job titles are vague. An ex-employer may say, "Make up any job title for yourself that looks good."

•   "Look for *progression* in a man's career," suggests a Duluth recruiter. "Ask: 'What kind of changes has the man made in going from one job to the next? Has each step been a forward one?' Where possible, I check by comparing his salary increments from one job to the next."

•   One recruiter says that *job tenure* can be the key to a man's background. "A man who has worked for only one company may be an outstanding performer, whose company wouldn't let him go. On the other hand, he may be a stick-in-the-mud, and a poor bet for employment. Examining his work record with this question in mind may help you decide which." Short tenure with a diversity of employers may indicate anything from an ambitious job hopper to an unstable neurotic. By checking tenure, and using any untoward finding as a question, you can examine the resume with a keener eye.

•   *Lapses in employment* are another significant point. One can't make snap judgments. But gaps in an employment record can provide helpful clues in determining a man's employability. If all other points of a man's background qualify him, the open periods should be investigated in the job interview.

Training a beginner in the fine art of reading between the lines of resumes may create a problem. Will he use such a technique intelligently or summarily? After all, he's being asked to pass judgment.

It goes without saying that anyone given a screening assignment should be chosen not only for intelligence, but also for maturity. The immature person is almost sure to lack the judgment necessary to make a perceptive evaluation of the "man on paper." And the man, young or old, with a weakness for playing God is poison for a screening job.

4. *"Are you screening for the job, or for the applicant's prospective boss?"* This is how a San Francisco personnel executive makes an important distinction. The fact is, there can be considerable differences between the qualifications as they appear on paper, and what the prospective superior really wants.

"There's no mention of height on the specification sheet," reports one recruiter, "but I know if an applicant is over 5 feet 8 inches, I might just as well save everybody's time and not send him along for an interview." In this instance, the employer's own height—or, rather, lack of it—made him allergic to taller men. It's a fact that won't appear on the job-man specification, but it's a fact of life the screener must contend with.

Other qualities may, in the same way, be especially desirable, or be knockout factors. Anything from an applicant's manner of speech to his hobbies can make him highly acceptable or unacceptable to the employer. Resumes that are screened by individuals who do not know the hiring executive's preferences may be wasting considerable time.

Should you screen for the job or the employer? It's a question that had better be answered by mutual agreement between the screener and the prospective superior, if false starts are to be avoided.

5. *Avoid mistaking "the symbol for the thing."* No matter how well an executive feels he performs as an evaluator of resumes, it's unwise to make direct comparisons between resumes as though they were the applicants themselves. For one thing, you always face the likelihood that a better man has written the poorer resume. For another, a bare-bones outline can never do justice to years of rich experience.

"No resume can show you the applicant's personality," is the way one recruiter describes the limitation posed by resumes. Remember that even the final stages of resume reading and evaluation are only preliminary to the job interview.

15

The Job Interview—
From Both Sides of the Desk

"The job interview is the climax of the entire recruiting process," says one executive who has conducted many.

He'd find little disagreement. The job seeker, after weeks or months of scouting, has his first shot at the target when he faces a prospective employer. The employer, who has invested time and money on recruiting, knows the interview may be his last step before selecting the final candidate.

For both job seeker and prospective employer, the ordeal of the job interview can be eased. Pitfalls can be avoided, challenges met more successfully by an understanding of what the job interview really represents. And effective steps can be taken by interviewer and interviewee to get the most out of the meeting.

Here again, it's strongly recommended that whichever side of the desk you occupy, you consider *both* aspects of the subject, as covered by this chapter. The man who understands *both* points of view will be able to anticipate his interview problems and solve them better.

How Reliable Are Interviews?

It may come as a surprise to many executives that behavioral scientists by no means agree that interviewing is an effective evaluation tool. Here's what two experts, M. C. Dunnette and B. M. Bass, have to say in the University of California periodical, *Industrial Relations:*

> The personnel interview continues to be the most widely used method for selecting employees, despite the fact that it is a costly, inefficient, and usually invalid procedure. It is often used to the exclusion of far more

168

thoroughly researched and validated procedures. Even when the interview is used in conjunction with other procedures, it is almost always treated as the final hurdle in the selection process. In fact, other selection methods (e.g., psychological tests) are often regarded simply as supplements to the interview.

Scientists' doubts about interviewing go back many years. In 1915, W. D. Scott conducted a study to find out the reliability of selection interviews. Six personnel managers interviewed thirty-six applicants for sales positions. Each manager ranked the applicants in order of their suitability for the job. The results have shaken interviewers ever since: The rankings made by the personnel managers showed little relationship to each other.

According to a case history supplied by Maxwell Harper, the same problem crops up in interviewing today:

John X, an experienced production executive, was interviewed and evaluated by two different companies. Company A reports, "He is definitely the best-qualified man we have seen. But we aren't hiring him because he isn't aggressive enough to deal with the union."

Company B reports, "We have seen other men who have been as well-qualified, but we're going to hire John X because he is aggressive and can deal with the union."

Despite criticism of the selection interview, however, there are few companies who would hire a key executive without one. At the very least, a man-to-man discussion gives the employer an opportunity to sense the mettle of the job candidate, assess his appearance, observe his manner, expressed attitudes, and so on.

Furthermore, the Scott study does not actually prove that interviewing is ineffective. What it points up is the fact that different interviewers may arrive at different conclusions. And psychologists and sociologists have been unable to come up with anything more specific or constructive about interviewing since. Accordingly, this chapter regards the theories of interviewing as a moot question, and emphasizes practical procedures and methods for avoiding the obvious and not-so-obvious pitfalls.

The Basic Situation

In the art of playwriting, there's something called the "obligatory scene." This is the scene the playwright *must* include. For example, if the play has a hero and a villain, somewhere in the course of the drama these two must be brought face to face.

The job interview is, in a sense, an obligatory scene in the hiring drama. The trouble is, too many think of it as a confrontation between opposing forces. "When an interviewer and interviewee face one another, the two sides of a desk become light-years apart," says one executive who's been through the mill. This view may be valid, but it is essentially unhelpful. There's a more constructive way to consider the job interview.

Some years ago, in a study on the sales interview, the Research Institute of America developed a concept that illustrates this viewpoint. It can be helpful to both employer and applicant. Here is a paraphrase of the part of the RIA study dealing with the attitudes of interviewer and interviewee:

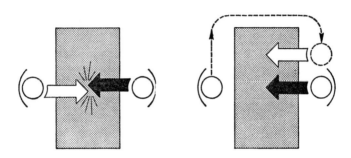

Imagine a desk as in the sketch, with the applicant on one side and the interviewing executive on the other. When the applicant exerts "pressure," it's as if he were pushing straight across the desk, as indicated by the arrows. Chances are, he will be opposed by resistance from the interviewer. The result is a conflict in which the applicant is usually at a disadvantage.

To exert pressure without generating resistance, the applicant must first get into the proper psychological position, as indicated by the dotted line in the second sketch. Here, when the interviewee exerts "pressure," it will be *with* the interviewer. The employer is aware of no pressure and accordingly has no reason to resist. Essentially, this change of attitude is achieved when the applicant realizes that it is not his objective to "put something over" on the interviewer or to "sell him a bill of goods." When the interviewee realizes that it is to his and the interviewer's *common interest* to arrive at a fair understanding of the situation, the interview should develop most constructively.

Mutual Interests of the Interviewer and Interviewee

The two principals in an interview naturally represent two different points of view, yet for each, the road to success involves an understanding of their areas of mutual interest:

• The applicant has two objectives: first, to discover whether or not the job for which he is applying is really the one he wants; second, if it is, to sell the interviewer on the desirability of hiring him.

• The interviewer also has two objectives. First, he must decide whether the particular candidate is the man for the job. If the answer is in the affirmative, he must then persuade him to take the job. These sets of ob-jectives have more in common than they have in conflict.

The principals must act in such a way during the interview that their mutual objectives will be met. This means, both must decide whether or not the applicant is right for the job. If both agree that the applicant *is* the man for the job, mutually satisfactory hiring arrangements must be made.

Three Basic Steps

Too often, the job interview is viewed as an isolated thing by itself. Actually, it consists of three phases; and an understanding of this by both applicant and interviewer is essential for an effective interview:

• *Preparation.* It's unwise for either individual to walk into a conference "cold." Each has homework to do if his role in the discussion is to carry weight.

• *The Interview.* This is the actual meeting, everything that is said and done when the two principals come face to face.

• *Follow-up.* These are the moves both interviewer and applicant should take as a result of what's developed during the interview. The nature of these follow-up steps naturally depends on the results of the meeting.

These steps will be developed as they apply to both principals in sections respectively titled: I. How to Conduct a Job Interview; II. How to Be a Successful Interviewee.

I. How to Conduct a Job Interview

In one of the better books on the subject, *The Executive Interview,* Benjamin Balinsky and Ruth Burger point out the range of types of interviews:

> While the employment interview is the most frequently used device in selection it is also the least standardized. There are patterned interviews, depth interviews, stress interviews, and even others. Apparently, the in-terview, like the chameleon, changes its complexion with whatever climate exists in the employing situation. But the real problem is that many different oral exercises in conversation go under the name of the inter-view.

In view of the breadth of the subject, the coverage of it here will be practical rather than theoretical. The ideas and concepts presented have been developed as the result of extended conversations with many expert interviewers: personnel officials, executives with considerable hiring ex-perience, employment-agency and executive-recruiting veterans.

A. *Preparation for the Interviewer*

Before he goes into an interview, the executive should be armed with three kinds of information:

1. *Facts about the applicant.* Major information source is usually the man's resume. If the man has been referred by an agency or a recruiting consultant, additional information may be available. If other executives in the company have already seen the applicant, the interviewer may or may not want to get their impressions in advance. Some interviewers prefer to *ignore* other evaluations, until they've had a chance to meet the applicant and form their own opinions.

Suggests King Whitney, Jr., of The Personnel Laboratory: "Get to know the applicant first on paper, before you see him, so that you can prepare for the interview and direct the course of the conversation along the lines *you* choose. Analyze his resume or application form and pinpoint the areas you feel need further exploration and clarification. You want to avoid, as much as possible, referring to a man's resume during the interview, because every time you turn to it, you put him on the defensive. Interrupting the conversation to look at his written record signals to him that you are about to query him and perhaps pin him down. This naturally puts him on guard."

Where the applicant is not the first one seen for the job, the interviewer should use his developing picture of other applicants, their qualifications, and so on, as a comparative measure of the present applicant.

2. *The job.* The interviewer should know in full detail the nature of the job he is trying to fill. This is for purposes of evaluation—"Will the applicant measure up to the requirements?" Dr. Mortimer Feinberg, well-known industrial psychologist and president of BFS Psychological Associates, has made the point that, "To evaluate a man in the abstract can be a waste of time. It is much more to the point to assess a man in relation to his qualifications for a specific job."

And also, you want to be able to describe the job demands to the applicant for his consideration.

In addition to the *responsibilities* of the job, the interviewer should be familiar with *special requirements,* and *problem areas.* For example:

• *Hours or places of work.* Not everyone will take kindly to working odd hours—Saturdays, Sundays. And unless the applicant knows in advance of special travel needs, a possible overseas or even out-of-state stint, there can be unfortunate repercussions after hiring.

• *Human-relations roughspots.* "You'll be inheriting an assistant," says an executive, "who is capable, but not the easiest man in the world to work with. . . ." Such facts should be discussed frankly, if the applicant is a serious contender.

• *Unusual technical requirements.* "A superficial knowledge of EDP isn't enough for this job. It requires a good working knowledge of programing procedures. . . ." Again, don't gloss over difficulties. The man who balks at them in the abstract is even less likely to be happy with them as a job problem.

3. *Checkpoints.* Knowing the critical aspects of the position—the reefs on which previous job holders may have foundered, for example—and the key qualifications, the interviewer should pinpoint the questions he particularly wants answered.

It helps to have some of the questions written down in advance. Some executives use a check sheet which contains the critical points, followed by a rating scale which gives the interviewer the opportunity to indicate his evaluation of the applicant with respect to these specifics. These may range from estimates of *maturity, tough-mindedness,* or *initiative* to such matters as *self-confidence* and *adaptability.*

It's unwise to use these check sheets during the interview. Many people tend to become self-conscious if each phase of the conversation is followed by jottings that obviously mean he's being rated. Check sheets are better used after the interview.

B. The Interview—from the Employer's Side of the Desk

Literally dozens of books have been written on the subject of interviewing, and it is not intended here, in a few pages, to give a complete description of the techniques and approaches. But the points below highlight some of the major considerations the interviewer must have in mind:

1. *Make the physical surroundings as appropriate as possible.* Privacy, quiet, arrangements not to be interrupted will help the interview proceed smoothly. And the old saw, "Put the interviewee at ease," is good advice. It works. That is, better rapport can be established.

2. *Choose your interview method.* Mentioned earlier was the large variety of types of interviews. Basically, your choice is between the patterned and unpatterned, or, as they're sometimes called, the *directed* and *flexible* interview. Your choice should be guided by the kind of information you're seeking. Here's a description of the two:

• *The directed interview.* The interviewer keeps a fairly tight grip on the reins, guides his talk along lines set in advance. An example of this method is the medical interview, in which the doctor gets the patient's history: age, height, weight, and so on.

• *The flexible interview.* The questions asked stem from the answer or reaction to a previous discussion. Typical example: The prospective employer is particularly interested in learning an applicant's motivation. He lets the discussion develop around various job moves the applicant has made, occasionally asking a question to sharpen a particular reply. Since the interviewer is unsure of the kind of answer he's seeking, his line of questioning must be flexible to permit follow-up of all possible angles.

Here's a comparison of the two methods:

DIRECTED INTERVIEW	FLEXIBLE INTERVIEW
Application	
Best for investigations with well-defined goals and clear-cut lines of questioning; verification of resume data.	Especially suitable for fact-finding in complex situations, or where the facts are likely to be on the foggy side.
Preparation	
Can be mapped out in advance, and in complete detail. May use a check sheet to assure touching all bases.	You can only decide on general objectives, and have to tailor the interview as you talk.
Time Limit	
The length of the interview is almost entirely in your hands.	You can't be too sure how long you'll have to stay with it to do a thorough job.
Results	
Likely to give you what you're after in routine matters where the objective is clear-cut and the interviewee cooperative. No help where a one-word answer won't suffice.	Best tool known for giving applicants a chance to open up. It's an ideal digging tool, effective in getting to the bottom of deep or complex matters.

3. *Give some thought to your personal style of interview.* An individual's method of interviewing is often as distinctive as his manner of dress or any other reflection of his personality. Different people conduct interviews in different manners. To name a few:

• *The friendly interviewer.* He attempts to get the applicant relaxed; his manner reflects a lack of pressure.

• *Reserved and objective.* This man, consciously or otherwise, builds a neutral climate, neither friendly nor hostile, neither warm nor cold.

• *Probing, sharp.* This man, under the guise of being businesslike (and sometimes under pressure himself) tends to create a certain amount of tension in the interview.

You yourself will have to decide which style fits you best. It's not intended here to uphold the virtues of the "relaxed fellow" type of approach over the "let's get down to brass tacks" method. What is hoped, however, is that whatever your approach, you use it knowingly and skillfully—with due respect for the feelings and intelligence of the interviewee.

4. *Distinguish between fact and opinion.* In talking to an applicant, a prospective employer will develop two types of material:

a. FACTUAL. This deals with such matters as education, background, compensation, age (certain states bar any direct questions on age, however). Material of this type will be developed to fill gaps in the resume.

b. OPINION. The interviewer must also develop opinions or evaluations of the candidate. As Gardner Heidrick, of Heidrick & Struggles, the Chicago executive-search firm, puts it:

"He must know what motivates the individual, what his strengths and weaknesses might be, how well he has managed, his sensitivity to people and to situations, whether he is a planner or a doer or both. The pattern of the past pretty well forecasts the pattern of the future. And," adds Heidrick, "all of this is obtained either through a directed interview where specific questions are asked or a nondirected interview where the individual is encouraged to talk. The higher the level, the more adroit the interviewer must be."

Assessments are often the result of complex impressions—what a man says, how he says it, what is implied, what is omitted.

In practice, the skillful interviewer attempts to check one fact by another, to firm up an opinion by a related fact:

"Mr. Smith, I have the impression that you're particularly interested in the creative aspects of your job. Is there anything in your last job that bears this out?"

Or, the cross-check may consist of getting a specific fact to verify a general one:

"Mr. Jones, I know that your resume indicates that you have had considerable experience in planning major programs. Can you give me a specific example of one such undertaking?"

5. *Avoid "cuing him in."* Interviewers sometimes unwittingly set out a track for the applicant to run on. They say something early in the meeting that the applicant seizes as a good line to follow. This can damage the usefulness of the interview.

One expert interviewer makes this suggestion:

"Get him talking about himself so you draw tentative conclusions as to what sort of a candidate he is *before* you describe the job and the company to him. If you first discuss the assignment and then ask him about his experience, he will slant his presentation to conform to what he thinks you want to hear. The rule is 'First evaluate, then elaborate.' "

6. *Ask questions that simplify answering—but avoid yes-no answers.* "But I thought you said you could type," exclaims the horrified executive. "I can," assures the newly hired stenographer, "with one finger." Questions that elicit a simple "yes" or "no" can yield partial truths that are extremely misleading.

One skilled interviewer makes this recommendation:

"Try to stimulate *conversation,* rather than conduct an interrogation, asking one question after another. For example, instead of challenging a man with, 'Why did you leave your last job?' try a more subtle tack with a *statement* such as, 'It looks as though you had a good future with your last employer. Why did you leave?' You are inviting a response that calls for more than a simple reply. You are opening up, in an unthreatening manner, a whole subject of conversation. If you continue to discuss this with the man, you are likely to find the real reason he left, rather than settling for a pat answer which he may have already prepared.

7. *Try not to form an overhasty first impression.* The experienced interviewer often regards the first few minutes as a warm-up period. He avoids the temptation of forming a quick impression of the applicant, either good or bad.

Says Maxwell Harper of the Harper Employment Agency: "The general pattern of executive interviews is such that a candidate is either mentally hired or not in the course of the first ten minutes' conversation. Then why do hiring interviews last longer? The balance of the time is spent in giving the employer a rationale for his already made decision."

If one is too quick in forming a positive or negative impression, it tends to color everything thereafter and destroy objectivity.

As one personnel executive puts it, "If you leap to a conclusion that 'this looks like a good man,' you invariably begin to whitewash the applicant. And it works in reverse." A more hard-nosed approach would make you more aware of both good and bad points that emerge throughout the interview.

8. *Don't interrupt unless it is absolutely necessary.* Whether you use a patterned interview or not, it is wise, at some point, to give the applicant free rein. An interruption may unwittingly stop him at just the point where he's going to say something significant. Remember that the more a man talks, the more he tells you about himself. "You only can learn when you listen," says one master of the art.

9. *Use silence.* Novice interviewers are often afraid to let the conversation lapse. Skilled interviewers, on the other hand, deliberately let pauses occur. They want to see what the applicant will do next: Does he talk about anything just to fill in the gaps because he is nervous? Does he clam up and wait for questions? Does he suddenly grab the reins and start interviewing you? In many instances silence is uncomfortable to the interviewee, and he will start to talk. What he says and how he says it can give you helpful insights into the kind of person he is.

10. *Be open and friendly, but avoid giving the impression that you are "sold" on him.* Some well-intentioned interviewers, because of a natural friendliness, give the applicant the idea that he has made an extremely favorable impression—even, by implication, that he has got the nod. If this is true, such an impression may be fine. But if not, and the applicant is

turned down later, he may have a severe reaction. A rejection after his hopes have been built up may cause an abnormal amount of anxiety. The applicant may fear that he failed in some damaging way, or that past employers have impugned his reputation. This is both unfair to the applicant and damaging to a company's public relations.

11. *Try to assess the man's motivation.* Perhaps one of the most revealing signs of a man's capabilities and qualification for a job is his personal motivation. Robert A. Huttemeyer of Thorndike Deland Associates defines two possible extremes between which a man might fall: "Does he have goals, or is he merely drifting aimlessly, taking this job or that one as an economic expedient?"

The importance of this key point is matched only by the difficulty of getting a reliable answer. A man's real reasons for doing something are often lost in the intricate maze of his psyche. We're sufficiently sophisticated nowadays to know that individuals themselves are often mistaken as to the reasons for their actions, or the relative importance they place on various life goals.

Too often the word "challenge" is used loosely, by both the employer and the applicant. The former wants to make a job more attractive—the latter desires to appear independent, venturesome, and with more on the ball than any ordinary job has yet been able to elicit. Accordingly, an employer will describe a job responsibility as "challenging," and an applicant will assert it's the "challenge of the job" that makes him want to accept it.

Perhaps the best one can do on this important point of motivation is judge an applicant on a simple three-point scale—highly motivated, medium, low, and let it go at that. But certainly, this point cannot be ignored in a final evaluation of an applicant for any important job.

12. *Watch out for the interview-wise applicant.* Some people show up extremely well in an interview situation, although they may be so-so performers on the job. The reverse is also true: A man may show up poorly in the interview situation and yet be an excellent executive. The interview is not a realistic job simulation. As one company president observed, "Some men are just good talkers. An interview is duck soup for them. But the same man who can waltz through a tough job interview may fall flat on his face when confronted by the pressures and responsibilities of a demanding job."

Best way to escape falling into the trap of the "professional interviewee" is to avoid registering approval or disapproval of anything he tells you. He is constantly watching you for cues as to what pleases or displeases. If you tip your hand, you only make it easier for the applicant to sell you—and avoid discussing the meaningful aspects of his work history.

13. *Don't be tempted by interview "gimmicks."* There is a segment

of management thinking, fortunately small, that greatly admires tricks in interviewing:

• One executive feels he's at his devastating best—therefore most effective in testing out an interviewee—when he puts his feet up on the desk, stares coldly at the candidate, and says, "Talk." A milder form of this form of inquisition has the interviewer say, "Tell me something about yourself."

• Another executive has heard of the "stress interview," and likes the idea. Accordingly, he shortly begins to toss questions at the job applicant in quick succession. Or, he suddenly brings in a query from left field, trying to "catch" the applicant at some disadvantage. Or, he puts on a show of wrath over some statement of the applicant's, "to see how the man stands up" to such browbeating.

• Another executive likes the "practical stress interview" gimmicks. He arranges to be interrupted at frequent intervals. He arranges for the candidate to sit in an awkward position, or in an uncomfortable seat. He hides the ashtray, on the chance that the applicant will be a smoker. He's heard, "It's a test of a man, to see how he reacts to this no-ashtray situation."

None of the approaches above are acceptable interview procedures, for two reasons: First, the candidate is at a disadvantage in the interview. It isn't fair to exploit the fact. Even more important, these methods may turn up very misleading evidence. The man who caves in under the stress interview may eat up pressure on the job. The one who comes through with flying colors may be able to do so because he knows the interview situation is, in a way, "make believe." The *real* thing might break him down easily.

14. *Don't get lost in details—see the whole man.* Mathew J. Beecher, of Price Waterhouse, has set down in writing what he describes as "his pet peeve about interviewing." He makes an insightful and helpful assertion:

> Most interviewers today don't interview the man for the position— they interview the technical qualifications for the job specifications.
>
> Interviewers seem to feel they have interviewed a man in depth when they have compiled reams of notes and faithfully completed the prescribed checklists. By the same token, the applicant feels he knows the position because he has been told in minute detail all the technical entailments of the position. The interviewer then fits the well-burnished technical qualifications of the applicant neatly into place meshing them with the precisely honed job specifications and you have what appears to be a perfect match. In reality, it is but an adequate match and an adequate job will be performed for an adequate period of time.
>
> There are thousands of the adequate adequates in management spots today—many of whom are drawing high salaries—who owe their present positions to the fact that they were detail-interviewed. These are the men of whom their bosses say, "He does his job all right—but I'd love to be able to get a real top-flight man in there." He is a man who won't be fired or replaced under ordinary circumstances—but let the "top-flight"

man appear on the horizon and the adequate adequate soon is promoted to "Vice President in charge of writing the company history."

There are interviewers today who look only at the technical experience of the man and the technical requirements of the job and then make their match because it is the easy way out. The script is faithfully followed and no decision really has to be made. Fact matching is not decision making.

Technically qualified people are not difficult to find—nor difficult to place. The true test comes when the nonfactual or gray areas are matched. That calls for matching the personality of the man with the atmosphere of the job. It calls for an appreciation of the intangibles of the man and an empathy for the nuances of the function. It calls for looking and feeling beyond the facts. A man's exposure and over-all background must be looked at in light of the climate in which he will work. It boils down to this—a "type" and personality fit between candidate and company ranks infinitely higher than technical qualifications. Potential rates higher than past detailed proficiency.

C. Follow-up for the Interviewer

You have shaken the interviewee's hand and bade him goodbye, giving him some idea of what your intentions are. Now comes the third step—summarizing your interview impressions in writing, while your recollections are still fresh. This is the time to take your check sheets out of the drawer and put them to use.

Discipline yourself to list both the strengths and the weaknesses of every applicant at the conclusion of each interview. This has another advantage: It forces you to look for both strengths and weaknesses *during* the interview—increasing your objectivity.

Comparing your written impressions with the opinions of other interviewers, test results, reference information, and even performance on the job helps you sharpen your judgment of people. It is an effective form of self-education and will result in increasing your confidence in your ability to judge people accurately.

II. How to Be a Successful Interviewee

Being successful in an interview doesn't necessarily mean you walk off with the job. As every good poker player knows, sometimes your smartest move is to fold your hand. An applicant's success in the interview comes about when:

He decides whether or not the job is one he wants.

If he does want it, the employer concludes from his behavior and statements that he is indeed the man for the job. Incidentally, *the employer wants nothing so much as to be sold!*

Here are the three basic phases the applicant must develop: *preparation, the interview, follow-up.*

A. How the Interviewee Prepares

There are good reasons for not walking into an interview situation cold. One is that it's unwise to lard a conversation with too many "I don't know" responses, or too many "Oh, I-didn't-know-that-about-your-company." Another is that the better informed you are, the more self-assured you will be.

There are three main areas about which you should have as much information as possible. One is *yourself.* The second is the *company* to which you're applying: its history, the specifications of the job, and the executive conducting the interview. Third, you want to get *the necessary information to decide* whether you want the job.

Ordinarily, you won't have to do much cramming to get your own record straight. If your memory occasionally plays you tricks, or if there are important details that can't be easily recalled, you may want to memorize these. Mark Twain may have had job applicants in mind when he phrased his famous rule: "Always tell the truth, and you'll have less to remember."

Almost all of what you will want on tap about yourself is in your resume. Read a duplicate of the one that will be in the hands of the interviewer, before the interview. If it seems likely that certain data or documents may strengthen your hand during the conversation, bring the material with you, preferably in a good-looking attaché case—but don't haul it out unless the need arises. Such supporting data may be anything from articles by you or about you to patents or material that specifically illustrate job or professional accomplishments.

Anticipate questions, particularly those that may be difficult to answer. Robert A. Huttemeyer, who does considerable interviewing in his recruiting for Thorndike Deland Associates, advises: "Have carefully considered factual answers for questions about past changes, performance, and so on." Especially the touchy questions.

1. *Getting a line on a prospective employer.* If the company you're interviewing is in an industry with which you are familiar, you may already have a good knowledge of it. Otherwise, it's a good idea to dig up as much information as you can: first, to make sure you understand the interviewer's point of view and, second, to make sure it's a company you'd want to be affiliated with.

Here are some of the techniques available to you:

• *Direct observation.* You can learn a lot from the appearance of the company's "plant," its size, location, the character of the signs on the door, etc. But keep in mind that appearances may be deceptive. With increasing automation, for example, the number of employees is no longer a direct indicator of a company's capability, or its annual dollar volume.

Similarly, due to acquisitions and mergers, you may not be able to tell a company's business by its name. "The United Specialty Metals Company" might export plastic jewelry, import wood carvings, manufacture art objects, or do heat treating.

"I can tell about a company," says an investment banker, "just by walking through it for a minute or two." You don't have to be an investment banker to develop this skill. Almost every work-wise individual is aware of the variations in work atmosphere possible among companies. You need only glance at a group of employees to sense that "this is a good place to work," or "there's an undercurrent of tension in the place," or "the place reeks of apathy."

Put out your feelers when you walk through the premises, and see whether you can't get some idea of the company "personality."

• *Advertising.* Does the firm say of itself, "Biggest in the industry"? "Founded in 1812"? Slogans and advertising often give a revealing picture of what a company sells, or how it sees itself.

Publicity stories, articles in trade or business journals signed by company executives also can be a tipoff to the areas of a firm's particular interests. Allied to advertising are the exhibits that a company may display at an industrial or trade show. Its brochures and pamphlets, even its handbook for employees, can yield valuable information about its history and areas of major interest. The company brochure often contains the names, responsibilities, even biographical sketches of key executives—possibly including the one interviewing you.

One successful job applicant asked the man who was to interview him to send along his company literature in advance of their meeting. Many will do this as a matter of course.

• *The receptionist.* Aside from what you can learn about a company by walking into its reception room (there may be a display of its products, awards, and so on), the receptionist herself is usually an excellent information source. Since it is usually part of her job to answer questions about the company, you should be able to get some of the blank spots filled in.

• *Printed reference material.* Standard and Poor's *Corporate Records, Moody's Manual, Thomas Register of American Manufacturers, Fortune's Plant and Product Directory* are usually available in any public library with a business reference section. Corporate history and current information may be obtained from sources such as these. There are many other such sources. A professional librarian can be helpful in guiding you to those available.

• *Credit rating.* The same logic that persuades a company to investigate a potential employee should encourage a job hunter to check on the reputation and reliability of a prospective employer. A Dun & Bradstreet report or other credit check as a starter can provide what is commonly known about an organization. A request to your bank can often bring you useful information about a firm's reputation.

• *Information through contacts.* You may know individuals who have contact with the prospective employer. Suppliers, employees, competitors —the list is as long as your ingenuity can make it.

2. *Getting a Line on the Interviewer.* Knowing a little about the man you'll be talking to can enhance that "I'm prepared" feeling. (It will also put you on a firmer footing—after all, he will know a great deal about you.)

It's obviously more difficult to get information about an executive than about the business organization. Your interviewer's title, for one thing, may or may not indicate what he does, or suggest the lines of his interest.

Take the general area of marketing, advertising, and sales management. You'd expect the management titles in this area to be sales manager, director of marketing, merchandising manager, etc. Yet a *Business Management* magazine survey recently found over 33,000 executives *without any hint of marketing in their titles* who said that they carried major function responsibility in advertising, marketing, or sales management.

Specifically, the magazine found:

    12,453   presidents
    16,931   vice-presidents
     1,583   secretary/treasurers
     2,244   general managers
       395   public relations directors

for whom sales or marketing was a major activity.

If you're called for an interview by one of these men, he may well want to explore your knowledge of sales management or advertising. Don't let the title fool you.

Credit reports often include statements about company officials. Also, besides the contacts previously mentioned, you often can fill in personal intelligence about the man who will interview you through community circles, professional trade circles, and printed source material, such as *Who's Who in Commerce and Industry.*

The alert job prospector can fill in the gaps about both company and executive, by everything from chats with bootblacks to financial reports in newsletters and magazines. A news item about a plant's being built, an old one's being remodeled; a "changing of the guard," i.e., a reshuffling of executive responsibilities, may mean changes of company activity, fortunes, image, or personality that can be of special significance to the job seeker.

And, of course, where your interview is the result of a referral, try to get as much information from the middleman as possible, be it a friend, employment agency, or executive searcher.

Your preparation for the interview won't be *emotionally* complete until you are clear on what you want from the interview. Remember, you don't *necessarily* want the job. You want to find out about the job, then to decide, on the basis of available information, whether you'd like to have it.

Keep these interview objectives in mind, and *in the order just given.* Don't start the interview with the conviction that you want the job. With this approach, you'll blunt your judgment. You literally won't hear any adverse facts that may emerge, and you'll overlook drawbacks that may make the job look very undesirable once you're outside the interview room.

Remember, then, you must gather the facts and impressions you need to judge whether or not the job is for you. Some of these facts are standard. They have to do with salary, responsibilities, future of the job, and so on. Others reflect your own personal attitudes and values.

You may want to write these question areas out as a list, circle the points that are decisive—"If the job requires extensive travel, I'm not interested" —these must be covered before the interview concludes, to avoid misunderstanding. It's embarrassing to have a job offered, then have to turn it down because of an obvious oversight.

B. *The Interview, from the Applicant's Side of the Desk*

Since the course of the interview is in the hands of the interviewer—and, within limits, should be left there—you should approach the occasion with an open mind. Your own experience as an executive should give you confidence because it will stand you in good stead in two ways. First, it is your stock in trade, the thing that has attracted the employer to you. Second, as an executive, you are likely to be far more at ease in the interview situation than other professionals who've not been used to dealing with many people.

The guide enumerated below can help you make the best of the situation regardless of the method of interviewing, or the skill of the man you'll see:

1. *Sometimes the interview starts before you know it!* States Jeremiah P. McAward, of Fidelifacts, whose experience with personnel investigations has exposed him to some less-well-known company practices: "You'd be surprised how often the impressions of a receptionist in the outer office count with executives inside. We know of several large corporations in which receptionists are asked for their detailed impressions of job applicants. For example, did Mr. Jones smoke in the reception area? Did he read a magazine? Which one? Was he relaxed? Did he engage the receptionist in conversation? Did he appear ill-at-ease? Where and how did he sit?"

You might justifiably take issue with this type of amateur surveillance. But the fact is, it's done. And the conclusion is clear: While waiting to be called for your interview, it's not a good idea to attempt a fast pickup of the young lady at the desk, or to impress her with an overfriendly conversation. You may be talking yourself right out of a job.

2. *Be sincere and direct.* Unfortunately, the word "sincere" was given a mortal blow in Frederick Wakeman's *The Hucksters.* But its meaning can be clarified by Roget's *Thesaurus:* Be "frank, open, ingenuous, true, honest, unfeigned, veracious."

In short, act in a way that comes naturally. It's a mistake to affect a manner, regardless of how attractive you may think it is. For example, an applicant for a sales manager's job, normally quiet and calm, may think he will make a better impression if he shows himself to be "aggressive." Or, a man being interviewed for a public relations job may feel it is to his advantage to exhibit a spirit of camaraderie. But as Prof. Benjamin Balinsky, author and chief psychologist of BFS Psychological Associates, cautions: "Be yourself, by all means. If you're not, you may be seen as inconsistent, or you won't 'jell' for the interviewer."

Actually, proof of the character traits that are desirable for the position you're considering should be implicit in your job achievements.

3. *Before the interview ends, be sure all your questions are answered.* Don't forget that you, too, are seeking information. You need certain facts to judge the acceptability of the job. In addition to questions you may have walked in with, others may grow out of your conversation. Perhaps you don't want to interrupt, or seem to steer the talk away from the areas of the interviewer's interest. Nevertheless, it's perfectly appropriate to bring up your questions with such preliminaries as these:

"Mr. Smith, before we leave the matter of responsibilities of the job, I'd like to get clear on a point. How large a personal staff will be made available to the man in this job? . . ."

"I'm glad you've gone into detail on that aspect of your company's interest. Do I understand correctly, then, that you expect to open an overseas branch that would fall under the new man's jurisdiction?"

"Mr. Jones, one point you've mentioned is of especial interest to me, and if you don't mind, I'd like to explore it with you for a few moments. . . ."

4. *"Sell the benefits"—what the company will gain by hiring you.* "I hired Millie," explains one executive to a colleague, "because when I interviewed her, she smiled and answered my questions pleasantly." That approach is fine for secretaries, but unsuitable for executives. The quick smile and the pleasant air are no sure-fire virtues for a manager.

As every salesman knows, the way to the sale is to convert *features* into *benefits for the prospect's company.* Insofar as the executive job applicant is concerned, his "features" are his past experience, things he has done for other employers. To impress a prospective employer, he must show what these assets will do for the company. Here are some examples:

"As you know, Mr. Black, when I was at J. B. North, I developed a system of paper controls for our field salesmen that boosted efficiency by 75 per cent. It seems to me that the same procedure, adapted to your company, would go a long way toward solving your field communications problems."

"Mr. Rogers, am I correct in concluding that lack of creative design ideas is a major problem for your company? If so, I'd like to spend a few minutes suggesting how my training and interests can be applied to your needs in this area."

"You have suggested that your company suffers from a rather murky image in banking circles, Mr. Worth. I don't want to represent myself as a PR expert, but as chief executive officer at Whirlaway, I worked closely with two men who took care of our financial public relations, and helped develop the policies that were so successful in building up present reputation in the financial community. I believe my experience with the Whirlaway PR problem could be directly translated for the benefit of your company."

5. *Remember that you and the interviewer are "on the same side."* "Take the position," says Professor Balinsky, "that the interviewer shares your objectives; that is, once he knows you as well as he can, he too is interested in your best possible placement."

In some situations this point may be made explicitly: "After all, we must both have the same understanding of this major point. It would be as catastrophic for you to hire the wrong man as it would be for me to take the wrong job."

This is not to say that you must continually agree with the interviewer. As a matter of fact, overwillingness to go along on every point is highly undesirable. First, it suggests a lack of positiveness and viewpoint. Second, although any trickery or manipulation is undesirable, it's not impossible that the executive may be testing you on this point of integrity. At any rate, one of the qualities a good interviewer looks for is a man's ability to form and express opinions. The man who places too much value on being agreeable may be judged inadequate for a job that requires firmness and the ability to say "no."

6. *Help the interviewer develop a picture of your ambitions and expectations for the future.* In the average case, this is something the interviewer will be interested in. As a matter of fact, it's routine for an executive to read through resumes to see to what extent and how rapidly a man has progressed in his career.

What you say should develop from your past experience, as recorded in the resume. It isn't quite convincing, for example, if an interviewee suggests great ambitions when his past progress has been slow or unimpressive. This isn't meant to damn such a man. He has as positive a story to tell of his hopes as anyone else, but his statement about his aspirations will seem more realistic if tied to previous accomplishments.

7. *Anticipate questions about your motivation.* Most interviewing executives are vitally interested in finding out what makes an applicant tick. Is the man too interested in the security factors of the job? How does he respond to challenge? How important is money to him? Would he do better with a low-pressure job, or is his drive strong enough to take pressure in stride?

To some extent what the interviewer is asking in this respect will emerge implicitly during the conversation. However, the conversation may turn in such a way as to make a direct statement appropriate: "I guess this word 'challenge' has been pretty badly overworked, Mr. White, but call it what you will, I think you can see from my record that I respond strongly to difficult goals."

However, even though "challenge" is a great big *yes* word and *security* is supposed to be a somewhat repulsive goal, one should try to be honest and accurate.

Professor Balinsky says, "Speak with as much understanding of self as possible." In line with this advice it would be a poor interviewer who wouldn't be struck by the honesty of the following statement:

"Much as I would like to represent myself as such, Mr. Gray, I'm not one of your management buccaneers. I believe and perhaps you do, now that we've discussed my previous achievements, that I could do very well in the job you're trying to fill. But I must confess that it is the elements that make for security such as the size of your company, its position in the field, and so on, that I find attractive."

8. *Understand the best way to represent a weak point or handicap.* Many job applicants are fortunate not to have any flaws or grey areas in their makeup or work experience. But some people do have, ranging from mental illness to a long period of joblessness. *The important point is, such flaws can be minimized.* A study by two psychologists in a veterans' hospital shows that *the manner in which a handicap was presented to a second person influenced the way he reacted to it.*

In a paper presented to the American Psychological Association in Los Angeles, Paul Rothaus and Philip G. Hanson demonstrated that an ex–mental patient "gains an advantage if he describes his hospitalization from a *problem-centered* rather than a *mental illness–centered* perspective."

Specifically, the psychologists reported that employment personnel rated patients as easier placement prospects if in interviews the patients said they entered the hospital because of interpersonal problems, rather than reporting they had been troubled with a "nervous condition."

What is suggested is that the kinds of questions asked by the interviewer depended on the approaches taken by the ex-patients in describing their situation. The problem-centered description seemed to lead to questions of how responsible the interviewee was for his own behavior. The *mental-illness* designation suggested to the interviewer an unfortunate path of inquiry focusing on the illness.

Perhaps the concept emerges even more clearly when a period of joblessness is used by way of example. Compare the more favorable first sentence with the weakness of the second:

"A variety of personal problems interfered with my ability to get and hold a job for a period of seven months in 1964. . . ."

"Yes, I was out of work for seven months in 1964. . . ."

The first statement suggests an understandable and acceptable cause for the job gap. The second statement merely raises conjectures—few likely to be favorable—as to the reason for the joblessness.

9. *Be prepared for "gimmicks."* You undoubtedly know about the "stress interview" technique. It consists essentially of the interviewer putting pressure on the interviewee. As mentioned above, it can be done a number of ways: by rapid-fire questions, incisive probing at particular points. Tricks such as staged interruptions, lack of ashtrays, a show of annoyance or anger at some statement, to see how the interviewee will respond—these and more are ammunition of the stress interview.

The capable interviewer isn't likely to resort to any such devices, for two reasons. First, it takes unfair advantage of a person who is necessarily locked into a subordinate or defensive position. Second, and more important: The assumption on which stress interviews are based is false. It's wrong, for example, to assume that the man who gets flustered in a stress interview situation won't be able to "keep his head when the chips are down." Or vice versa, for that matter. The interview, it must be repeated, is *not* a dependable simulation of a real-life situation. Many a man who does beautifully in the interview because words and verbal fluency are his forte, may perform miserably in a job that demands action, creativity, or organizational ability. And the opposite is certainly possible.

What recourse does the interviewee have? He has two: One is to go along with the obnoxious tactics as well as he can. The other is to break in and tax the interviewer with a blunt statement: "Mr. Doe, I understand what you're trying to do at this point. And I must tell you that it's a kind of test to which I'd rather not submit. Few authorities feel that ability to withstand stress in an interview is a measure of that ability in general. . . ."

Shocking? Likely to lose you the job? Perhaps. But at least you'll be able to maintain your dignity in your own eyes—and probably in the eyes of the interviewer as well.

Perhaps the key to recovering the situation, should it have gone into such a path, is to show that you bear the interviewer no ill will or resentment. Although you leave the course of the discussion in his hands, you can perhaps gently steer it into more constructive and worthwhile channels: "As far as stress is concerned, I'd like to point out especially that the pressure I was forced to work under in my last job was tremendous, but I found I could ride with it as part of the job. . . ."

10. *Don't try to deprive the interviewer of the reins.* It's up to the interviewer to guide the course of the conversation. It's unwise to usurp this prerogative.

However, it's not impossible that the interviewer will be a poor practitioner of the interviewing skill. Or, he may want to see how you will respond to the subtle hint that you take the initiative.

In either case, it's perfectly all right for you to pick up the conversation and head it in an appropriate direction. *But*—two cautions:

• If the interviewer permits a period of silence to develop, don't be *too anxious* to fill the gap. As pointed out in the section on how to interview, the point is made that silence can be an effective method for getting an interviewee to let down his hair. After a while, you may say: "Mr. Y, would you mind if we get to the matter of . . . ?"

• Avoid the reaction of the young interviewee who sought to break a silence by blurting out, "I must say, Mr. Z, your secretary is quite a dish." If you want to take the initiative, your choice of subject should be to the point of your serious interest, and that of the interviewer.

Special note: Money talk. "Should I name a figure if an interviewer asks what salary I expect?"

That question, in its many possible variations, is frequently asked by job seekers. Not without reason, for hiring or rejection often hinges on the success or failure of candidate and prospective employer to agree on compensation.

Here's one counselor's advice on the matter of money in the interview:

"Treat the negotiation of salary as one in which you and the interviewer are trying to reach a fair arrangement. If possible, do a research job in advance, to determine the 'going rate' for the company and industry. If you're forced to be specific, relate the figure to 'worth' rather than to want or need. Avoid talking minimums. Never turn down an offer. If you feel it's low, use it as a basis for upward negotiation. Don't overlook other forms of compensation: profit sharing, stock options, executive bonus and benefits. If appropriate, negotiate for future salary levels."

Strength of demand—the eagerness of the company to hire a man on the one hand, or the candidate's eagerness for the job on the other—may be a factor. To some extent it's a poker game. Neither party will want to seem overanxious, to avoid weakening its bargaining position.

However, there's another consideration. Individual salaries, in most cases, must integrate logically into salary levels that exist in the company. In other words, a company may be anxious to hire a man, but may not be able to go above a set limit, to have the salary conform with others being paid to executives in comparable jobs.

Occasionally, a company may be able to adjust a salary—in the event that it's completely sold on a man—by changing a job title, or adding an additional responsibility to the job content. In most cases, the executive candidate will be aware of these possibilities in connection with his own administration of salaries among past subordinates.

Finally, don't forget that salaries at higher management levels, in some respects, are flexible. An outstanding man can often set his own price, or get it eventually, once he's made good at the job. This latter fact suggests that it may pay to take a job at a figure below expectations, with the understanding that proved success will win stated increases.

C. Follow-up

Your interview may end up in any one of a number of ways. Some executives have had the pleasant experience of hearing those heartwarming words, "You're hired," at the conclusion of an interview. More likely: If you're interested and they're interested, there'll be additional executives for you to meet; or it will become clear that although they're interested, other candidates are being evaluated. A final possibility, of course, is that either on your part or theirs, the decision is that you're not meant for each other.

Whatever the case may be, go as far as you can to bring the interview to a positive conclusion.

Some of the possibilities: If the job prospect has been ruled out, see whether you can get the interviewer to provide you with referrals. In this case, the end of the job interview and the exploration for referral contacts might be worded:

"Mr. Rose, I want to thank you very much for this opportunity to talk with you. Too bad the possibilities didn't pan out for us. However, do you happen to know of any company or individual executive that might be interested in someone with my particular experience?"

A sticker: If the interviewer is noncommittal, should you leave it up to him to get in touch with you? Such indecision is likely to be hard on the nerves. It is perfectly appropriate to adopt this low-pressure approach:

"Mr. Scott, do you have an approximate idea as to when your next move on this matter will be made?" If he gives you a date or an approximate time you may then say, "In that case, I'll get in touch with you in about—" and add an approximate date.

There are three specific follow-up steps that usually may be taken in addition:

• Make a record, however brief, of the interview. This should include the name of the company, the interviewer, the date and place of the meeting. Any impressions you have developed in the interview that you may either want to try to duplicate or avoid in subsequent interviews should be noted. These facts may come in handy in connection with developments in other parts of your job-finding program.

• If the chances are that you want the job, and are still in the running, make notes of any additional things you should do as preparation for future interviews. Perhaps the discussion made you aware of key facts about the company you would profit from knowing. Or, some particular aspect of your experience might have proved of interest. You might want to get more details from your records, to prepare for the second go-round. Your notes will be most helpful if they're made as soon after the interview as possible, while the details are clear.

• Any job leads that arise out of the interview either explicitly or implicitly should be noted and followed up.

16

The Give and Take of Testing

"Mrs. Smith," the head of a chain of beauty shops is asked, "did you use psychological tests in selecting your executive vice-president?"

"Of course," says the lady executive. "Wouldn't dream of hiring a key man without testing."

"And did the man you picked score the highest of all the candidates?"

"Not quite," says Mrs. Smith, "but he did have the bluest eyes."

Moral: Many companies and recruiting executives use testing—but exactly which tests are used, and how they are used, vary greatly.

The Status of Testing

Testing in business has been and will continue to be a controversial activity. As is often the case, the opposing parties rush to extreme positions, and, in the resulting clash of contentions, it is difficult to find hard facts.

Suffice it to say, the state of the art is undecided. There are groups strongly in favor and groups strongly against. But between the two stands a large number of businesses that use tests and, it must be added, to their own satisfaction.

There is no doubt about the widespread use of tests. *Harvard Business Review* recently made a survey on the question, "Who tests?" The answer was, "Every sort of company, from small businesses to the industrial giants. Tests are used by publishing houses, advertising agencies, and management consultants; electronics firms, insurance companies, steel companies, airlines and banks; in short, the butchers, bakers and candlestickmakers of modern business." Over half of the executive respondents reported that their companies were at the time using tests for selecting or promoting, transferring, and developing salaried personnel.

Types of Tests

The job seeker who sets out to explore the world of psychological testing soon finds himself bogged down in names and descriptions of literally hundreds of individual tests. This is because the term "psychological test" covers a broad spectrum of types. After all, the field is almost a hundred years old—early studies of individual differences were first made by Francis Galton in the 1870s. An idea of the major kinds of tests—and their limitations—can be gleaned from a study, *Psychological Testing—A Businessman's Appraisal,* made by the Research Institute of America:

Achievement, performance, skill, job knowledge, and proficiency tests— measure the present adequacy of learned knowledge or the skill of an individual in a particular job area. Examples are numerous: tests in shorthand or typewriting for secretaries; in the use of business machines for accounting clerks; tests for painters, electricians, motor vehicle operators. The United States Employment Service uses a battery of job aptitude and proficiency tests for some 250 occupations.

Limitations: A high degree of reliability and validity is reported for this type of test. However, they are most often limited to job areas that require a specific knowledge of, and ability to do, certain physical operations—atypical of most executive activity.

Intelligence, mental ability, "brain power" tests—are designed to measure an individual's general capacity to learn. The IQ test is most familiar because of its wide use in schools and in the Armed Forces.

For business use, the original tests have now been revised and validated for several hundred occupations or job areas. Consequently, the score of any given individual can be checked against the level of mental ability usually required for successful performance in a specific job area. Thus, in considering job applicants and candidates for promotion, one can determine how their measured capacity to learn fits the required range.

Limitations: No one doubts that some individuals have a greater capacity to learn than others. A tug-of-war, however, results whenever the question is raised as to the primary abilities included under the general heading "capacity to learn." Another battle rages over the degree to which learning capacity is inherited or the results of one's educational, social, and economic background.

Businessmen need not enter this battle. If the results of selected tests jibe with successful employment practices, that's all that should concern the executive evaluating the usefulness of testing procedures.

Aptitude or learning ability tests—are designed to measure an individual's capacity to learn (and thereby perform successfully) in a specific job area known to require specialized abilities.

Limitations: Aptitude tests are primarily used to determine a person's probable success in a job area new to him. But even if the person has had experience in an area, aptitude tests can supplement demonstrations of proficiency. For older ex-executives, findings of this type of test are of questionable value.

Attitude, interest, and preference tests—indicate the work areas in which an individual is most likely to apply himself enthusiastically and find satisfaction or enjoyment. Other things being equal, an individual will probably be more successful in a job he likes.

Limitations: The consensus is that, in business, these tests have relatively little value because the executive being tested can make them come out any way he wants them to. There is nothing subtle about their design, and they are easy to slant. Accordingly, they can't be relied on to distinguish between a man who is genuinely interested in a particular job, and a man who is only pretending to be.

It is conceded these tests may have validity when used in vocational guidance since it is to the individual's benefit to be frank. But even in such instances, some more objective measure than expressed interest may be used, such as past activities, knowledge of the field, or similarity of present interests with those of others now in the field.

Personality, temperament, personal or social adjustment tests—Everyone is familiar with the popular stereotypes conjured up for different occupations—the extrovert, hail-fellow-well-met salesman; the jut-jawed, Brooks Brothers executive. Regardless of the inaccuracy of these popular conceptions, it is recognized that traits of personality or temperament, and the degree of personal and social adjustment, are important to job success. The importance, of course, varies with the job.

These tests are designed to measure traits or behavior tendencies against those found most frequently among persons who presently hold down jobs in the field and perform them successfully. Whether valid or not in predicting successful job performance, they do tend to rule out the non-conformist and the non-average—which sometimes means ruling out extraordinary people.

The following are among the traits which are supposedly measured by these tests:
Aggressiveness
How well one gets along with others
Stability
Confidence
Sociability
Initiative
Extroversion-Introversion
Dominance-Submission
Objectivity
Agreeableness
Cooperativeness
Masculinity
Emotionality

Decisiveness
Persistence
Tolerance
Drive
Depression
Selfishness
Judgment

Limitations: Because personality tests provoke extreme opinions, in assessing their probable value to his company, the businessman must first consider four factors:

1) The extent to which successful job performance can be sharply defined. (A company that has had experience in evaluating jobs for compensation plans based on performance will be especially aware of the extent of the problems involved.)

2) The difficulty in defining the extent to which job success is due to specific abilities rather than to personality traits.

3) The difficulty in defining and weighing personality traits against the needs of a particular job.

4) The difficulty in measuring the extent to which an individual has these traits—especially in the degree to which answers can be falsified. Even though the individual does not consciously falsify his answers, he certainly will take the benefit of any doubt.

If the manager believes these difficulties can be overcome, extensive investigation and analysis, with the advice and assistance of highly trained personnel, will still be required. (Even ardent enthusiasts won't put personality tests in the "do-it-yourself" category. Services of a qualified psychologist are generally required to administer and interpret personality tests.)

"Projective" methods or techniques—have not been used extensively in personnel practice and, for business purposes, are considered by some to be in the experimental stage.

The projective tests—Thematic Apperception Test or TAT, the Rorschach or "ink blot" test—are combined with analyses and interpretations to give an elaborate and detailed picture of an individual's emotional state and personality. They differ from the usual personality tests in that they do not measure an individual against normal or predetermined dimensions.

Some Pros and Cons

An objective observer of the business scene might be surprised by the popularity of psychological tests, considering the many handicaps to their use:

• Testing derives from the field of psychology, still regarded by many businessmen as "that sex-and-bathroom nonsense."

• Alternatives to testing—interviewing, past performance, etc., are less "technical" and involved as evaluation tools. (Those favorably inclined toward testing consider these to be complementary rather than alternatives.)

• Job candidates, particularly those in upper echelons, often resent being asked to submit to tests.

• Test findings add just one more factor to be considered in making a hiring decision—and often they confuse rather than help—because they seem to conflict with past job performance. For example, the psychological evaluation of one job candidate read, "He is slow to grasp new situations and, in some cases, fails to grasp the significant facts surrounding a problem." Yet the man's work history clearly indicated that he had successfully handled many difficult situations. How could these findings be reconciled? One possibility is, of course, that what the candidate lacked personally, he compensated for by his skill in delegating and mobilizing the capabilities of subordinates.

• Testing has been assailed from many quarters. Psychologists themselves argue about theory and application. Observers of the management scene have taken potshots—"hurled blockbusters" might be a more accurate description—at business's use of testing (William H. Whyte in *Organization Man* and Martin L. Gross in *The Brain Watchers*, for example). Yet, even after the furor created by Gross's attack—he asserted that tests are invalid, an invasion of privacy, that they reinforce conformity, and that they are easily faked—publishers stated that tests were selling better than ever.

• Tests often represent an additional cost in the recruiting process.

Despite these negatives, there are a variety of reasons for the continued use of tests:

• Experience has often been favorable. Many companies that use them claim that tests have been a major factor in improving the performance of personnel, reducing turnover, and maintaining a high level of executive competence.

• Testing has attained status as part of today's "scientific approach," a new element in the tradition of the larger "scientific revolution" in management.

But overriding the common-sense pros and cons is another, perhaps dominant, reason for the use of tests.

• *"It's the right tool for the job, even if it doesn't always work."* This is the statement of a staunch advocate of testing, the president of a food-products company who has a realistic view of testing.

His view has strong professional backing. Consensus of psychologists is that although tests are fallible, they are far more valid and reliable than personal judgments or subjective assessments.

Facts such as these also seem to back up the food-company president's view:

A survey of 177 industrial organizations by F. J. Gaudet and A. R. Carli, entitled "Why Executives Fail," showed that for every manager who fails to make the grade because of incompetence or insufficient knowledge, there are seven whose failure stems from personality problems.

Management has got the message from surveys such as this that personality is *the* key to an individual's job performance. And, to this time, psychological testing is the only known tool for analyzing and evaluating personality.

Another test-minded top executive remarks: "When I get a report from our psychologist on a job applicant, I feel that at least it talks about the right things. It may not be 100 per cent accurate, but it will probably raise questions that I would otherwise not consider."

Better insights into the uses and abuses of testing lie in pursuing the answer to the following question.

What's Wrong with Testing Practices?

To understand the uses and the limitations of tests, it will help to run quickly through some of the problems and misuses of testing. For example:

1. *Tests are sometimes poorly administered.* A recruiting firm was anxious to submit a highly qualified prospect to a client. As matters stood, the candidate had only half an hour free between planes. He was given a quickie pencil-and-paper test, and the client then received a "comprehensive" analysis of his "mental qualifications."

In other words, in addition to doubt about testing done under the best circumstances, there is room for doubt about test givers.

2. *The wrong qualities are tested, in terms of the specific job.* In a recent issue of its publication *Alert,* the Research Institute of America gave this example:

> Every company wants to hire the best salesman it can find. But sometimes companies confuse "best" with brightest. This was dramatically demonstrated when consulting psychologists were called in to solve a high turnover problem in a 150-man sales force. They discovered that the prime culprit was an intelligence test.
>
> Psychologists found that the company's most successful salesmen actually made low or moderate scores on I.Q. tests. Yet, in hiring new men, the company was rejecting all but those in the higher ranges.
>
> Result: the selection of over-qualified men led to an expensively high turnover rate.

The Institute goes on to observe that intelligence tests are particularly susceptible to misuse. Not only are the test forms easily obtained and administered, but the temptation is great to favor the high scorers almost regardless of what it is he scores high in!

Another common error is to assume that a man's interests and abilities will match. As the *Harvard Business Review* said in an article on the subject of selection of salesmen by tests:

> This assumption (that interests and abilities match) is wrong on its face. Psychologically, interest does not equal aptitude. Even if someone is interested in exactly the same specific things as Mickey Mantle or Willie Mays, this of course does not in any way indicate the possession of a similar baseball skill. Equally, the fact that an individual might have the same interest pattern as a successful salesman does not mean that he can sell. Even if he wants to sell, it does not mean that he can sell.

3. *Test scores seem easy to fake.* Manuals are available on the market now that tell test takers how to beat the tests. Even without such help, many tests are such that the average person can tell what the "right" answer should be.

For example, if one is applying for an executive job, there should be no doubt as to the correct answer on this question: "Would you rather lead a group discussion or be a forest ranger?"

Psychologists minimize the faking possibility, and studies have been conducted that seem to show faked results are not easily produced. But at best, the pro-test forces only score a draw on this point.

4. *Tests isolate individual traits of a man rather than test the whole dynamics of the individual.* The *Harvard Business Review* article on its survey continues:

> Most personality and aptitude tests are totally traitological in their construction and approach. They see personality as a series or "bundle" of piecemeal traits. Thus, someone may be high in "sociability" while being low in "self-sufficiency" and "dominance." Someone else may be high in "personal relations," but low in "co-operativeness." Somehow, the whole (or the *Gestalt*) gets lost. The dynamic interaction that is personality, as viewed by most modern-day psychologists, is buried in a series of fractionalized, mathematically separable traits.

5. *Test results are overweighted in selection.* Even those who understand and accept testing agree that companies sometimes give test results too much weight. Psychological testing is only one of three major decision-making factors in recruiting, the others being face-to-face interviews and the applicant's work history. Many organizations weight the tests out of proportion to the other two factors.

6. *Tests are often misused substitutes for decision making.* Says Mathew J. Beecher of Price Waterhouse & Company: "One of the problems with psychological testing is the fact that it has become a 'decision haven.' It is too frequently used as the main element in deciding whether or not a man is to be hired. This means a personnel department

or top management abdicates its responsibility for decision making by hiding behind the skirts of test results."

7. *Some firms use testing as a means of keeping up with the "business Joneses."* "For some companies," said a recruiter with a consulting firm, "testing is a status symbol. It is used not because it is understood or needed, but because many organizations feel it is the 'sophisticated management thing to do.'"

Two Case Histories

Case histories will demonstrate what's right and what can be wrong with testing:

A chemical company was looking for a manager to head up a new division. He had to have outstanding technical ability and yet be a diplomatic individual, because he had to train a new staff and work well with others in the organization. The problem could be summed up as a search for "a very bright, aggressive, imaginative chemical engineer with a record of successfully handling people."

The search proved difficult since the company was rigid in its insistence that an applicant meet all the qualifications. But finally, a recruit appeared who apparently met all specifications except one—there was some doubt about his ability to get along with people.

A check with the applicant's previous employer confirmed this suspicion—he had a poor record of work relationships. However, since his other qualifications and experience were on target, the company decided to give him a battery of psychological tests.

Test results confirmed that the candidate was poor in his job relationships and that he tended to be an exacting martinet. Yet he seemed to be aware of his shortcoming and was making a concentrated effort to overcome it. His former employer verified this impression, but qualified it with "he still has a long way to go."

The situation was reviewed by the top executive staff of the chemical company. The decision was made to hire the man. The president told the candidate that his difficulty in dealing with people was a negative factor, but that he was being hired because he possessed the other qualifications to an outstanding degree. The candidate was further told that his actions involving others would be minutely scrutinized, and, at the first sign of any serious mishandling of people, he would be in trouble.

Three years later, the new executive had completely proved himself. True, there were some trying moments in the early stages. As he himself agrees, he is not the most lovable man in the organization, but he has few "people problems." He is well-respected and in many instances admired by his colleagues.

The significant fact in this thumbnail history is the company's wise use of tests to verify key facts in a man's work history and its decision to watch the weak points uncovered. Top management properly used the test findings as just one more factor to throw in the balance of its considerations. Events proved its decision had been a good one.

Case history number 2 also has a happy ending, but involves an instance where the company took action contrary to that indicated by the psychologist. These facts were supplied by an individual who was involved in the case as a top manager in the company involved:

A tool-making concern of medium size planned to consolidate several plants into a single Midwest location. It began looking for an executive who would assist during the period of consolidation and who would then assume control of operations.

An executive who had some years before done consulting for the company was considered for the job, since he had the technical qualifications, as well as the liking and respect of many of the company officials. The president, to "put the pink ribbon on the package," as our informant phrased it, had the man interviewed by an industrial psychologist.

The psychologist recommended that the man *not* be hired because "he did not understand the job." This finding was based on the answer to the question, "What do you think the job entails?" The candidate answered, "The consolidation of several plants, and the judicious handling of the personnel."

A problem was created because the psychologist wanted an answer summing up what the job would be in ten years, and the candidate had replied with a "first things first" approach.

The psychologist also concluded that the candidate "wasn't aggressive enough." This opinion was based on the fact that the current president was exceedingly so, and, comparatively, the candidate was "weak." Finally, the psychologist stated that the candidate "had little imagination" and that, overall, he was not a "potential president of the company."

A friend of the candidate went to bat for him. His past record was emphasized, along with his acknowledged technical ability, knowledge of the company's operations, and so on.

Final chapter: The man was hired. The consolidation proceeded smoothly under the new top executive. The morale and operating efficiency of the company have settled down to a slow but satisfactory growth.

Of course, there are unresolved questions. Did the president make the correct decision? Might not another candidate have done better? Unfortunately, such questions are unanswerable. But what does emerge is the inappropriateness of the psychologist's recommendations.

Against this admittedly lean background on a broad subject, some key points will be made about psychological tests for the benefit of the company who may use them, and for the job candidate who may one day be tested.

Twelve Key Questions on Testing, for the Company

1. *Should you test?* Yes, *particularly* under these conditions:
• For key personnel, where the more you can learn about your final candidates, the better off you're likely to be.
• If job performance depends heavily on the "human relations" factor —as opposed to technical know-how, for example.
• To resolve a "tie" between two closely matched finalists for a job.
• Where you're going to invest considerable time and money in training a man for a new or expanded responsibility.

2. *Should you use professional help?* Yes, particularly if you're going to use personality tests, because the amateur test administrator can quickly get in over his head. Keep in mind that the competent psychologist will avoid making hiring decisions for you. He will provide you with an analysis of a person, and relate it to key requirements of the job in question.

3. *Should you have a psychologist set up a special battery for your company (an involved and expensive procedure) or use "off-the-shelf" tests?* To a large degree, it depends on the size of your company, and the number of executives you hire. If the answers are "large" and "many," it will pay you to have a tailor-made job. If the answers are "small" and "few," a competent psychological consultant, made conversant with your needs, will be able to use prepared tests effectively.

4. *Should you hire a man who refuses to be tested?* That's a tough question. Best answer is, first try to find out the reason for the refusal. There are three possibilities:
• An independent-minded individual may, rightly or wrongly, refuse to stand still for a test because he feels it's an invasion of privacy.
• An insecure individual may be reluctant to "expose himself," for fear that a probing of his psyche will come up with derogatory findings.
• An individual may be afraid that some existing personality flaw—it might be anything from a past mental breakdown to deviancy—will be exposed.
In the first two instances, a candidate may change his mind when management stresses the limited weight given tests, and otherwise minimizes the process, so that it's not an "ordeal" or a "threat." In the third case, it's likely the refusal will be unchangeable. In the case where you have two candidates running neck and neck for the job, and one refuses to be tested, whereas the other gets a reasonably satisfactory rating from tests, the latter should get the nod.

5. *Is there anything that can be done to maximize the services of a*

psychologist? Yes. In addition to hiring a firm or individual of assured qualifications, take the steps necessary to get reports from him in the most usable form. You should ask for reports in practical, everyday language. There's no need to wade through technical lingo, such as ". . . the individual ranks toward the higher end of the average range of executive-level people"; or ". . . the ambivalence of the individual has not been adequately resolved in a way to make superior functioning probable."

Also, have the findings related to key qualifications of the job. If you need an executive to take on a tough production job, you'll want to know what the psychologist feels about the man's ability to work under pressure.

Of course, it's up to the company retaining a psychologist to establish rapport so that there is a good understanding of job qualifications and the background circumstances surrounding the job—key relationships with superiors, subordinates, and colleagues.

6. *Is there any way to tell a dependable psychologist from one who is less so?* In part. Personal recommendations from satisfied users are obviously important. There are also objective reference sources: professional affiliation, certification, and university associations. The American Psychological Association, 1333 Sixteenth Street N.W., Washington, D.C., can help here.

It is generally agreed that of equal importance to the quality of a test is the integrity and skill with which test results are interpreted and presented. A reputable practitioner will satisfy both requirements.

7. *What are the more common indications of misuse of testing?*

• *Use of "untested" tests.* A variety of situations account for the use of questionable tests. One company had a battery of tests devised for it by a personnel assistant without qualification or experience in testing. There was real doubt as to what the tests actually tested for, or how they related to job needs. In another case, a psychologist tailor-made a battery of tests, but subsequently was unable to demonstrate any reliability or validity for the battery. Company executives continued to use it, however, because they "liked the tests."

Finally, some companies make use of nonscientific approaches that reflect a personal whim of someone at the top. The president of a small laundry chain made up his own "leadership test," based on his ideas of what an executive needed, to be effective. A sample question: "What would you do if a good employee came to you and said, 'I quit'?" "One of the best answers I ever got to that one," he confides, "was 'I'd fire him before he could finish his sentence.' It was clear to me that the man who thinks like that would make an effective, hard-nosed manager."

• *Going along with the same battery, year after year.* This doesn't refer to the tailor-made battery that has been validated and is continually being updated by the psychological staff. But in all other cases, note must be taken that psychological centers are continually putting out new—and presumably better—tests. At the very least, a periodic review of testing materials is called for.

8. *What should the company, going to run its own testing operation, watch out for?* These points touch some of the critical areas:

• Select tests from a reputable test publisher. If you have any doubts about the firm you are thinking of buying from, consult the American Psychological Association (1333 Sixteenth St. N.W., Washington, D.C.). You can also find reviews of specific tests in the *Mental Measurements Yearbook,* available in most libraries.

• Draw only tentative conclusions from a person's test performance, if you have had no formal training in this area. Suggests one professional tester: "Read the test manual carefully, and be sure you know exactly what the test purports to measure and what it is not intended to measure. Otherwise, you may make an assessment which is off base—detrimental both to your interests and the examinee's."

• *Don't* regard tests as the scientific way of making a "hire"-"no hire" decision. Tests aren't designed to provide a complete picture of an individual, only those aspects which are difficult or impossible to obtain from other techniques, such as interviews, work-history checks, and so on. The final decision should be made on a "whole-man" basis.

• Be sure the tests are administered under proper conditions. The surroundings should be relatively quiet, well lighted and ventilated. And make sure prescribed time limits are rigorously observed. Otherwise, the entire procedure is a waste of time—or worse, completely misleading.

9. *Who should see the test results?* As few people as possible and only individuals of authority and discretion. King Whitney, Jr., of The Personnel Laboratory, makes the point this way: "An individual's test results should be shown to only a few top people in the company, and should be kept under lock and key. This is information which can be misused and abused when it gets into the hands of people who have an axe to grind or who simply do not appreciate its confidential nature."

10. *How can disparities between test results and those from other sources be resolved?* You should start with the premise that tests are not infallible. They can be off base for a number of reasons, from incorrect interpretation to the examinee's misunderstanding of the instructions. Nevertheless, if the discrepancy is important, two steps should be taken:

• Dig into the point of conflict—with further tests, for example, or further interviews, or by fuller investigation of work history in the questionable area.

• Include the unresolved question along with all the other findings, and see whether putting it in context tends to suggest an answer. If not, consider the question as a moot element, one that will have to be accepted as part of the "gamble" inherent in any hire.

11. *Should the examinee be told how he made out?* There's a great temptation to level with an individual, either because he's hired—and it's then done out of a feeling of closeness—or because he isn't—and the thought is, "Why not?" However, it's a good temptation to *resist*.

Don't be fooled by *your* feeling that you're objective and calm about the whole thing. *He* can become quite impassioned. As King Whitney, Jr., puts it: "It's not that some people *can't* take this kind of knowledge and should be kept in the dark; it's because they don't know *how* to take it, and must be properly prepared in order to be able to take it."

12. *How much time and money does testing require?* As far as the *time* element, an effective battery of tests usually takes a day to administer, often a day and a half. As to the *cost*, it's a question that deserves a direct answer, although it seems to be in the same category as, "How much does a lady's coat cost?" It depends on whether you're talking mink or muskrat, cloth or chinchilla.

Psychological-service firms charge somewhat higher rates than the free-lancing psychologist, who operates without benefit of overhead, and often with minimum staff assistance.

A capable individual psychologist is likely to have a fee basis that starts at about $100 for a single evaluation. (What we're talking of here is a comprehensive battery, including personality evaluation.) The service-firm rate starts about $150 and may go as high as $300 or $400, especially if projective tests are used.

Twelve Key Questions on Testing for the Test Taker

For the company, to test or not to test is generally just one more policy question that has to be decided by the regular corporate decision-making machinery that operates in the personnel area. But for the individual job seeker, testing is a threat or, at best, one more hurdle in the job race. Here are some problems that commonly confront test takers, and some suggested solutions:

1. *What kind of tests do employers use today?* There are two sets of answers to this question. One has to do with the categories of psychological tests. These have already been described at the beginning of this chapter, starting on page 192. Now as to the second answer, there are generally three kinds of tests:

• Pencil-and-paper tests.

• An interview examination, usually conducted by a psychologist. This may be of either the patterned or flexible variety.

• Projective tests, in which you are shown material and asked, "What does this look like to you?" "What kind of a situation does this suggest?" and so on.

2. *Can I "cram" for psychological tests?* Not in the ordinary sense.

Aptitude tests, for example, are designed to reveal natural talents rather than knowledge or acquired skill. Probably one of the best things you can do is to review the twelve Key Questions on Testing for the Company, starting on page 200 in this chapter. This will help give you some perspective on the approach or attitude the average company is likely to have toward testing.

Aside from the matter of developing a realistic perspective on testing, the best thing you can do is try to develop a relaxed view about the whole thing. It's the rare company that will have you stand or fall on test results. And if you've got to the test stage, you can be sure your qualifications are pretty impressive.

Suggests one test-wise executive: "The best way to prepare yourself to take psychological tests is to adopt the frame of mind that now you're going to have an opportunity to show how good you are."

3. *What should I do if on the day of the test I don't feel up to par?* If the ailment isn't sheer nervousness, and likely to recur each time you face the testing situation, ask for a postponement. Explain your problem—whatever the reason for your not feeling physically or mentally fit—and suggest that a substitute date be decided on, to avoid giving the impression that you're dodging the test. Tests allow for some mistakes due to pressure, so don't be too concerned if you feel nervous. Almost everyone is.

4. *Can I expect any help from the examiner?* Within limits, yes. Advises Dr. W. E. Kendall, director of the Psychological Corporation:

"The examiner is instructed to do everything he can to put you at ease. Take advantage of this to find a comfortable location in the testing room, where light and ventilation are good, and possible distractions are at a minimum. Immediately bring to the examiner's attention any special situation that arises." Occasionally, you may even query him about the proper procedure when the instructions seem unclear or ambiguous.

5. *Any specific suggestions about how to answer questions?* A few:

• Read test directions carefully. If solution of the sample problems is not clear, ask the examiner to explain. Also, read each test item carefully.

• If the test has a time limit, do not spend undue time on problems for which the solution is not readily apparent. Seldom is an examinee supposed to finish all items. You'll do much better skipping a tough one, giving you the chance to answer two or more easier (for you) questions. Usually, the more correct answers, the higher your score. As Dr. Kendall points out, "Most tests of verbal and quantitative skills have unit scoring —that is, each correct answer is worth one point—so the emphasis should be on obtaining the maximum number of correct answers."

• Where machine-scored answer sheets are used, be sure you understand the mechanics of their use.

• To the question, "Should I guess at answers I'm not sure about?" the reply depends on the scoring method of the individual test. If there is a penalty for wrong answers, make only judicious guesses. On the other hand, on some varieties of tests you are encouraged to guess. Don't get the two mixed up.

6. *Should I try to outsmart the tests?* So much has been said about the "fakability" of tests, there's the general feeling that it's better to be wised-up and give phony answers than to play it straight. Here's what the experts say:

A Denver psychologist advises: "Don't try to outsmart tests—especially personality tests. Your assumption that you know what the test interpreter is looking for can be dangerous and may result in your putting yourself in a bad light, if your guess is wrong. You're safer being honest."

A test-wise personnel director: "You can outfox yourself by faking answers. I know one man who lost out on a job because he tried to make up responses that he thought would paint him as a free-swinging, creative type. Since the employer was looking for an organizer and detail man, his attempt didn't have much chance of paying off."

Dr. W. E. Kendall: "Test items relating to attitudes, opinions, and interests don't have 'correct' answers. Research has shown that certain patterns of answers are characteristic of specified classes of respondents. The well-constructed tests have built-in checks. Therefore, it is to the advantage of the respondent to answer questions as directly as possible."

7. *Are there likely to be any "catch" questions?* Probably not. Says Dr. Kendall: "Standardized tests have been carefully prepared and pretested. Therefore, take each question at its face value. There should not be 'trick' questions in a well-constructed test."

8. *How much do tests count?* There's no single answer. Some companies or executives give them more weight than others. Generally, says one executive recruiter who invariably uses testing for final screening: "Most companies use tests as one of many sources of information about you. If by chance you don't rate as high as you should—and tests occasionally do miss—you can still land your job by proving your mettle on other of the evaluative techniques."

9. *What if I feel tests are invalid?* That's a tough question—and you have a lot of company. But the fact is, many an executive who faces a test session hides a vague fear of "exposure" behind the rationale that he "isn't afraid" of tests.

If the only thing that bothers you about the tests is the intellectual belief that they are unscientific—à la Martin L. Gross's *Brain Watchers*—you may still be able to go along with them on the basis of expediency. Test taking becomes just one of the several hurdles you may have to face to get a desirable job.

10. *What if I'm afraid of taking the tests?* This feeling may be based on

a simple fear of the unknown—"I don't know what those fancy tests are," says one old-line executive, "and I sure don't like the idea of their digging around inside my skull with 'em." Or it may be based on a perfectly sound realization that a test may turn up some information an individual would rather not have generally known. If the fear is based on lack of understanding of the tests, it's perfectly in order for you to have a talk with the psychologist or test administrator in advance, so you can have spelled out for you just what the tests will cover.

On the other hand, if an individual has good reason to know that the test may reveal information he would prefer kept secret, he has two alternatives. Either not to take the test and forget about the job or to have a talk with the prospective employer, and try to get a hiring decision on the basis of past performance and other factors that are a matter of record. However, this may not be too easy to do, since an employer who customarily uses tests might be unwilling to go along with such a request.

11. *Who gets to know the test results?* Some job candidates don't mind taking tests, but they shy at the idea of such personal information's being generally available. It should be made clear that in the typical case, particularly in large companies that have a considerable amount of such data, tight security is placed on psychological test results. The information is kept under lock and key, and sharply restricted, to keep the results from a loose-tongued or inquisitive secretary or clerk.

Further, there are some executive recruiters who, in transmitting psychological data to clients, will put only the routine material in writing, convey any critical or highly personal intelligence orally. This is done to prevent any slip-ups in case of mergers, or any other shift in management and control of personnel files.

If you have any fears, or any doubts about who is to have access to test results, this is a matter you can legitimately take up with the executive who is your liaison within the company. In ordinary circumstances, he should be able to tell you precisely what will be done with the highly personal descriptive or diagnostic elements of your test results.

12. *Should I ask to see the test results?* If you're interested. But whether or not you will depends on the nature of the tests you take, and who administers them.

One executive got to know that he scored in the "top 3 per cent for financial executives" in intelligence, by telling the executive, "I don't mind taking the test, but I'd like to know how I make out." However, when it comes to personality elements, the candidate shouldn't expect to get a "personality reading" in return for taking the test. In the first place, if the test administrator isn't a professional, he'd be very foolish trying to act like one and discuss such results with the subject.

Even a professional, in the employ of the hiring company, will hesitate to risk the danger of involving the company in a damage suit by discussing "findings" that might be taken as libel, or an invasion of privacy.

Where a company has employed a testing firm or an outside psychologist to do the screening and evaluation, the individual, if he's interested, may request a counseling session with the professional on the basis of the tests. This may not be available free of charge, but it's likely that reasonable fee arrangements can be made. In most cases, specific understanding would have to be made that the prospective employer is not in any way involved.

One exception: When the tests have brought out a problem area and the candidate is to be hired, the company may actually suggest that the problem be made the subject of one or more counseling sessions.

Sample Test Reports

Customarily when a job applicant is tested, the psychologist or testing service submits a written report appraising the candidate to the prospective employer. Examples of this kind of report may be found in the appendix, page 254.

17

References, Reference Checking, and PEI

Charles Y., a junior executive in a mail-order house, was fired for stealing cash remittances. Had his company contacted the place he worked before, it would have learned that he had quietly "resigned" after being caught in a similar offense.

Henry Z. had a nervous breakdown after a year on the job with a publishing firm. The firm's insurance carrier paid the $5,500 medical bill. But the company suffered at least as great a loss in higher insurance premiums, lost working time, and disruptions in working schedules. Here, too, a query to the man's previous employer would have uncovered a record of instability.

Employers today are far more aware than they used to be of the need for checking an executive's past history before undertaking a permanent bond. Says Jeremiah P. McAward, executive director of Fidelifacts, Inc., a personnel investigating service:

> About 25 per cent of job candidates can be expected to falsify their answers to some application questions. The most misrepresented area is the individual's employment record. Typical falsifications: the individuals don't hold the jobs described; their salaries were not as high as claimed; major difficulties with superiors are completely covered up.

Educational background, too, is often falsified. One survey of a group of engineers uncovered the startling fact that on their employment applications, 10 per cent had claimed more or higher degrees than they actually held.

The results of such misrepresentation may be innocuous or damaging. The highly competent female executive who chops five years off her age is hardly a threat. It's a different story when an ex-embezzler seeks to hide a prison record. One realistic employer says that when a man's been hired

208

on the basis of a falsified record, "If the misrepresentation isn't extreme, we give the employee a chance to perform successfully on the job." But not all employers are as generous. *Industrial Relations News* reports that of a group of thirty-six companies studied, seventeen said that they generally dismiss any employee who has falsified information on his application. Many firms feel that inaccurate background data could lead to false assumptions about a man's capabilities, with job failure as a result.

At any rate, it's important for both job applicant and employer to follow some consistent policy on the matter of data furnished in applying for a job. This chapter can help both principals to develop realistic, trouble-minimizing policies.

The Rub for the Job Seeker

For most executive job hunters, references are no problem. "My record speaks for itself," they feel, and they're perfectly willing to make the record clear. But occasionally, a job seeker has a blemish, either real or fancied, on his escutcheon. Aware that his statements may be checked, he thrashes about in his mind, trying to decide how to handle the negatives with least danger to his job campaign. Although this is one of the more difficult problems to handle, it's not insuperable. Three suggestions are especially important:

1. *Expect an "investigation," not merely a reference check.* Employment people make a clear distinction between a *reference check*, in which persons named by the applicant are contacted for information, and a *pre-employment investigation*, in which an applicant permits a prospective employer to probe more deeply into his background.

2. *Avoid misleading statements, no matter how trivial.* One employment-agency head will never forget the time he sent a man out on a sure lead. "Our man was perfectly qualified for the job, and got it, pending a check of references. His prospective employer had asked him to submit five references. He put down four, and then, momentarily stuck for a fifth, made up a fictitious one. Of course, it was the phony one the company checked. P.S., he lost the job."

3. *If you feel capable of handling the job, despite some flaw in your qualifications, make this point in your job interview.* First of all, the interview, where you encounter your prospective employer face to face, gives you your best chance to explain away or minimize a questionable point in your background. Secondly, if you say nothing and the facts are subsequently discovered by the employer, the point in question may be exaggerated out of all proportion. As an employer admitted in one case, "It didn't make a darn bit of difference to us whether the guy had been a lieutenant or a major in the Army. But the fact that he had lied about

it implied a sense of inadequacy, if not dishonesty. The job we were trying to fill required a very self-confident type." The chapter on interviewing, page 186, has some helpful advice on how to present a weak point in the best possible light.

The balance of this chapter, *directed to the employer*, is also must reading for the *job applicant*, since it tells exactly what the problems and practices of pre-employment investigation are, in which the applicant is likely to be involved as a precondition to being hired.

What Every Employer Should Recognize about References

"It has been said that gunman John Dillinger had three glowing letters of reference in his pocket on the day the FBI finally closed in on him and shot him down," says Rawle Deland, of Thorndike Deland Associates. "True or not, the story illustrates the danger of accepting references without going beneath the surface to check their reliability."

Deland adds an arresting statistic to support his point: "We find that fully half of all executive candidates who survive intensive screening up to the reference check are disqualified at this juncture. In other words, if you don't check references in depth, you stand a 50-50 chance of hiring someone who won't work out 'as planned.'"

The average person named as a reference has bland good intentions— and that's the trouble. His attitude is summed up in this classic statement about an ex-employee one company was glad to get rid of: "This man is eminently well-qualified for any position for which he is suitable."

Procedures for Checking References

"We rarely get derogatory material from references on a man we're hired to investigate," says McAward of Fidelifacts, "Not even a previous employer who's had bad experience. Very often a well-intentioned employer will go along with a falsified tale by an ex-employee because he doesn't want to 'stand in the way of the man's earning a living'—or be open to a libel suit."

Needless to say, the hiring company wants the truth, and not a shaded version. Fortunately, there are steps that can lead to the truth.

1. *Send out letters of inquiry and compare answers.* A California service organization swears by this method. It sends a letter to all references given by the job applicant, and then analyzes the answers, stacking one reference's view against the others. Here is a sample:

Dear Mr. Smith:

Mr. William R. has applied for the position of treasurer in our company. In so doing, he has offered your name as a reference.

Would you be kind enough to provide us with your appraisal of Mr. R.'s qualifications, both personal and professional? We should be greatly obliged for your evaluation of his qualifications for the position designated. Thank you in advance for your assistance.

Truly yours,

Warren R. F. Dee

"It's been our experience," says the personnel executive of this firm, "that a definite and fairly accurate picture of the man can be obtained this way. Seldom do all the letters say the same thing. Accordingly, we use a number of key questions to evaluate the answers:

• "What is the tone of the reply?" Often, it's not so much *what* is said, as the *manner* that is revealing. If, in an otherwise matter-of-fact reply, you were suddenly to read as a summary statement, "Mr. X is one of the most dynamic, enterprising world-beaters I know," you might sense that the letter-writer meant well, but wasn't really stating an accurate fact.

On the other hand, if the writer sounded really enthusiastic, "I've seen Mr. Y run a meeting of high-level executives, and his ability to get the most out of a group is outstanding," you'd probably feel that Mr. Y really had the skill described.

• "Is there agreement among the letters?" If four or five men all mention Mr. Z's fine organizing ability, then it may be concluded that Mr. Z is indeed a good organizer. Sometimes replies will differ on the same point. For example, one may state that "Mr. White tends to favor the broad aspects of his responsibility and to delegate details," while another observes the opposite. If the doubts raised are about an important point, it's up to the employer to resolve the question by a follow-up interview with the applicant.

• "Does the letter give off too rosy a glow?" Replies that go all out to boost an applicant may be written by a good personal friend, anxious to further the job seeker's career, or an individual eager to lessen the threat of being stuck with an impecunious relative. Such replies need not be ruled out, but they should be read in comparison to others.

Most dependable, perhaps, are the replies that mention strong points, but also suggest weaknesses: "I can recommend Mr. Grey unqualifiedly for honesty and dependability. However, I should also point out that administrative detail seems to floor him, and if his job responsibility includes considerable detail, it would be helpful if this area were backstopped for him."

• "Have facts asked for been given, or evaded?" If your letter of inquiry has asked for specific information—how long has the man worked for the company, exactly what were his responsibilities, and so on—you'll want to observe how clearly your questions are answered. If they are answered satisfactorily, and back up what the applicant has said about himself, fine. But evasion, or disagreement among the replies suggests further probing of the area with the man himself.

A philanthropic organization with overseas branches says that reminding the reference of the importance of an accurate appraisal usually brings a helpful reply:

> Dear Mr. Jones:
>
> *Re: S. F. B.*
>
> We solicit your help with respect to our consideration of the above-named person for an overseas post. We know that you realize the importance of having capable, stable and reliable persons carrying out our program overseas. Any weakness or shortcomings, quite tolerable in a domestic situation, may be magnified in a foreign assignment and thereby jeopardize an entire vital program. We should appreciate getting your candid evaluation of this candidate's suitability in these terms.
>
> Your comments will be kept in the strictest confidence. We should also be grateful if you would suggest the names of others who might be acquainted with the work and character of Mr. B.
>
> Yours truly,
>
> N. T. Granger

It goes without saying that those answering a letter of inquiry should be shown your appreciation. A two-sentence message may be adequate: "Thank you for your response to our request for information concerning Mr. C. B. We find your information very helpful in our consideration of Mr. B."

2. *The phone check.* One expert strongly prefers the phone to the letter for reference checking. He says, "Few people will commit themselves on paper, partly because they are too busy to compose a written reference, but primarily because they are reluctant to be specific when they can be quoted directly."

Some checkers feel they can get the reference to open up more easily on the impersonal telephone—if they can succeed in establishing rapport. One way to establish a good relationship is by being businesslike, friendly, and aware that you're asking the man at the other end to be helpful: "I realize you're a very busy man, and I'm sorry to impose on your time like this, but we should find it extremely helpful if you could spend a few minutes giving us the benefit of your knowledge and opinions of Mr. Black."

One experienced phone user says: "I often find that saying something neutral, or even downright negative about an applicant will get a more useful answer than just asking an open-end question, such as, 'What would you say of his ability to work with people?' " The approach he's suggesting involves statements such as:

"I have the impression that he gets flustered easily. . . ."

"He sometimes seems overly aggressive. . . ."

The reply you get is likely to be more positive—either in agreement or disagreement, than if you leave it up to the reference to phrase an opinion in the abstract.

3. *The telephone checklist.* Companies that use a telephone check on references usually develop a standard list of questions to make sure that the ground is adequately covered. A sample of one such checklist is reproduced below.

TELEPHONE CHECKLIST

Name of Applicant	Person Contacted	Position

Company	City & State	Telephone Number

1. I'd like to verify some of the information given us by Mr. ———— who has applied for employment with our organization. Do you remember him?
2. What were the dates of his employment? From———— 19—— to———— 19——
3. What type of work was he doing for you? ————————————————

---

4. He says he was earning $———— per———— when he left. Is that right?————
   If "No," what were his earnings? $————
5. How much of this was salary? $———— How much was commission or bonus? $————
6. Was he a dependable, responsible executive? Yes———— No———— Did he lose any time because of drinking, gambling, financial or domestic problems? What specifics?————————————————
7. How did his performance compare with others'?————————————
8. How closely was he supervised?————————————————
9. What did you personally think of him? ————————————————
   Did he get along with other people? ————————————————
10. Why did he leave?————————————————
11. Would you rehire him? Yes———— No———— If "No," why not?————————

---

12. What are his outstanding strong points?————————————————
13. What are his weak points?————————————————

Checked by———————————————— Date————

4. *Face to face.* It's time-consuming, it can't be done from deskside, as is the case with a phone call, but most reference checkers assert that meeting with a reference, such as an ex-employer, face to face is worth the time it takes.

"Only face to face," says one personnel manager, "can you observe the facial expressions—hesitations, uneasiness, or enthusiasm, for that matter. These can tip you off better than words can."

Along with the advantage it gives the interviewer, the person being called on has the reassurance of your presence. He's not likely to worry about what's behind the disembodied unfamiliar voice at the other end of the phone.

It goes without saying that whoever performs the personal visit should satisfactorily represent your company. And to ensure a businesslike call that doesn't string out into a loose gabfest, it may be useful as well as reassuring to the man being called on if the same type of checklist described for phone use be employed.

After going through the routine questions, the face-to-face meeting lends itself particularly well to a few concluding open-end questions in which the information giver can really let his hair down, if he is so inclined.

Getting the Truth

The problem in reference checking isn't to get an answer, but to get an accurate and helpful answer. The reference who doesn't want to hurt an applicant by revealing his drawbacks may have good intentions, but it can be argued that kindness in this situation harms rather than helps. Assisting a man to get a job for which he is unqualified is seldom a service to him. Second, an employer who hires an applicant on the basis of misleading information is more likely to dump him than one who knows his strong and weak points, and can thus make an intelligent decision. Few employers look for a paragon. Being realistic, they can make a hiring decision with an easier mind, feeling that they know the applicant's capabilities for what they are.

Rawle Deland warns of four types of reference givers that are likely to distort the truth about an ex-employee:

The legal eagle was once sued by a former employee about whom he gave an honest opinion. Now he's so gun-shy that he'll never tell the truth, even on a confidential basis. He instructs everyone in his company to give only favorable or noncommittal references. There's no effective way to beat this one, but you've got to recognize him in order to discount his comments as worthless.

The hatchet man is quick to tell faults first. This isn't bad in itself, but after a dozen comments that never get warmer than a mild recommendation, you begin to wonder. The way to get around this fellow is to ask his opinion about someone you know yourself. The extent of his disparagement will enable you to judge the value of his comments from then on.

The unforgiving one is the employer who thinks that anyone who ever left him is *ipso facto* no good. He'll never say anything favorable about a former employee, because he believes that anyone who couldn't see the terrific opportunities in his company must be quite stupid. Once again, it's the adherence to a single pattern—the same type of reference for all former employees—that sends up the warning signals on this kind of reference.

The bag of wind is a fellow we all know. No matter where he is— giving references, at a cocktail party, or in a business meeting—he's always the same. He's full of words, but when you ask yourself later what he said, you realize that it was just that—words. Repeating what this fellow says—or reading it again—will make the meaninglessness of his remarks apparent.

To overcome attitudes of this kind, the experts recommend that the reference giver be put on the spot, firmly but subtly, by an appeal to his sense of moral responsibility. Approaches such as the following can accomplish this:

"I know you wouldn't want him to get into a job that he couldn't handle, so I'm sure you'll give me a frank answer to this question."

"Suppose *you* were hiring him again. What questions would you want to have answered?"

"I know you recognize how important it is—both for the company and the executive—to have a compatible job fit, and I'm sure we can rely on your judgment."

To these approaches add another that is helpful in certain circumstances. Try to take the pressure off the reference giver by noting that it's not a this-job-or-none situation:

"We're trying to evaluate him in several areas and don't have any particular position in mind for him at the present."

Use Pointed Questions

Experienced personnel executives are keenly aware of the effectiveness of incisive questions for uncovering facts. Rawle Deland of Thorndike Deland, the executive-search firm, has written his views on this matter:

Don't be vague. You can't expect good answers from bad questions. Be specific; a general question invites a general answer. Specify the job you're considering the man for, and tell what qualifications have proved important in it previously. By the time you're asking for references, you should have a pretty good idea of what you want to know, so come right to the point. If you sense that the candidate has had trouble with the people under him, don't ask, "How were his human relations?" Come right out with what you want to know: "How did his subordinates like him?"

Other specific questions to be asked if appropriate: Why did he leave you? Why didn't he move faster with you? Was he more at ease with other executives or with shop employees? Would you rehire him?

One Milwaukee executive reports that he stumbled onto an effective technique for getting around evasive tactics. He said, "I was checking an applicant's background with a previous employer. I'd gone through all the routine questions, and then I remarked: 'You know, Mr. Brown, I should tell you that I have the impression that your ex-employee is still very much in love with your company. I think I could work on him so that he'd be willing to return. Would you like me to try?'

"Up to this point, the man had given a uniformly favorable recommendation. But now he blurted out, 'I wouldn't hire back that so-and-so for anything in the world!' "

The Libel-suit Danger

It's important for all hiring companies to understand the libel-suit hazard that makes ex-employers wary about giving out information. Of course, as a hiring executive himself might be someone's ex-employer, the information can be helpful two ways.

The following explanation is paraphrased from an item in File 20 of the Research Institute of America's *Labor-Personnel Report*:

> The president of a wholesale bakery called in his Purchasing Agent one Friday afternoon and told him he was through. The purchasing man asked how come. The president said, "Let's just say business is bad." But when the executive wouldn't accept that reason the president said, "You've been getting kickbacks from suppliers." As matters developed, the president was sued for slander, and the saving fact was that nobody else was present during the conversation. To prove slander, one must show "publication" and there can't be any publication unless a third person is informed.

Clearly, "publication" exists in the reference-checking situation because a third person is involved. It isn't necessary that an ex-employer call a man a thief, for example. If that implication can be drawn from what is said, the employer is open to legal action.

The Research Institute gives this example of the possibilities:

> Personnel Manager A dismisses a man who passed bad checks. When Manager B calls on the phone, A implies that the man is a poor risk for any job requiring the handling of money. B quotes A in turning the man down. The employee sues the former employer, calling B as a witness.

One state unemployment agency has cautioned employers about reporting dismissals for intoxication, dishonesty, and other acts of misconduct. The following recommendations may help you read between the lines when you get what seems to be a somewhat less than explicit answer:

Don't say, "He was drunk" or label acts as dishonest or immoral. Say instead:

"Reported to work under apparent influence of some intoxicant, and was not in my opinion able to perform his job satisfactorily."

"Removed property from company premises without proper authorization."

"Engaged in conduct unbecoming an employee on the job, to the embarrassment of management and fellow employees."

One official of an investigating service makes this added suggestion: If you get derogatory information about an applicant, use it circumspectly. First, you want to protect your source. Second, don't, under the guise of frankness, tell more than you should about the information you've uncovered, since you want to avoid getting into an argument.

Pre-Employment Investigation

PEI takes several steps beyond reference checking. It usually requires the specialized skills of a professional investigator, and it is expensive. But it is likely to provide you with considerably more useful information than is available through any other means. Many firms use PEI where the applicant is a key employe with a salary in the higher brackets, and his performance and character are vital to the company's destiny.

Other good clients of investigating firms are companies whose transactions require a high degree of confidentialness and who cannot risk hiring an executive who may be susceptible to bribery, or whose ethics are so low that he might try to capitalize on his inside knowledge of company secrets. Although these weaknesses may not be easy to detect, it's much more likely that a man with a spotless past—who shows no propensities toward excessive drinking or gambling, for example—will be a better bet than one whose habits are questionable. And it is the personal-habit area that is susceptible to investigation.

The same need for special screening also applies to companies whose research, design, and marketing policies are such that they become valuable competitive information.

Several points are important to observe, however, if you plan to get involved in PEI:

1. *Let applicants know that they will be investigated as a precondition of employment.* "And be sure," says one advocate of the approach, "that you tell the man early enough in your contact to keep him from getting out on a limb with some ill-considered 'strengthening' of his qualifications." Some companies ask for written permission from applicants to make investigations.

2. *Make it clear that PEI means more than a reference check.* In the minds of some, "investigation" simply means a checking of references. But when PEI is undertaken, particularly by an outside agency, it may in-

volve not only a check of academic background and work experience, but also a probing of social contacts and personal life. This latter area often requires what is professionally known as a "neighborhood check."

Failure to tell the applicant what's involved can lead to trouble, as witness the following:

A firm looking for a treasurer finally found the right man. Everything was perfect: education, experience, personality. The employer told the man they were going to "investigate" him. He agreed. But when he learned that some of his neighbors had been interviewed, he hit the roof. His complaints to the employer were so bitter, the employer decided to reverse his hiring decision. "I have troubles enough without another hothead on the staff," was the conclusion—fair or otherwise.

Companies operating in towns or smaller cities generally find that the social qualifications and habits of prospective employees are especially important. Many an executive has "failed to make it" because of a marital problem, or a problem wife who couldn't adjust to the community. These personal matters, too, may figure in a PEI, if the executive position being filled is sufficiently critical.

3. *Consider using an outside agency.* You may not want to go to the expense in all cases, but for a particularly critical hire, an outside professional investigating agency can yield results beyond what might be available on a do-it-yourself basis.

Every major city has at least one reputable organization able to run personnel checks. Rates vary, depending on the service required. One firm quotes a price of $8.oo for each "experience area" per man. At this rate, a routine check into an applicant's work record, credit standing, and educational background costs $24.oo. Cost of investigations for upper-echelon executives runs much higher, of course, because they usually include a neighborhood visit, investigation of social contacts and standing, and so on. Costs for this type of check may run from $200 to $1,ooo per executive.

4. *Make sure that investigation reports are read.* Two years after a West-coast firm had hired an assistant office manager, he made the headlines by embezzling $75,ooo of the company's money. What the newspapers didn't print was the fact that the company had in its files at the time of hiring a PEI report stating that the man had been discharged before because of "irresponsibility." He had also misrepresented his previous salary and marital status on his job application. He had been hired simply because no one in management had bothered to read the report.

In *any* case, whatever material a company gets, be it a letter, a report, or simply notes on a telephone conversation—none will do any good unless a responsible executive reads and acts on it. See page 245 for examples of PEI reports.

18

The Mystery of the Knockout Factor

"How did I make out in my tests?" asks the applicant for a junior-executive position.

"Fine, fine," said the personnel manager, "but we won't be able to use you. Trouble is, you scored 100 per cent in your honesty rating. The job we have in mind requires an outstanding liar. But if we ever need someone with integrity, we'll get in touch with you right away."

Pure fiction? Yes, but not so far from the fact. Despite all the rational job specifications, the carefully designed psychological tests, the precise definitions of what is wanted, the final hiring decision may hinge on a factor the job candidate never dreamed he'd encounter—and frequently never knows. To cite just one recent example:

An international corporation was screening candidates for key managerial positions in its Latin American affiliates. One of the major problems it ran into was the typical American attitude toward paying officials to get things done. Yet, in some countries, a polite form of bribery is not only customary but part of accepted business practice. The ability to handle such situations gracefully was a key qualification for the job. Yet on indirect questioning, most of the candidates expressed horror at the very idea.

This chapter takes a look at some of the possible answers to the question: "The company considered dozens of people; why did they finally select—or reject—executive A?"

This is not an idle question. It's important that company recruiters face up to the question of why they hire or reject. The company that pins down the answers is far more likely to select the right candidates than one that doesn't.

Similarly, the job hunter who understands the real basis on which company choices are made will be able to relieve his mind on two points: First, he'll not spend sleepless nights wondering why he didn't get a particular appointment; second, he'll be able to make a more realistic evaluation of his own areas of weakness and strength.

The Inner Flaw

Although they wouldn't admit it, many executives feel defensive about some aspect of their qualifications or background: "I won't be able to get any further in company X because of my religion," or "I don't stand a chance because I didn't go to the 'right' university." Such reasons may touch on anything from age to accent, from place of birth to physical appearance. And certain factors may indeed be handicaps. But the fact is, handicaps often become problems only because the individual *believes* they are.

The Mouse in the Lion's Mask

An executive job seeker tells his friends: "What do you think of that so-and-so at company Y? He ruled me out for a sales job because I happened to be wearing a white necktie. I know that was the reason because he mentioned it in the course of our conversation."

Perhaps it was the white tie. But it might have been any one of a dozen other reasons—*or none at all*. Applicants are too prone to believe that hiring decisions rest solely on the interviewer's personal preferences, prejudices, and predilections. Other nonpersonal factors are just as often at work. Two examples:

• *Committee hiring* is a common practice at the ABC Company. ABC's executives like it because, individually, it gets them off the hook. No one man can be blamed for hiring a staff member, should the latter fail to make the grade. As a result of this practice, the maverick, the unusual candidate, is unlikely to be hired. Generally, it is the "neutral" man, the one to whom no one objects, that gets the job.

• A company, as an individual, can *change its mind*. Company BCD had run a blind ad for an assistant to the president. Many good men had applied, sure that their qualifications were sufficient to get an interview. All were disappointed. The word had come down from the top: "Stop looking. We've decided not to fill the job for the time being."

But what about the feelings of the rejected candidates? Nearly every one of them seized upon a personal "flaw" as a reason for being eliminated. The man over fifty felt it was his age; the one born overseas felt it was his place of birth; the one who had gone to a city college decided that his lack of Ivy League credentials had cut him out of the competition.

In other words, rejection is often a capricious rather than logical outcome. The job seeker who feels he has been victimized by a biased recruiting process often fails to consider more innocent, even if no more commendable, reasons: poor screening procedures, poor judgmental ability, pure chance.

Worst Foot Forward

There is another manner in which an applicant may lose out. Given a particular attribute that he feels is a handicap, he presents himself in such a way that the quality actually *does* harm his chances:

"A. Z. Smith," the resume read, "Age, fifty-nine. . . ."

A veteran recruiter attests to the truth of the incident. A marketing manager of unusual capabilities states his age right at the beginning of his resume. Age was not necessarily a handicap, but it was hardly an asset. *He knew better.* As an outstanding marketing executive, who had devised many successful campaigns, he knew that you don't sell anything by making the buyer aware of its drawbacks. Why had he done so when he was marketing himself? In a perverse way, perhaps to give himself peace of mind. Feeling his age to be a flaw in his qualifications, he might have thought, "If they're still interested after learning my age, O.K. But if they see that first, I won't have to worry about a last-minute turndown for that reason." Logic was against him, of course. If the man were selling a product, he would expound on its virtues, minimizing or even turning around the drawbacks. For example, if you're selling white tuna in a market that prefers pink, you can assert: "Won't turn pink in the can."

Similarly, in interviews many job seekers are often unnecessarily defensive when the talk turns to a sensitive area:

"I see you went to Hardknocks U," says an interviewer.

"Yes, what about it?" responds the applicant belligerently.

"So did I."

Or, "That's a rather unusual name you have, Mr. Sysz."

"I guess it is. You know, some of those old-country names. . . ."

"I mention it because my wife's maiden name was Sislick."

The "Truth" About Company Bias

Does bias exist? Do companies select staff for reasons other than ability or superior qualifications? There is no single "truth" about company hiring policies. The facts are often lost in:

The fog of *ambiguous company practices*—the written policy and the practice don't match.

The fog of *self-delusion*—"My company invariably hires the best man for the job, regardless of race, creed, or color" (yet religion *is* a key factor).

The fog raised by *contending factions*—one company's vice-president of sales won't hire men of a particular national origin; the vice-president of engineering favors them.

There are two kinds of knockout factors that cause screeners to rule out job applicants:

Explicit. These factors stem directly from the job description and related specifications. A qualified man is ruled out because someone comes along who is better qualified.

Implicit. Knockout factors in this category aren't likely to appear in either the job description or man description. They reflect preferences based on company tradition; for example, the generalized image of a type, that will prompt an executive to say: "He looks like our kind of guy." Or the qualifications represent the bias of the recruiting executive or the superior of the man being sought. As already mentioned, recruiters sometimes run across an executive who won't hire an applicant because of his height—or lack of it.

A bias may appear in negative or positive form:

One executive says: "I can't stand people who affect mustaches. Candidate A is out."

Another one says: "I'm looking for a clean-cut, well-spoken individual who would be at home either at the opera or the racetrack. I hired candidate B because he had that flexibility."

A recent cartoon tells an appropriate story: At an executive desk sits a bald-headed man with a walrus mustache, looking up at a job applicant similarly bald-headed, with walrus mustache, etc. The executive says, "Mr. Jamison, I like the cut of your jib. You're hired."

What of the WASP?

With wry humor, the foreign-born research manager for a New England electronics firm says, "I guess the founder of this company would do a couple of nip-ups in his grave if he saw my name on the office door. But there it is, and I must say, it's not so much a testimony to the end of prejudice, as to the fact that I'd made some discoveries that this company badly needed."

We do not yet live in a world where the Cohens, Kellys, and Kents or the white and nonwhite have equal acceptance. However, the preeminence of the WASP—the White Anglo-Saxon Protestant—is fading. In a recent study the American Jewish Committee reported that discrimination against Jewish engineers, researchers, and economists in major American industry has "largely disappeared." The decline in bias is slowly spreading from the professional to the managerial circles.

Louis Caplan, of Pittsburgh, president of the committee, stated the result of the AJC study in these words: "The current technological revolution in the United States has made possible a major and widespread breakthrough against discrimination" in the technical and research branches of industry. Further, a brief reading of almost any roster of top executive personnel will show an ethnic diversity of names unlikely fifteen or twenty years ago.

Some prejudices reflect local traditions and attitudes. Minority groups, made distinctive by race or culture—for example, individuals of Irish, Italian, Mexican, Asiatic, and American Indian background—may be at a disadvantage in particular localities. By and large, such obstacles are fossilized attitudes of the past.

True, the realities of the business situation rather than idealism or the departure of bigotry from the human soul explains the growing tolerance. But for whatever reason, the day of the WASP as the sure choice for top appointments is slowly disappearing. The country as a whole set a note of broad acceptance when it elected Catholic John F. Kennedy to the Presidency in 1960. Company after company has made similar choices, selecting the nontraditional candidate when he seemed to have more on the ball than his competitor.

Trends in Knockout Factors

Patterns of discrimination—and the word is used here not in its pejorative sense—are merely a reflection of our changing society. In this decade, the advent of the Negro executive is raising new questions for some companies. Changing age patterns of the general population are influencing hiring attitudes. Here is a brief rundown of trends with respect to a number of qualities:

Age. Sophisticated companies have stopped looking for "a man of thirty-five with thirty years of experience in the mining industry." This reflects not merely a triumph of arithmetic over chronophobia, but several other factors as well:

• Increasing average age of the population.

• Increasing longevity.

• Increasing span in which the individual retains his mental and physical capabilities.

• Increased time necessary for an individual to acquire the experience and technical knowledge to run today's intricate corporate organization.

What these facts mean in actual practice is this: If the final choice narrows down to two men, one forty-five and the other fifty-five, the younger man is likely to have an advantage. But the man of fifty-five, with ten productive years ahead of him, now seems like the good bet, since the accelerated business process makes ten years seem a long tenure. A good executive can easily earn his keep, and then some, in that period of time.

Hergenrather Associates, West-coast recruiting consultants, made a survey of successful executives to determine a salary level appropriate for given age brackets:

Age	Salary, $
27 – 30	9–12,000
30 – 35	12–18,000
36 – 40	18–25,000
40 – 45	20–30,000
46 – 50	23–35,000
Over 50	28–50,000

The relationship between age and salary is sometimes used as a measure of capability. For example, a man of fifty, who has been earning under $20,000, tends to be automatically tagged as "not having much on the ball." The presumption is that if he were a comer, his performance would be reflected in a higher salary.

The Hergenrather survey further showed that candidates for president of a corporation are mostly in their early fifties and are usually tapped at about fifty-five.

Education. Two factors are included here. One is how far a candidate has gone educationally—college, postgraduate degrees, and so on; the other has to do with *where* the studies were undertaken.

The editors of *Factory* (April, 1963), reporting on an interview with Vance Packard, author of *The Pyramid Climbers,* came to this conclusion: "How important is a college or graduate degree? It depends in part on your age. If you're 40 or less, you'll be under a definite handicap without it. If you're up in your 40s or 50s, they couldn't care less. Your work record tells the story. However, there's more of a chance of a production man advancing without the sheepskin than any other candidate—with the exception of the salesman."

At the same time, the increasingly technical nature of business operations is making advanced education a must for other than prestige reasons. The traditional up-the-line advance, starting from the supervisory ranks, is growing less frequent each year, especially when the individual starts with less than a college degree. In short, the old "rags to riches" career in management is likely to occur only when the "rag" is a diploma.

The "where" of the education continues to be a consideration. The reputation of the individual college or university lends its aura to the graduate. A Harvard Business School graduate holds shinier credentials for an administrator's job than a graduate of some unknown business school. An engineering executive gets an extra impetus in his career when he's a graduate of MIT.

There is some logic to the extra weight given the prestige colleges. Harvard *does* have an outstanding business school. MIT graduates *are* likely to be among the best-educated engineers in the country. The Ivy League graduate tends to have the edge when the hiring corporation is prestige-conscious.

Where does this leave the qualified job seeker whose schooling unfortunately lacks the glamor label? The same place *every* job seeker finds himself, when he is matched against competitors. He must point to other compensating qualifications—achievements in previous jobs, outstanding capabilities, unique experience.

Marital status. The *Factory* article mentioned above has some intriguing observations to make about a candidate's spouse. Although these are made in the context of promotability, the considerations cut the same way in hiring:

> Your marital status can vitally affect your chances of advancement especially if your home office is in a smaller city. If you're a bachelor past 35, you have two strikes against you before you start. If you're divorced, it's a handicap—but not nearly as big a one as if you had never been married.
>
> It's important to establish that you're reasonably happily married, though not excessively so, says (Vance) Packard. Some corporations shy away from the man who is too attached to his home. They feel he will avoid extra work for fear of disrupting his family life.
>
> Companies often expect the wife to be adaptable enough to move to another section of the country in case of transfer. Your spouse doesn't have to be highly sophisticated. She should be wholesome and not overly conspicuous in behaviour, dress or conversation. And she should be capable of growing with you as your responsibilities increase. She will be required to act as your hostess in business-social situations.

The question of the executive wife as a "job qualification" of her husband's is decidedly controversial. *The New York Times* of March 9, 1963, carried this front-page headline:

NAVY TO GRADE OFFICERS' WIVES AS A KEY TO HUSBANDS' CAREERS

Commentators both in print and on the air made considerable to-do about (1) the injustice, (2) the impracticality, (3) the lack of logic of having a man's wife rated as one of the elements of his acceptability.

But the world of management has far outdistanced the Navy in its consideration of the wife as a potential factor in an executive's promotability. In big-company politics, a wife can often make or break a man's career. An executive is rarely elevated to a top spot until his mate has cleared the inspection of top brass. Corporate thinking on the matter is simple:

"It doesn't matter too much in metropolitan centers," says one management-consultant recruiter, "but in a small town, a company feels that the social acceptability of a wife and her ability to adjust are critical factors in her husband's career. In some cases, the wrong religion, the wrong politics, the wrong values are considered knockout factors. Unfair? I don't think that's the point. In the small town, any problem the executive's wife or children pose for the community becomes a reflection on the company."

Place of origin. Austin Hall, in his book *How to Get a Better Job*, poses the question: "If you were not born in the United States should you state in your resume or job interview that you are foreign-born?" In his opinion, the answer is "no." There is no point in emphasizing your place of birth, whether it is Paris, Missouri, or Warsaw, Poland. The prospective employer wants to know *you*, not where you came from, and a statement about being foreign-born may sound defensive.

One can certainly agree with Hall, as far as he goes. But, as in the applicant's marital status, the attributes of "foreign origin" that stay with the man may mark him as "different" and, in some localities, thereby less acceptable.

You don't have to cross borders to awaken xenophobia. Northerners tend to be viewed with suspicion in some sections of the South, and vice versa. In some business offices in Manhattan, a "Brooklyn accent" is considered "low class" (paging Prof. Henry Higgins) and a drawback to its possessor.

In general, the determining factor is the company's sense of its own image, and the extent to which applicants, as potential representatives of the company, enhance or tarnish that image—with employees, customers, and the public at large.

This problem, as that of religion, is fading as our culture changes. The localized culture itself is disappearing. More widespread education, greater mobility, TV and radio are exerting a homogenizing effect on the population. The day is coming when even a Professor Higgins might have trouble discerning whether an executive was born and bred in Boston, Baltimore, or Seattle.

In this problem area, companies tend to be altogether pragmatic. A good production man who can deliver results will be hired regardless of any traces of an undesirable "local culture." But where the job to be filled calls for critical contacts with customer or the public, a company ordinarily will avoid handicapping itself. "He was a crackerjack sales manager," admitted the president of a furniture company, "but he'd be badly hobbled calling on customers in Louisiana, with that Midwestern twang of his."

Manner, appearance. Most of us tend to have two self-images. One is the realistic, unglamorized way we see ourselves in the business context. The other is a somewhat idealized figure of our phantasy life. The *Factory* editors seem to blend these two in prescribing desirable appearance for a job applicant in the eyes of a hiring "board of review":

> How do you look to top management? . . . Have you got enough poise and self-confidence to be at home in the executive suite? In addition to being good at your job, you need to have a certain amount of sophistication and worldliness. You must acquire at least a working knowledge of the arts, economics, and the national political scene. . . .
>
> How articulate are you? Keep in mind that as a member of top management you can be called to Washington to testify before committees or to attend conferences. This means you have to be a walking and talking advertisement for your company.
>
> As for physical characteristics, large corporations have a tendency to choose tall slender men for top spots. Although you do not have to be a movie star to qualify, a rough-cut, lined face on a squat, round figure can hurt your chances.
>
> The old truism that clothes make the man goes double in the corporation world. Executive candidates usually try to look the part—although there are a few companies where top executives wear sport shirts. Some men even check the latest illustrated business publications when in doubt about clothes. Argyle socks can lose a candidate his big chance.

One suspects considerable tongue-in-cheek in the above paragraphs. Granted the appeal of masculine good looks over a Frankenstein monster, usually it is only the company looking for a "front man"—in public relations, customer relations, or sales—that gives serious thought to the more advanced types of masculine pulchritude. For the average executive job, physique doesn't much matter. Dress, of course, does, except in some rare cases where management may feel like the advertising-agency president who said, "I find my customers are favorably impressed by an art director or a copy chief that looks nutty. A beard, unkempt hair, loud clothes seem to say, 'This guy must really have it, or they'd never keep him around.'"

Residence. Just two or three points to be made here. A man's home address may be considered an indication of his social situation, his financial stability, and his sense of how to spend money.

Many application blanks ask a man to provide the address and estimated cost of his dwelling. Or, such information may be provided in the course of a pre-employment investigation. The hiring executive will use this information to decide whether the applicant lives "on the right side of the tracks," or in the "right part of town." If the evidence is affirmative, it is likely to favor the man's chances. If negative, it tends to nick his chances somewhat.

If a man's home suggests that it has got its fair share of his income, that is taken as a mark of stability—as opposed, possibly, to the individual who skimps on his home in favor of a large boat or expensive car.

The applicant's home surroundings are sometimes taken as an indication of salary requirements: "He'd need over $50,000 to live at the level suggested by that house of his," remarked an executive in a recent selection conference. "We can't afford it."

Health. Few companies hire executives without expecting the preferred candidate to have a complete medical checkup. As a matter of fact, some companies follow this policy right down to the rank-and-file level.

The executive who is suffering from a major health problem is fortunate if he can continue a long-time tenure in his existing company, much less advance his career in another company. It all depends on the nature of the impediment. Organizations representing almost every kind of disease ailment have campaigned to make the victims acceptable to the business community. Groups have sought to make employers aware of the special loyalty and dedication often forthcoming from the physically handicapped. From mental health to heart disease, the same message has been conveyed. Some employers are persuaded; others are not. For some executives with health handicaps, self-employment is often the best answer.

On the other hand, many employers are open-minded on the subject. This is particularly true of those reaping the benefits of superior performance from handicapped executives or those who have had nervous breakdowns, polio, heart attacks, and so on.

Gaps in the employment record. Said an employment agency executive, "I have a tough problem. A man came in here today. He was a qualified accountant, had been an office manager. He's fully capable of turning in a good performance. But he's spent six years in prison for embezzlement. How can I get a job for a man with that kind of record?"

Experienced personnel people are adept at detecting a soft spot in the chronology of a resume. An unexplained gap in employment may suggest alcoholism, mental problems, a criminal record.

Said one bitter executive job seeker: "I've stopped making the rounds. I'm going to set up some small business of my own. Every time I talked to a prospective employer and my stay at a mental hospital came out, he lost interest. That was never the reason given for rejection, but I'm under no illusions."

There's no doubt, the odds *are* stacked higher against the applicant with a problem in his background. Aside from the suggestion made in the chapter on interviewing (page 186) on how to deal with a handicap in qualifications, the only thing that can be added here is this. There have been many instances where persistence and willingness to be realistic paid off: "It took me eighteen months to find a job," says an ex-alcoholic art director. "But eventually I came across a man who was sufficiently impressed by the fact I'd been sober for a year to take his chances. Believe me, I make it up to him in every way I can."

Recent developments, including those on the legislative front, suggest that two categories of executive deserve special mention, the female executive and the Negro executive.

The lady executive. The total number of women at work—in all jobs— has risen dramatically in recent years. Fourteen million women were in the workforce in 1940, 23.5 million in 1960, an estimated 25 million in 1962. By 1970, government manpower experts predict the total will reach 30 million.

Meanwhile, what of the lady executive?

According to Assistant Secretary of Labor Esther Peterson, the traditional reluctance of business to put women in high-level administrative jobs shows no significant sign of easing.

Nation's Business offers these figures: "In 1940, four percent of the executives in the United States were women. In 1950, the figure had risen only to five percent." It was still at that level when the 1960 census was conducted.

Actually, the penetration of women into the executive echelons varies considerably, depending on the industry. In some industries, lady executives are no strangers: cosmetics, retail merchandizing, banking, insurance, real estate, and credit jobs have opened up for women in recent years.

But generally a sex barrier exists. States *Nation's Business:* "Many companies shy away from giving women top jobs because they fear the effect this will have on other employees—particularly men."

The most constructive advice that can be given to the career-minded woman is to pick the industry and company. Although occasionally you hear of a woman heading up a trucking company, or a construction firm, investigation usually reveals that such positions have been inherited from a deceased spouse. But the executive job, particularly one that includes a high technical element—engineering or manufacturing for example— seldom falls to the woman contender unless she is willing to compete on male terms and proves superior.

The Negro executive. One of the country's outstanding recruiting consultants was recently asked: "If a client asked you to find a Negro to fill an executive vacancy, what would you do?"

"I should hesitate to accept the assignment for two reasons. First, I should suspect the motivation behind such a request; and second, I don't know how I should go about finding a 'Negro executive.' "

In a few years, the same question is likely to draw an entirely different answer. But set in its time context, the recruiter's response points up some of the interesting and conflicting situations resulting from the Negro emancipation of the middle sixties.

"NEGRO COLLEGE MEN SOUGHT FOR HIGH-LEVEL JOBS." This headline appeared in *The New York Times* on September 12, 1964. The story indicated that the United Negro College Fund, a biracial organization, was supplying operating funds to thirty-two accredited Negro colleges for the purpose of qualifying Negro graduates for positions of responsibility. An official of the fund stated that many important concerns had been seeking Negro college graduates. Many were said to be sending recruiters to Negro colleges to interview graduates.

Developments of this kind dramatize the fact that the prospects for the Negro aspiring to an executive career face a brighter future.

Yet, it would be naive to assume that the employment path will be strewn with roses. Two months earlier than the item in *The New York Times*, *Newsweek* quoted Herbert Hill of the National Association for the Advancement of Colored People as saying, in connection with Negro opportunities for higher-echelon jobs: "All we get from the management community is apathy. The white corporate power structure must take the initiative, but as yet they're ignorant of the profound social change that's going on."

One of the problems facing both the business community and the would-be Negro executive is *tokenism*. Although many large corporations—such as Western Electric, Lockheed, R. J. Reynolds—make sincere desegregation efforts, others merely seek out a "showcase Negro" as a symbol of their "open-mindedness."

However, the obstacle to employment posed by the tradition-bound corporation is sometimes matched by the poor education of aspiring Negroes. For example, in 1962, 2,100 Negro college men took Federal civil service examinations. Only 86 passed. Commissioner John W. Macy, Jr., puts the blame for the showing on the low quality of segregated schooling the Negroes have received.

There is no mystery about the rarity of the qualified Negro in the past. With no prospect of a job, there was no reason for a Negro to prepare himself for the executive life. A Negro engineer, mathematician, or business administrator had little hope of finding a job. The ambitious Negro college man usually planned to become a teacher, minister, dentist, doctor, or social worker.

"The future will undoubtedly see changes," says Hobart Taylor, Jr., of the Commission on Equal Employment Opportunity. "I think we are reaching the end of another day, the day when the Negro had to be better. I think we are coming to the day when a man has to be simply as good." Hopefully, it may not take decades for the educational system to grind out Negro executives capable of holding their own in the executive suite. As is true of other minorities, the schools, government bureaus, and non-profit institutions are incubators of Negro executive skills. When the opportunities are developed, the qualified men will appear. Then it will be up to individual organizations to develop policies in keeping with the times.

What Every Company Should Know about Its Selection Factors

Every organization and every hiring executive, consciously or otherwise, uses standards, values, or qualities on which to hire or reject executives. The cues below can be helpful in this connection:

1. *Know what your knockout factors are.* It may take some soul searching or some intensive analysis, but a review of past recruiting activity and the posing of some probing questions can turn up useful information:

Exactly why was applicant A hired?

Exactly why was applicant B rejected?

What factors am I aware of using as a basis of evaluation and judgment that *don't* appear in the descriptions for hiring?

2. *Reassess the knockout factors that have been identified.* Obviously, some knockout factors are logical and legitimate. No one would fault an executive for turning down a man with a poor health record for a tough, demanding job. Nor is it unreasonable for a president, recruiting a top staff member, to look for a man with certain educational and social attributes.

However, where analysis reveals an illogical bias in hiring, the company or executive must ask, "Can we continue to indulge ourselves in the luxury of such attitudes?"

3. *Ask, "What am I hiring for?"* The executive who decides he wants to hire a man who will "fit in" may be making a sound decision. But so may the executive who thinks: "What I really need here is a maverick, an aggressive, creative individual with a compulsion to achieve, who doesn't mind treading on toes in the process." Pinning down the general hiring objectives in terms like these can help confirm or question present practices.

4. *Ask, "Are all executives following company policy?"* It's as true in the recruiting area as it is of other management practices: The fact that a company has a policy doesn't mean it's being followed. If time and thought have been given to devising an effective hiring approach, the responsible executive should see to it that (1) all staff members who implement the policy *know* what it is and *understand* it and (2) follow it in all but the exceptional cases.

What Every Applicant Should Know about Knockout Factors

To the executive seeking a job, the "knockout factor" concept is important, particularly if it seems to focus on a questionable aspect of his background, appearance, or personality. Thinking in terms of possible drawbacks can help avoid needless problems.

1. *Are you avoiding the "defensive-aggressive seesaw"?* Keep in mind that people often react to a feeling of inadequacy by becoming either defensive or aggressive. If the former, the natural tendency is to cover up or disguise a weakness. If the latter, the attempt is to "bull it through" should the sensitive area come under discussion. Either of these attitudes can be more harmful to the job seeker than the weakness itself.

2. *Can you eliminate the weak point?* There's a good deal of wisdom in Shaw's *Pygmalion* for the executive laboring under a social handicap. Here's what can happen:

"Do you know how I landed that job?" a successful applicant asks a friend happily. "Those speech lessons I've been taking for the past six months finally paid off. It wasn't just a matter of my foreign accent, but that squeaky, breathy quality in my voice was a real prospect cooler. The speech lessons overcame all that."

Not all liabilities can be eliminated. But in some cases, minimizing a weak point can make a difference. Many a prematurely grey executive has landed a desirable job with the help of a bottle of hair-color restorer.

3. *Can you turn liabilities into assets?* Superficial handicaps can sometimes be converted into positive assets, especially if the possessor can accept the quality himself. For example:

"You do seem to be well-qualified, Mr. Jones," says the interviewer. "But frankly there are several other very capable candidates for the position, and I don't feel I can give you any real encouragement. . . ."

Says Mr. Jones, "May I be very frank, sir? I have an idea you think my height would be a handicap. Isn't it true that you feel a sales manager who is five foot four might be at a disadvantage?"

"Uh—well . . ."

"You may be right. But I'd like to remind you of two things. First, Napoleon was exactly my height. And second, my friends tell me I have a personality that's six feet tall. Now, if you don't mind, I'd like to go into a little greater detail about what I think I can do for your company. . . ."

Two Saving Thoughts

"One mental obstacle I find standing in the way of many applicants," says one employment agency official. "They don't seem to realize that this matter of qualification is always *comparative*. Sure, the man with only three years of college may feel at a disadvantage. But perhaps his strongest competitor has only two years of college."

Another point on which most veteran recruiters agree: Weakness in any quality can be compensated for by outstanding strengths in other areas.

None of us are perfect in all details. And the experienced executive knows that he hires a *whole man* rather than a bundle of traits. He knows that the results he gets on the job stem not from one quality or another, but from the *total performance* of the individual.

The job seeker, aware of his strong points and a history of past accomplishment, should be able to face any review of his qualifications with the confidence that if he is sufficiently interested in a particular job, and the opening is appropriate for his skills and background, his chances are as good as the next man's—better, if he can present himself with effective self-confidence.

19

The Job Market of the Future

Obsolescence of executive skills. Here, in a phrase, is the key to the executive job market of the future, its problems and opportunities.

The changing nature of executive activities not only puts greater pressure on the individual executive to refurbish his professional capability, but creates a strong need to reappraise his field for its career implications: An expected promotion may be blasted by any one of a number of changes in his company. An aspiration that was years in the making may be suddenly rendered impossible by a major change in a man's industry or organization.

For the company, too, executive obsolescence poses tough problems: "How can we keep our executives abreast of their specialties?" "Where can we get the new blood we need to maintain the high quality of our managerial staff?" "What will our management needs be tomorrow— and how will we best meet them?"

This final chapter suggests some of the problems and solutions available to both the career-minded executive and the company concerned with executive manpower, in the face of a developing job market.

Old Problem, New Face

Obsolescence of job skills is not new; it goes back to the Industrial Revolution. In our recent past we have seen the process of human obsolescence continuing. You'd have to search hard to find a blacksmith, a buggy-whip braider, or a hand turner today.

But what *is* new is the phenomenon of obsolescence reaching up the organizational ladder to managerial ranks. "The accelerated rate of progress in automation and technology has generated job obsolescence," said

234

Lester J. Weigle of Humble Oil & Refining Company in a speech at Northwestern University.

The Obsolete Executive

Innovations in the world of business and industry—"progress in automation and technology"—are changing conditions of work at the top. A number of shifts are taking place:

• *Work-method changes.* "We had to transfer the head of our mixing division," says the head of a Colorado food products firm. "As long as we used the old type of batch mixing, he was fine. When we switched to a continuous, electronically-controlled system, he was just out of his depth."

• *Changes in methods of doing business.* An office-equipment firm maintained a large department to handle used and rebuilt machines. It was headed by a capable executive. But when the company began selling on an international scale, the additional problems of marketing abroad were more than the department head could cope with. A new man had to be brought in.

• *Functional specialization.* "Our treasurer was adequate for the job as long as it was mainly a matter of keeping track of income and outgo," says the president of a food chain. "But the character of financial operations in our company has changed drastically; the job now requires highly specialized knowledge in a number of areas, including taxes, new concepts of liquidity, investment, and so on. New problems and opportunities in his field kept slipping by him. We had to bring in a better-educated, more highly trained man for the job."

• *Higher standards of management performance.* Largely because of stepped-up competition, many companies have been forced to demand better results from their executives. Accordingly, the practice of "letting old Ed stay in his job until he retires in two years" is rapidly fading. Few organizations can afford the luxury of such sentiment. They prefer to express their good will in the form of early retirement with generous separation arrangements.

What the Executive Can Do

The executive planning his professional future today must keep his eye on several dynamic factors:

• *New management techniques.* Says Willys H. Monroe, of Booz, Allen & Hamilton, as reported in *Nation's Business:*

> The biggest changes in the job of the average manager in the next five to ten years will stem from both new techniques and differing organizational concepts. Such tools as PERT, game theory, business simulation,

computerized information systems and reliability engineering will enable executives to do their work with increasing precision.

Not all industries or companies will feel the impact of such innovations within the next months, or even years. But over the long haul, only a mere handful of companies will be operating without them.

For those who are concerned about the consequences of such innovations, the words of John T. Garrity of McKinsey & Company are pertinent, particularly since they shed light on the impact likely to be felt at various management levels: "Some people see the computer as a kind of middle-management doomsday machine. I disagree. True enough, there are likely to be substantial dislocations in the middle-management echelons when computers come on the scene. But it's been my experience that veteran managers can stay on top by acquiring a practical working knowledge of computer operations and capabilities."

• A *higher level of education and training among management personnel.* Peter Drucker has hailed the sixties as the decade in which we shall see "the management of the educated." From top to bottom of the average company, the staff will reflect our skyrocketing educational standards, our demands for more-advanced technical training.

• *New organizational relationships.* The fuzzing and even disappearance of the traditional line-staff distinction has been under way for some time. Changes of this character will continue with automation and EDP. Prof. Leonard Sayles of Columbia University points out: "New 'combination jobs' will develop as the computer ties activities together." He provides an example: The customary superior-subordinate relationship will phase out; lateral relationships and communications will become more important in the computerized firm.

• A *continuing increase in the professionalism of management.* For years the experts have been heralding the professionalization of the manager. What they generally mean is the growing systematization of techniques by which managers manage. But there are allied factors. One of special importance in the career context, is the fading out of some of the old ideas about the connection between an executive and his company. Perhaps "company loyalty" will never become outmoded in a literal sense. But to the extent that it was supposed to forge a bond between executive and company, it is rapidly becoming a relic of the past.

A survey on executive mobility reported in *Dun's Review* by Donas Haymes states: "Since World War II, and particularly since 1950, sociologists and business analysts have noted the beginning of a new trend: more and more executives are switching jobs, and switching more and more often."

In a business world in which job hopping is more readily accepted, the individual executive's career objectives can be considerably more wide-ranging.

• *Transferability of skills.* Another consequence of executive professionalization requires special mention. As management methods become more systematized, as executive techniques become more sharply defined, managerial skill loses its parochialism. A marketing executive who knows chain-store operations can function as well for a drug company selling to chains as for a food company. Financial operations of a large chemical processor may be handled by the executive whose experience has been largely confined to advertising. EDP operations are about the same, whether the input concerns textiles or textbooks.

With these facts in mind, the executive may turn to some of the specific facts relating to job opportunities of tomorrow, and what he can do about them.

Shaping Your Career Program

The executive looking ahead to his next step up the ladder, and the one after that, will find his thinking and planning made easier by key considerations such as these:

1. *Expect change.* Perhaps your company will be one of the few that will be operating tomorrow just as it is today. But it's unlikely. You'll be in a much stronger career position if you anticipate change. The importance of this point lies in the fact that it helps you become emotionally prepared. Many an executive has faltered and foundered in his career because he tried to resist tomorrow, instead of trying to exploit it.

Dr. Samuel Johnson, eighteenth century wit and author, said: "Change is not made without inconvenience, even from worse to better." Executives, from their own observations of the business scene, will readily agree with the wisdom of the statement. On the work scene, every innovation is almost invariably met with opposition—overt or otherwise. The man who feels he's being steam-rollered by progress isn't likely to be able to ride with it.

One company president was able to help a member of his staff see the light: "That's the end of the good old days," was the subordinate's bitter remark when a company reorganization was announced.

"And good riddance," said his boss. "I'll agree with you that they were 'old' but I can't go along with the 'good.' The new setup will be better in almost every way."

2. *Watch your industry.* Not all industries will feel the effects of change in the same way, or at the same time. Pay particular attention to the rate and nature of progress in your company's industry. There are a number of opportunities for checking up:

- Trade shows, displaying the newest equipment and services available.
- Trade journals—articles and advertising alike reflect the latest trends.
- Seminars and conferences sponsored by trade and management associations.
- Talk shop—with salesmen, purchasing agents, colleagues, who can add their observations to yours.
- Keep your eye on the industrial leaders. What they do today, others will be doing shortly.

3. *Watch your management function.* Whether you're a production executive or operate in engineering, financial, marketing, or other areas, advances in techniques and increased specialization are undoubtedly taking place in your field.

- Keep up with the changes by attending conferences and seminars sponsored by professional associations.
- Keep up with the literature. Publishers of trade journals and texts are maintaining a steady flow of new material in most fields. You can't read them all, but you can, by careful selection, stay in touch with the significant developments.
- Take refresher courses. In some cases, they're made available by companies. General Electric runs a six-week course "Modern Engineering" to give engineering managers a refresher in science and technology. In some cases, trade associations or management associations sponsor sessions designed to update executives in their special disciplines.

4. *Watch your company.* For many managers, the brightest future lies in their present affiliations. Even where this may not be the case, the executive may consider his own firm a significant weather vane of industrial change.

The advantage you have here is that when your company innovates, you are in a strategic position to observe the background against which it has taken place. You know the pressures that have caused the change, alternatives that were considered, problems arising in connection with the innovation, and its eventual results. With this information, you may enhance your own capabilities as an innovator, either in your present job, or in a future one.

5. *Can you add to your skills?* Although some of the implications of this point have already been covered, additional points exist. The executive may, in some cases, improve his skills aside from any considerations relating to technological advances in his company or industry. For example:

One oil-company legal executive was able to bring about a decided advance in his career by language study. He was a good enough lawyer. But he added a familiarity with Spanish to this capability. He put himself at the forefront of the candidates eager to manage the firm's South American operations.

An engineering executive took a writing course in his local community college. As a result, he not only improved his written communications to others in his organization, but he was able to write publishable articles for trade and professional journals. Outside recognition of his expertise added considerably to his professional standing and desirability.

In many cases, when executives develop skills associated with their basic technical proficiency, they round out their overall managerial capability.

6. *Remember the elements that don't change.* Says Willys H. Monroe: "No matter how esoteric management systems or techniques become, the task of motivating, challenging, rewarding, creating a cooperative environment, organizing efforts and setting demanding goals still remains with the future manager as his primary challenge."

One might quibble over the phrase "primary challenge," but the gist of Monroe's thought is unassailable. Call it human relations, or management leadership, the executive's ability to work with people effectively—subordinates, colleagues, superiors—will continue to be a major factor for his success.

7. *Keep up to date on the job market.* The market for executive skills fluctuates almost as much as the stock market. At one period, financial executives may be in demand; at another, marketing men are the most eagerly sought.

Methods for keeping informed on the state of the market are suggested by earlier chapters of this book. For example: Sampling the ads from time to time will provide a good idea of what type of executives companies are hiring, and for what areas.

How about the executive who's happy in his present job but curious as to how he'd fare in the marketplace? Contact with employment agencies can bring some clear-cut information here, since it's based on the observations of experts. The executive who doesn't mind a small investment might want to go further and put himself on file with an executive registry. This, too, will bring specific answers to the eternal question: "How much am I worth on the market today?"

New Job Possibilities Ahead

Where will the new jobs be tomorrow? An answer sometimes overlooked by the business-oriented executive: in government. *The Wall Street Journal* recently reported on the employment situation throughout the nation. An outstanding fact was that "the biggest increase is on the rolls of state and local governments." Of course, government hiring tends to be tied to the availability of tax money. And in specific instances, there exists the question of access to jobs—either by civil service or official appointment. But the point here is the obvious need for executive talent—in Federal, state, and municipal organizations.

Since by far the greatest interest lies in private industry, in part because of greater salary and advancement opportunity, here are some facts that can clarify what's ahead for tomorrow's job seeker.

There are job titles today that didn't exist yesterday. There will be new ones tomorrow. Here is a brief run-down of some newer categories of jobs, suggesting the shape of things to come. Stanley Schuler, in *Nation's Business*, attributes the designations to the American Management Association and various consulting and recruiting firms:

• *The product manager.* Born in the packaged-goods industries, where he still is often known as the "brand manager," the product manager is responsible for the marketing of a particular product or product group.

• *The project manager.* He carries through the creation and development of a new product. He runs a team usually made up of technically trained people.

• *The operations-research manager.* Objective of this job is to find, through mathematical analysis, the answers to such complex questions as whether the return will justify the cost of keeping a department store open at night, or what is the cheapest distribution pattern for a line of products.

• *Manpower development director.* He concentrates on manpower planning for future needs as well as manpower development in the company.

• *Director of communications.* He is in charge of communications from management to employees. He may also direct public relations activities.

• *Materials manager.* This is a specialty splintered off from the production job. It's concerned with the acquisition and use of all materials used in the production of finished products.

The list may be continued at length, but the jobs indicated are sufficient to suggest the refinements and specialties developing from the traditional "production executive," "personnel director," and so on.

In general, it may be said that the two major influences affecting the nature of tomorrow's jobs are, on the one hand, specialization and, on the other, growing technical content. To the extent that the executive can keep up with both these factors in his job area, he'll be able to develop the brightest prospects for marketing his job capabilities.

You May Not Be a "Product," but . . .

The president of an Indiana grain-products company sees the matter of executive skills in a rather down-to-earth way: "The executive who wants to advance might well think of himself as a product he's putting on the market. Everything he can do to add to the product's sales appeal—everything from improved appearance to unique 'special features'—will make the buyer more eager to get him, and at a favorable price."

It is the acuity with which the executive sizes up the market, and best prepares himself to satisfy what's needed, that is most likely to propel him in the direction he wants to go.

What the Company Can Do—Short Term

There are both short- and long-range aspects to the problem of maintaining performance levels among executive personnel. Here are some short-term considerations:

1. *Consider the personnel implications of change.* The technical advances, said by some to be constantly accelerating, obviously mean changes in work procedures, equipment and machinery, and general methods of doing business. In addition, there are obvious consequences in terms of the human element. Putting it briefly, companies will have to face the problem of dealing with lagging executive capabilities.

Lester J. Weigle, in his talk at Northwestern University, suggested that management has four possible ways to handle the problem of executive obsolescence:

Featherbed—keep the executive in his job, make it as easy as possible for him, cut out tough assignments, give him an assistant.

Relocate—transfer the executive to a less-demanding assignment.

Terminate—retire or separate him from the company roster.

Retread—help him improve his capabilities so that he can continue to function.

Of these four methods, the first is costly, the second is not always practical, and the third is painful or clearly undesirable. The fourth, "retreading," appears to be the best solution. Where it can be applied, the following points suggest implementation for the "retreading" solution.

2. *Develop and promote programs for updating executive skills.* It is not intended to go into the broad considerations of management development programs here. This author, among many others, has treated that subject at length in a previous book—*The Management Makers*, Macmillan, 1962. Appropriate at this point are a few specifics for smaller companies that may lack formal training projects.

Helping your people stay abreast of changing job demands is essentially a matter of training and education. In some cases, the training can be very specific. For example, if your company's procedures have been modernized, you can help the old-timers understand and master their new assignments by on-the-job training.

In many cases, such training is undertaken by the manufacturers of the new equipment installations. Where the changes are procedural and have been recommended by consultants, the consulting firms will usually undertake to train the people you designate.

Where new knowledge is required, and it is available outside the company—engineering and technical schools, local colleges, universities—encourage your managers to take courses that will help them. Some companies make it a policy to partially or wholly pay tuition fees for this type of training. You may want your personnel officer to see whether your company has a viable policy on this point.

3. *Keep training job-oriented.* As much as possible, relate training and educational programs to actual job needs.

For example: The executive in charge of training for a Chicago bank felt that teaching machines and programed instruction might be important aids in the bank's training programs. He assigned two department heads to investigate the field and asked them to submit reports by a given date. "I have two things in mind," he says. "First, it's important for us to have the information. But also, preparing the report will help these two men keep abreast of an important training technique. They will probably be using it with their own subordinates."

What's Ahead for the Company—Long Term

For the company whose organization planners would like some insights against which to check their own expectations, a statement by Gardner Heidrick of Heidrick and Struggles, Chicago firm specializing in executive search and personnel consulting, may be helpful:

> The executive demand of the future can be predicted, but it is difficult to pinpoint the exact time that some of these changes will develop.
>
> On a general basis, within the next ten years there will be greater demand for top management executives and less for those in the lower middle management group. Professional management will be reaching its peak and the supply, because of ages and events, will be low. Automation will require fewer supervisors, which in turn minimizes the source of senior executives.
>
> The executive opportunities of the future will require the successful candidates to have a general understanding of the use of scientific and mathematical methods of solving management problems. The surface has not been scratched in the use of operations research, computer technology and other techniques which are being developed. Hence, the executive of the future must have a sounder education in the tools of management, whether in the broad general administrative area, or in the functional areas of engineering, manufacturing, marketing, and finance. The ability to adapt new and changing concepts to a business will be essential.
>
> On a general basis, too, is the increasing worldwide viewpoint. It is an attitude and understanding which more and more organizations must

develop and accept, which means the successful executive will have had experience and/or a good understanding of international trade and activities.

Emphasis will be on research and development, with particular attention to new products and improvements of the old. This, too, will require administrative executives with scientific and engineering background, and also expands itself into the marketing area, where greater emphasis will be put on the position of corporate market planning, with its attendant aspects.

Communications will become more important, both internally and externally, meaning that properly-trained public relations executives and sounder advertising men will be required. Personnel executives must have a broader understanding of human values, motivation and management development, as organizations will be concentrating on getting more effective results from the people within their companies. Financial executives of the future will be the business manager type, not just the accountant, statistician, or money-man alone.

More presidents will have a scientific and engineering background, but will arrive primarily through marketing, financial or legal management. They will be college graduates, many with advanced degrees.

The view of another expert in the area of executive recruiting sheds further light on the shape of tomorrow's executive job market. Here are the views of Wardwell Howell of Ward Howell Associates, New York:

Eighteen years ago when I entered this field, the company that had to look outside its own ranks for executive talent felt that it had failed in the aspect of management training. It also felt that to take men from a competitor was rather underhand—in fact, piracy.

Today both of these feelings have changed. To bring in a man of stature signifies a growth situation and an interest in new or different business techniques. It is also realized that men are not "stolen," they move only if their present position doesn't offer worthwhile opportunities.

Eighteen years ago recruiting was still a rather haphazard profession, with the recruiter attempting to discover by the shotgun method of approach who might be available. Today research of those companies which would be the logical place for the needed talent is made, followed up by a rifle shot at the particular individuals who, based on a study of their backgrounds, should prove of interest. In effect, the best man obtainable is being sought, not just "Mr. Available Jones."

The changes mentioned above point to a trend that should continue. Rather than just finding a man who can handle a particular opening, a man with specific abilities who can realize definitive goals is required. Executive skills are becoming more clearly defined. One sees the table pounding sales manager replaced with the marketing vice president. Educational degrees are becoming more important, not as much in themselves, as in what they indicate. In short, there is a growing tendency to seek *trained* executives.

There is a good deal of talk about specialist vs. generalist. Certainly most positions, and increasingly more so, will be filled with specialists. These men have a depth of knowledge in a particular facet of business. Recruiting of specific experience should then continue at an accelerated pace.

But the generalist is one who started out as a specialist and who was able to see beyond his own field. He could see the proper relationship between his area and the others it abutted. He developed sufficient breadth to direct the work of those concerned with specific problems. In short, he is a Manager.

In 1970, as today, the generalists should continue to be the ones to hold the senior management positions and will be sought out by recruiters to become chief executive officers.

The Ultimate Factor

There are many factors that will determine the kind of executive who will be running your company tomorrow, and how you get him. The single basic factor is the American economy, that vast, fascinating, unpredictable entity that is both the envy and hope of the world.

When the economy moves ahead undisturbed, the executive job market moves along with it. When the economy hesitates, the executive job market develops dislocations. For example, in recessions, financial executives tend to come into greater demand, other types less so.

But, as has been said, "The business of America is business." As far as the economy is concerned, the business leaders are both the feeders and the fed. In a greater sense than may be said for any other profession, they create their own opportunity, and their own future.

Appendix

A. Pre-Employment Investigation

Companies considering final candidates for key positions often want to know more about a man than is available by the mere checking of references. Private investigators usually make this type of investigation, sometimes referred to as "personnel reporting." Below are samples of two reports resulting from such pre-employment investigation, as developed by Fidelifacts, a company with offices in most of the large cities in the United States. Both reports are, of course, completely fictitious.

Sample Report

BACKGROUND INVESTIGATION

Name		Date of Report
Jones, Sidney Tanier	Born: 9/5/35	4/5/65

Employment
Self-employed
26 Main Street
Smithville, Okla.   (App. Dates)   11/60 - Present
We were advised that although applicant maintains his Main Street office, applicant has been residing and working in Tulsa for the past three or four months. We were also advised that applicant's mail is sent to P.O. Box 1836 OCS, Tulsa, Oklahoma. Applicant is self-employed as a consulting geophysicist and lease broker.

Residence
203 N. Gavin Street
Smithville, Okla.
This is a brick, one-story, Colonial-type house in excellent condition and is about ten years old. It would be valued at approximately $25,000 and is located in an area comprised of wooden-frame and brick homes that are valued from $10,000 to $50,000. The location is excellent to the oil center and trade area.
J. T. Donlon, 65 Poole St.; J. H. Elkin, 1060 N. Main St.; and J. S. Thim, 10 Lee St. have known the applicant for ten, three, and five years, respectively.
These people advised that the applicant owns this home, but has not been

seen at this address for the past four months. His wife's name is Andrea Z. Jones, and they have a fourteen-month-old child. Applicant is not too popular with his neighbors, and none have ever visited his home. They feel that he is a "social climber" who thinks he is better than his neighbors. They also feel sorry for applicant's wife because of his affair with the wife of a geologist with whom he is reportedly residing in Tulsa. They further advised that applicant has been having an affair with this woman for the past year, and both are supposedly living together in an apartment in Tulsa. This woman left her husband and four children, and rumor has it that applicant left his wife immediately after the birth of their son. We were further informed that because of a suit filed by applicant's wife, the oil people are reluctant to deal with the applicant at this time. These people further informed us that applicant's father was formerly the vice-president of Amalgamated Hardware Company of Smithville, who left his first wife to marry Betty Y. Jones, mother of applicant. Applicant relies on his mother to help him when in financial difficulty.

These neighbors stated applicant is self-employed as a lease broker and consulting geophysicist. As far as they could determine, his moral character and reputation are bad, as are his habits. He sometimes drinks at social functions, and his weak points would be that he is prone to get himself involved with other women. He has a good education and is a capable oil man.

Credit

Usually reliable sources report a satisfactory credit record for applicant in Smithville. However, on 10/16/64 there was a suit filed against applicant by his wife, Andrea Z. Jones, for legal separation and $1,000 per month. Suit #29106.

Criminal

Usually reliable sources report no record identifiable with the applicant could be found in Smithville, Okla.

Cities covered in investigation:	Period of Investigation	File #
Smithville and Tulsa, Okla.	12/29/62 - 1/4/64	201 - D325

The information contained in this report is for the SOLE AND CONFIDENTIAL use of the subscriber and is provided only under the terms of the subscriber's agreement.

Sample Report

BACKGROUND INVESTIGATION

		Date of Report
Jackes, Victor Arnold	Born: 9/24/38	9/30/64

Employment

DUGAN BROTHERS & COMPANY
932 AMERICAN NATIONAL BANK BUILDING
DENVER, COLORDO 80202   June, 1963—April 2, 1965

MR. FRED WRIGHT, manager, stated that the applicant was employed during the above period as a mathematician and in this capacity figured income rom stocks and bonds. His date of birth was in file as 9/24/38 and his Social Security number is listed as 124-44-8553. Mr. Wright would not divulge the applicant's salary. Prior to this, applicant was employed by Peters, Writer & Christensen, Equitable Building, Denver, Colorado.

The applicant was rated as average in his job performance and ability to get along with others. Mr. Wright stated that the applicant had difficulty communicating with people. His attendance record was good, and he was described as the type of person one could depend upon. Mr. Wright stated that the applicant's services were satisfactory, but added that he would not be eligible for rehire due to the fact he was slow and lacked self-confidence. Wright said that applicant had worked for a man of whom he was slightly afraid.

There was no evidence that the applicant indulged in excessive drinking, and there were no garnishments or other difficulties. The applicant did not participate in company social organizations, and the only outside activity of applicant's known to Mr. Wright was skiing.

Mr. Wright said that in the summer of 1962 the applicant had lung trouble and was absent from work approximately thirty days. This trouble never occurred again, according to Mr. Wright, who said that he would recommend the applicant for a position of trust and responsibility as he was honest and "wanted to do the right thing." Mr. Wright added that because of the applicant's shortcomings, he resigned by mutual agreement.

Present Residence

266 COTTON STREET
DENVER, COLORADO 80203   September 1961—Present
This is a five-year-old apartment building consisting of unfurnished apartments. It is known as the Cotton Apartment House and is located in a middle-income residential area composed of single-family homes and apartment buildings.

MR. THOMAS DRADUBA, manager of the building, MRS. THOMAS DRADUBA, and MISS RICH, all of the above address, have all known the applicant approximately three years.

The neighbors advised that the applicant resides here with his wife, Dorothy, and that they have no children. The applicant and his wife are described as very lovely people who are good neighbors and tenants. Their rent is paid on time, and they are quiet and cause no trouble.

The applicant and his wife both work, but the details of their employment are not known. However, neighbors stated that applicant works in "some brokerage house." The neighbors did not know whether applicant is active in any civic organizations or if he has any hobbies. They said that he does not drink to excess, is of good repute, and has never been involved in any trouble. The only further information known regarding applicant and his wife is that they own two cars.

Credit & Criminal

Usually reliable credit sources report the following which may be identifiable with the applicant in Denver, Colorado:

Victor A. Jackes is shown in file as residing at 266 Cotton Street in Denver and as formerly living at 32 Nash Street, Denver. The last inquiry was on

7/6/61 at which time the files were revised. He is shown employed with Peters, Writer & Christensen and then with Dugan Brothers.

On 7/6/61 the American Furniture Company showed a high credit of $740.02—manner of payment AA. Mr. Jackes has been in file since 5/2/60, and his credit rating is satisfactory. A bank reported a savings account of up to $300.

Usually reliable criminal sources report no record identifiable with the applicant in Denver, Colorado.

Cities covered in investigation: Denver, Colorado	Period of investigation 9/22/64 - 9/30/64	File # 1283 F 79

The information contained in this report is for the SOLE AND CONFIDENTIAL use of the subscriber and is provided only under the terms of the subscriber's agreement.

B. Position Descriptions

When a search for an executive is undertaken by an employer, or on behalf of an employer by a search firm, a description of the job to be filled and, sometimes, of the type of man to fill it are necessary prerequisites.

For this purpose the executive-recruiting firm of Antell, Wright & Nagel uses what it calls an "executive sketch." This pins down in black and white both a description of the position to be filled and the education, background, and experience a candidate must have to fill the job. Here are two executive sketches for positions which Antell, Wright & Nagel successfully filled.

EXECUTIVE SKETCH A

THE POSITION:

Operations manager, reporting to the vice-president and general manager of the division. He will be directly responsible for the profitability of this division through his subordinate organization. This includes:

General sales manager
　　Plant managers at branch plants
　　　　Product engineers
His specific responsibilities include:

A. *Production*

　(1) Production, forecasting, deliveries
　(2) Inventory controls, purchasing
　(3) Manufacturing costs
　(4) Quality of products

B. *Sales*

　(1) Sales programs for automotive products in OEM and resale markets
　(2) Sales forecasts to permit plant scheduling and control

(3) Advertising programs
(4) Customer contacts

C. *Profits*
(1) Profit forecasting
(2) Pricing policy

D. *Engineering*
Product improvement, modification and development through engineering research

E. *Personnel*
(1) Constructive employee relations
(2) Maintenance of adequately trained personnel to protect the company and permit advancement of qualified persons

QUALIFICATIONS:

A degree in mechanical engineering or business administration is preferred, although the equivalent in manufacturing experience will be considered. Although the man selected will have charge of operations, the emphasis will be placed most heavily on his manufacturing know-how. He must be a good manager and be able to anticipate production problems with practical solutions. He must be thoroughly familiar with the manufacture of small, low-unit-cost, high-volume products and be conversant with the demands of automotive OEM sales as well as aftermarket needs.

OPPORTUNITY:

There will be ample opportunity for the man selected to demonstrate his ability to run this division in his own way and to qualify for greater responsibilities with the parent company. Compensation is composed of an attractive salary plus profit-sharing bonus.

EXECUTIVE SKETCH B

THE COMPANY:

This is a long-established, profitable operation doing roughly $50 million in annual sales, located in an attractive, medium-sized city in the Midwest. It employs approximately 3,000 people.

THE SITUATION:

The general management of this operation is reorganizing its marketing activity to provide more-effective market planning and new-product development.

THE POSITION:

This is a new position in the organization and will report directly to the vice-president and general manager. He will have supervision of, and responsibility for, market planning, sales, advertising, new-product planning, and field sales operations. He will develop plans and policies to expand sales in present and new markets; analyze sales and sales-cost performance; develop corrective programs as necessary; and administer and coordinate programs for product maintenance, new-product development, advertising and sales promotion, and training and development of a field sales organization.

QUALIFICATIONS:

Preferred is a college graduate with a degree in marketing or sales administration. A Master's degree in business administration, training, or mechanical engineering would be a desirable addition.

His record should reflect successful responsibility for a sales operation in the machinery and equipment fields, administration of a field sales organization, and knowledge of engineering requirements in such equipment.

It is assumed that in such a capacity he will have had experience in sales and marketing management, as well as advertising, market forecasting, and product planning. An administrative background of planning in capital-goods sales will be expected.

He should be sufficiently aggressive and articulate in expressing his ideas verbally and in writing to exert a decisive influence on top management, yet be resilient and flexible in his job attitude. He should have the personality, appearance, and poise to represent the company at the highest levels in contract negotiations. His personal warmth and good human-relations sense are importantly desirable attributes.

OPPORTUNITY:

He should be of a caliber and have the interest to permit promotion in the foreseeable future to the position of a division manager.

There is an attractive base compensation with a bonus and stock participation as well as most attractive fringe benefits.

Below is a typical position and candidate description as developed by Brennan Associates of New York City for a client, in the course of an executive-search assignment.

POSITION SPECIFICATIONS

DATE: JANUARY 2, 196__
CLIENT: CONSUMER PACKAGED GOODS
LOCATION: MIDDLETOWN, U.S.A.
IN CHARGE: WMB
TITLE: DIRECTOR OF MARKETING
SALARY: to $30,000

THE POSITION

History of the Position: This is a new position established to provide marketing support to the line-sales organizations.

Major Functions: The director of marketing will be responsible for developing, in conjunction with the line-sales organizations, marketing plans for each of the company's product lines. These plans should include sales and profit objectives, advertising plans and budgets, sales-promotion programs (including sampling), new-product development or acquisition.

Recommend pricing strategy and structure for all products including counter-measures necessary to meet competitive conditions.

Coordinate all advertising carried on by the company, act as the prime contact with the advertising agencies, and recommend ad themes, copy approaches, and media structure.

Receive, screen, and evaluate new-product developments and acquisition opportunities and recommend attractive ones to top management.

Recommend packaging, labeling, or product changes to improve marketing effectiveness, and follow through to see that changes are carried out.

Relationship: The director of marketing reports directly to the president, who is also the chief executive officer.

He must establish good working relationships with the other members of the top executive group as well as with the line-sales organization to assure his effectiveness.

Financial Incentives: Salary up to $30,000, depending upon past performance, experience, and earnings.

In addition, the director of marketing will participate in the executive incentive compensation plan, which provides an annual payment depending upon company profits. This may range up to 20 per cent of the annual salary.

Also, he will be included in the management benefit programs such as hospitalization and major medical, pension, life insurance, etc., as he qualifies for each.

Opportunity for Growth: The opportunity for growth and advancement is excellent. Since the director of marketing will be largely responsible for the increase of the company's sales and its moves into new products, his success will be of direct and significant benefit to the company.

Outstanding performance as director of marketing could lead to a vice-presidency.

THE CANDIDATE

Essential Minimum Experience: The ideal candidate for the director of marketing position must have a proved record of successful performance in the manufacturing of consumable products. He should be knowledgeable in advertising, packaging, pricing, and sales promotion.

He should know successful methods of marketing through supermarkets and independent chains.

His experience should have been with a line-and-staff organization.

Age: From thirty-five to forty-five years old, but age limits should be flexible when considering a candidate outstanding in other respects who is not within this age bracket.

Education: College degree required. Business administration or liberal arts preferred. Advanced study in marketing or business management desirable.

Personal Qualities: The candidate must have a keen mind, a mature grasp of essentials, and sound judgment. Southern background preferred since his work will largely be done in Southern states where the company's major markets are today. The candidate must be personable and persuasive to carry out his plans working through others.

Family Background: Should have a good family with community standing to provide him with advantages of social contacts.

Professional Affiliations: None required. However, membership in American Marketing Association or other appropriate organizations would be an asset. He should be willing to join key organizations when necessary.

Civic and Community Participation: Should be able and willing to participate in civic and community affairs when this is timely and proper. An interest in golf or other sports would be an asset.

Also developed by Brennan Associates is a sample form used for detailing a job and candidate specification. A form of this kind can be of use to a company planning to undertake its own executive search. The "company" section at the end of the form gives a company the chance to describe itself in terms that will be of interest to prospective candidates.

JOB SPECIFICATIONS

DATE: IN CHARGE:
CLIENT: TITLE:
LOCATION: SALARY:

THE POSITION

History of the Position: (Why position is open)

MAJOR FUNCTIONS: (Specific duties and responsibilities)

RELATIONSHIPS: (Reports to and reporting to him)

FINANCIAL INCENTIVES:

OPPORTUNITY FOR GROWTH:

THE CANDIDATE
ESSENTIAL MINIMUM EXPERIENCE:

EDUCATION: (College degree—general, technical, or special)

PERSONAL QUALITIES:

FAMILY BACKGROUND:

PROFESSIONAL AFFILIATIONS REQUIRED:

CIVIC AND COMMUNITY PARTICIPATION DESIRED:

AGE:

ANY OTHER FACTORS:

THE COMPANY

Products, Size, Ownership, History:
PROCESS:

How Products Sold:

Headquarters:

Number of Employees:

Annual Net Sales:

    Annual Net Profits after Taxes:
Plants:

Subsidiaries:

Ownership: (Family, closely held, management control, public stock, listed, or other)

MANAGEMENT: (Officers)

Union or nonunion:

C. Executive-recruiting Consultants

An association of firms doing executive search has been in existence for several years—its name, Association of Executive Recruiting Consultants, Inc. Here is a list of members as compiled at the beginning of 1965:

MEMBERSHIP LIST
ASSOCIATION OF EXECUTIVE RECRUITING CONSULTANTS, INC.

Antell, Wright & Nagel, 230 Park Avenue, New York, New York 10017

Canny, Bowen, Howard, Peck & Associates, Inc. 405 Lexington Avenue, New York, New York 10017

Clark, Cooper, Field & Wohl, Inc. 200 Park Avenue, New York, New York 10017

William H. Clark Associates, Inc. 300 Madison Avenue, New York, New York 10017

Elmer R. Davis & Associates, Inc. 60 East 42d Street, New York, New York 10017

Thorndike Deland Associates, 1440 Broadway, New York, New York 10018

DeVoto Associates, Inc. 11 South LaSalle Street, Chicago, Illinois 60603

Fordyce & Dole Associates, Inc. 420 Lexington Avenue, New York, New York 10017

Hardy Jones, Smith, Dingwall & Associates, Inc. 342 Madison Avenue, New York, New York 10017

Heidrick and Struggles, 20 North Wacker Drive, Chicago, Illinois 60606

Ward Howell Associates, Inc. 122 East 42d Street, New York, New York 10017

Richardson, Bellows, Henry & Co., Inc. 355 Lexington Avenue, New York, New York 10017

Joseph L. Rodgers & Co. 155 East 38th Street, New York, New York 10016

Paul Stafford Associates, 155 East 50th Street, New York, New York 10022

L. F. Stowell & Associates, Inc. 400 Park Avenue, New York, New York 10022

Spencer Stuart & Associates, Inc. 200 Park Avenue, New York, New York 10017

Wright-Porter, Inc. 230 Park Avenue, New York, New York 10017

Needless to say, many firms not members of AERC are reputable operators, and live up to ethical and performance standards equalling those of association members.

D. Psychological Reports on Executive Candidates

Companies seeking executive talent often depend on psychological tests to assist in their appraisal of candidates. The usual procedure is for the final candidates—the two or three being weighed preliminary to a decision—to be exposed to a battery of tests. The results of these tests are usually given in a written report.

BFS Psychological Associates, a New York psychological-services firm, provides its clients with a covering "instruction sheet" that suggests a realistic approach to the use of a test report:

How to Read and Use This Appraisal Report

These pages contain psychological findings on the named individual insofar as modern scientific methods allow. This report can be a powerful tool for improving each individual as a performer on the job. But by the same token, the potential for good inherent in these facts can do immeasurable damage if the findings are misused.

Before reading the report, be sure to study the following instructions:

1. *Keep the whole man in focus.* Every human being has both strengths and weaknesses. You will be misled if you allow the weaknesses to obliterate the strengths, or vice versa. Read this report with the expectation that you will find negative and affirmative values. And remember that no isolated element disqualifies a man or woman. The important thing is the balance that is struck

between strengths and weaknesses. Moreover, a psychological report, as distinguished from a performance report, is a picture of the individual's potential. Some people are equal to their potential; others fall below and are still to be brought up to it.

2. *Keep the job in mind.* For your purposes, the central issue is not how an individual's qualities measure up against an abstract standard of perfection but how they relate to success in the job at hand. A man's weakness may be the very element that spurs his performance—e.g., a negative trait may be exactly the kind you need for that work. On the other hand, a man's strength may be entirely irrelevant to the job he has to do.

3. *Keep this report confidential.* Examination of the contents by any unauthorized person, discussion of the findings with anybody who has no direct and legitimate interest in them, may have serious repercussions. Rumors may be initiated and reputations damaged. Word of mouth may attach unfounded connotations to items taken out of context. Future psychological studies are certain to be impaired if there is any suspicion that absolute confidence is not observed.

4. *Use the report to strengthen the individual.* The purpose of a psychological report is to improve performance, not to shatter the psychological defenses that all of us build up over the years. While the subject of the report is entitled to know the conclusions, they must be presented to him constructively so that he is encouraged to achieve his full potential as revealed by the findings. It is therefore recommended that the report be discussed with the subject by the psychologist who made the study.

By observing the four principles indicated above, you can make this report an invaluable management tool that serves the needs of both your company and the individual.

Below is a sample report, as developed by BFS Psychological Associates. Note particularly the specific areas that are covered.

EXECUTIVE APPRAISAL REPORT

MATTHEW WILKINS, JR. April 13, 196–

Address: 715 Grove Street
Bloomfield, Connecticut
Phone: 203 - 115-9006
Date of Birth: March 4, 1922
Birthplace: Hoboken, New Jersey
Marital Status: Married—Four children Ages 25, 23, 11, and 10

PSYCHOLOGICAL ANALYSIS

INTELLECTUAL FUNCTIONING

Mr. Wilkins has very superior intelligence. He ranks at the top 1% of the general population and above the average of executive-level people. He was friendly while taking the tests of ability and fully cooperative. Although a little tense, he was mainly composed and poised while working on the varieties of test problems. Occasionally his pace was a little inconsistent, especially when the items were relatively easy for him. He seemed to be a little impulsive in working on some of the easier items but handled them very quickly and rapidly.

His vocabulary is very much above the general average, and he can express himself well, especially in relation to areas of experience. His spelling could be improved. It is similar to the relatively inadequate spelling of many engineers. His fund of general information is superior, and he can use it in a variety of situations.

Arithmetical reasoning is very superior. He is a natural in this area and finds reasoning with numbers relatively easy. He can think well with abstract verbal concepts and especially well with problems of space and design arrangement. Apparently he has a great facility in seeing how things might look even when they are not concretely before him. He should be able to plan well and deal easily with complex materials. His memory for recent events is exceptionally high, especially for a person of his age.

He is relatively slow in building up new associations and takes a deliberate approach in new areas. He is very good in discriminating between essential and less-essential details. He sees them very clearly and reacts to them with accuracy. His mechanical-technical aptitude is very high. His comprehension of what is expected in social situations is very much above the general average but not outstanding. Apparently he is not very adroit in getting all the small nuances in social situations. He is straightforward and may miss some of the subtler elements.

WORK CHARACTERISTICS

He is a hard-working person and, when he gets involved in a particular set of circumstances, tries his very best to work up to a good level. Although somewhat tense in unstructured situations, he is quite quick and most of the time effective. Sometimes it seems as though he were not really pushing himself hard enough, but the quality of his performance is good nevertheless. He might seem to take it a little too easy at times but, once he meets a difficult problem, he really applies effort. He meets situations with a good deal of decisiveness.

In new situations he shows no particular elevation of tension. He seems to be able to mobilize his efforts quite well and is stimulated by the difficulty of the task. Occasionally he might leave out some details in easier situations. He likes to see the "big problem" and to work at it and thereby may gloss over some of the lesser aspects. However, his great experience pulls him out of any difficulties. Apparently he knows enough to go back and to analyze in greater detail. He is quite analytic and methodical when working on the more difficult problems. He has some imaginativeness and displays it when he really gets into the swing of things. He is a practical person, however, and generally works on the problems at hand rather than leave himself free for imaginative endeavor. He has high standards and is able to put them into effect. Under pressure he may occasionally miss out, but he is capable of review and improvement.

His initiative is appropriate to the occasion. He does not take large strides into new situations. He tries to meet a standard and after he does moves onto higher levels. His drive energy is quite constructively applied even though there may be some wavering while getting the situation in hand.

INTERESTS AND VALUES

His major interests are in the persuasive and social-service areas. He perceives himself as an administrator and manager rather than a research person. He has had many years of experience in varieties of manufacturing establishments and has had direct experience in some crafts. Also, he has seen himself as being good in mechanical-technical operations and functions. School teachers told him that he might be a good engineer. He was apparently adept in shop work, drafting as well as mathematics.

He is oriented toward practical matters to a large enough degree, and he sets value on theory and the search for truth. Although he has a social-service interest, he is not oriented toward just being a helping social-service person. The social-service interest is related to his high regard for religious values in which he sees people as important. He wants very much to get ahead and has ambition left, as he put it. Especially he would like to become more secure financially. He has two married daughters and two younger children whom he would like to educate and bring to the point of independence.

As a youngster he played football, basketball, and lacrosse. He was quite large for his age. He participated in scout work. He has been interested in community and church activities. Also he did not neglect advanced studies and took courses in physics, thermodynamics, and metallurgy as well as in business administration. He enjoys relaxation and wishes he were at the stage where he could entertain himself more frequently in relaxing activities. However, he feels the need to continue to work and earn a good living.

WORK PROGRESS AND ASPIRATIONS

In summers during high school and in college he held varieties of jobs. He worked as a ditch digger and common laborer and later learned welding. He had a variety of manufacturing positions and at one time was a consultant for McGrath & Co. He might have stayed longer with McGrath but the travel was too great, and he liked his home too much to be away so frequently. His last position was somewhat unstable. Apparently he had thought it would be a steadier position, but there were many things going on, and eventually his division was spun off. He and others lost their positions.

During the course of his working career, he has done labor-relations work, apparently with some degree of success. He believes that he has a "tough hide" and can take rebukes. Apparently also he knows how to handle himself so that he can win points for management. He feels that his training in mechanical engineering was an excellent start for his career. He had never expected to work as a "pure" engineer and always was hoping to get into the manufacturing and management end. He aspires to a top division managerial position in a multi-plant corporation and wants very much to participate in corporate planning. He believes that the first thing he must do in any job is to do it well and that compensation will follow if he does his job well.

RELATING TO PEOPLE

He is a very pleasant man with somewhat of a rough exterior but a softness underneath. Although he is fairly conventional he still has quite a sense of independence. He can grapple quite well with varieties of interpersonal situations. He is not the most resourceful person and sometimes overtalks a point. However, he is quite impressive and apparently has learned to balance firmness and fairness fairly well. He is not averse to getting into action with people on the "workman" level to show how things can be done. He believes in using himself as an example. He thinks he is seen as "a good guy." He will work hard to have himself accepted but not go as far as to make himself that popular.

He may have some tension in new social situations, but he seems to be able to remain in control. Also, he is able to assert himself without much overt tension and to enter into give and take with superiors. He is quite businesslike in new and difficult situations. When he feels more at ease, he shows an attractive sense of humor. He is quite outgoing for a person with engineering background but is not "back-slapping." He is somewhat introspective. Although feeling independent himself and being fairly assertive, he can use an occasional show of encouragement from his superiors. He will respond well to encouragement. He will try to train and coach his subordinates and has been known to bring them together in small groups for talk sessions to arrive at a consensus.

FAMILY BACKGROUND

His father died in 1955. He was a marine engineer for the Central Railroad. When Mr. Wilkens was younger, he occasionally helped his father at work. Apparently they were fairly close. His mother is eighty-four and still quite active. Both of his parents were church workers, and his mother taught Sunday school. She is able to manage fairly well with whatever income she has, and he helps by contributing some money. He felt that his parents gave him quiet but strong support. He describes them as fine people and church leaders.

He speaks well of his wife. Apparently they get along quite well. He is devoted to his family. They make friends wherever they go. He is not averse to moving and believes that the job is more important than the residence. Apparently his wife is quite willing to move if it means a good job for Mr. Wilkens. They have four children, apparently two families. His two older daughters are both married and he has four grandchildren. He has two younger children, a ten-year-old girl and an eleven-year-old boy, were postwar. Apparently he believed that his wife was finished having children but was surprised by the first young child and then had a second. He wants to provide well for his family.

PERSONAL ADJUSTMENT

Mr. Wilkens makes an adequate personal adjustment. He seems to be able to handle himself in the usual situations and to come through without much difficulty in more trying situations. He has anxiety but manages it quite well. It does not overwhelm him. Occasionally anxiety breaks through in new and difficult situations, but it also serves the purpose of driving him on. He is getting a little older and occasionally has to mobilize his energy to continue at a good pace. However, he thinks quite well of himself. He is also quite able to see himself clearly and is not adverse to criticism. Generally he is a good-natured person who can apply a sense of humor that reduces tension in difficult situations.

SUMMARY AND POTENTIAL FOR GROWTH

In overall intelligence Mr. Wilkens is very superior. He is capable of handling very complex problems of space and design arrangement, an ability directly related to manufacturing and plant management. He also has a good memory that will serve him well. His arithmetical reasoning ability is very sharp. He might learn how to spell better but his vocabulary and fund of information are quite high.

He is a hard-working person and over the years has learned to work hard. As a youngster, he worked while attending school. He also learned skills such as welding. He is a mechanical engineer by training but mainly interested in manufacturing management. He believes that his progress has been quite good and that he can continue to make progress. He believes in his capability to do divisional management work.

He has a wealth of experience which he can put to good use. He may not be the most adroit person socially, but he is an honest, forthright person with good feeling for people. He shows no hostility or need to twist matters and will behave in a sincere manner. Once he gets used to a situation, he shows a good deal of warmth.

He rises to the occasion. Sometimes his work does not seem up to his innate level of capability, but he can improve on his own. Also a little encouragement and a little challenge push him upward. Apparently he is quite a devoted family man. He has two younger children whom he would like to educate. He wants to be more secure financially and, although he would like to relax more or at least begin to relax, he also feels the need for greater financial security. He makes an adequate personal adjustment and does not have any special problems.

Potentially he has many years of accomplishment before him. He has a wealth of experience, a good mind, and special aptitudes for manufacturing operations and management. He is not the most assertive and resourceful person socially but he is quite able to handle himself in difficult situations. He can work along well with people on different levels. A little pat on the back occasionally will pay dividends in his case.

There is no optimum length for a psychological appraisal report. Here is a report based on a battery of psychological tests as submitted by The Personnel Laboratory, Inc., of Stamford, Connecticut. In circumstances where the appraisals of several men are to be compared, the relative brevity of the report form used by TPL in this instance can prove helpful:

STANDARD APPRAISAL

of   Frank C. Cody   for   A Leading Manufacturer
purpose   Applicant for a Position as Sales Supervisor   project #   620778
age 31   sex M   education High School Graduate   date March 22, 1962
consultant L.Z.

SUMMARY

This is indeed a man in a hurry! His ambition is almost overwhelming—he has a constant need to be on the go, to keep active, and to keep progressing. In fact, no matter how well he is doing, he is always worrying that it is not enough. This both provides a good deal of incentive and motivation for him—and the constant possibility that he will become restive and move on to another organization if he decides he is not going ahead as rapidly as he wants to.

DEVELOPMENT OF POTENTIAL

Cody is well endowed with intellectual potential, energy, drive, and ambition. If his restlessness does not become unrealistic, there is no reason to doubt that he can go on to assume higher-level managerial responsibility for you in the future. He has excellent understanding of selling methods as well as basically sound talent for organizing and planning. It is probable, however, that he will be an impatient and demanding supervisor—because he is impatient and demanding in his expectations of himself.

STRENGTHS

1. Hard-driving ambition. Full of tension, restlessness, and ambition, he is capable of working hard and enjoying it. As long as he is convinced that his efforts are getting him somewhere and leading to even greater future rewards, he can keep up a pretty consistent pace.

2. Mentally quick. Learns rapidly—and may be impatient with people who do not think as fluently and perceptively as he does.

3. Exceptionally good command of most of the tricks of the trade in selling—and a few ideas of his own on persuasion as well.

4. Efficient with arithmetic and paper-work, although like most salesmen, he prefers to keep it at a minimum.

WEAKNESSES

1. It is almost inevitable that a man with this much drive, ambition, and impatience is going to step on a few toes here and there. In this instance, it is evident that although he is perceptive, he does not have the kind of sensitivity to other people that would make him able to recognize when he is permitting his own aims and interests to become so intense that he is failing to consider other people's feelings. He is far more an aggressive, persistent salesman than an easy-going, service-minded one.

2. Fundamentally, he is much happier when he is on his own and does not have to account to anyone else. He probably chafes at the bit under company or supervisory restrictions.

COMMENTS

While Cody has the talent, intellectual acuity, energy, drive, ambition, and determination to be an exceptionally successful salesman, his own impatience may get in his way now and again. Since he cannot function comfortably or productively under close supervision, it is necessary to give him as much freedom in operating as is possible. However, because his enthusiasm is such that he can be carried away by it, you will want to be very decisive and very explicit in laying down company policy for him. You will also want to keep in mind that this is a man who will do his utmost for the company—as long as his own best interests coincide with those of the company. Although loyal, he does not have the kind of devotion that will make him stick it out if not satisfied with the attention, rewards, or advancements he is getting. He needs a great deal of challenge—and it has to be constantly renewed if he is to remain absorbed.

E. Resumes

As a matter of common practice, resumes come in a broad range of sizes and forms. As suggested in Chapter 14 on resumes, the simplest and generally most acceptable form consists of a one-page summary, followed by two or three backing pages that fill in the details.

The French word "résumé" unfortunately has no direct English counterpart. A summary of the professional or work history may be called, in addition to "resume," anything from a "catalogue of experience" to "personal data," plus a few dozen other phrases, sometimes well chosen, occasionally otherwise.

Below are a number of sample forms that may be adapted to the particular needs of the job applicant. Select the form that presents your particular experience in the clearest, most-inviting terms.

CONFIDENTIAL

ROBERT J. BROWN
212 Cedar Lane
Kismet, Ohio 10023

Telephone:
216 666-2384

PERSONAL

40 years old. Born 1923, Flint, Michigan
Married. Three children, ages 8, 11, and 16
5 feet 10 inches tall. 180 pounds. Excellent health.
Fluent German. Fair French.

EDUCATION

University of Michigan, Ann Arbor, BSME 1947
Columbia University, New York MBA 1949

EXPERIENCE

1959–present   *Vice-president*
                              Arind Corporation

Joined this manufacturer of liquid filling equipment for food and drug industries as general sales manager, headquartered in Kismet, Ohio. Increased
sales 17 per cent during first year.

Planned and organized new-product task force, resulting in my appointment
in 1961 as general manager of a new division for development and production
of automation equipment for the candy industry. Direct, personal sales effort at
top corporate levels brought volume to $7.5 million by the end of the second
year, and pretax profits to $832,000. Also set up joint manufacturing and cross
licensing venture with German manufacturer. Have just completed negotiations
for sale of division assets to an investment group, with substantial profits for
Arind.

1953–1959   *Manager, Eastern region*
                             Darin Associates

Responsible for both sales and technical supervision of client projects for this
engineering consulting firm, including concept, design, and fabrication of production and packaging equipment. Increased billings 450 per cent, with only 250
per cent increase in staff, by upgrading performance of professional personnel.

Previous Experience Design engineer and field sales engineer on the West
Coast for Naird Machine Company.

Comment Objective is line or general management position in engineered
capital equipment or in technical services.

                                      —Executive Register, Inc.
                                      New Canaan, Connecticut

Here is an example of a covering letter accompanying a resume, as submitted by a counseling service, Executive Career Development, Inc., of
Chicago. The brief "Facts at a Glance" resume that follows shows how
essential information can be streamlined. ECD invariably follows its
"Facts at a Glance" data with three pages of data filling out the picture
suggested by the "facts."

August 25, 1964

Dear Mr. Amos:

We are representing a young executive of unusual ability who can become
available to join your organization if the challenge is sufficient.

Richard E. Spaid is thirty-four and currently employed at the general-manager
level of Amalgamated Corporation where he is director of planning for the fast-
growing refrigeration group.

This man has excellent references, including the head of one of the nation's
largest retail firms. The facts and conclusions in the enclosed biography—which

we think is rather impressive—have been verified by our long personal conference and background investigation of this man.

A former Big Ten athlete (swimming), Dick Spaid is a big, aggressive man in excellent health. He gets along well with people, is a leader, and has shown that he can inspire men to maximum effort.

His education (B.S.M.E. Purdue, M.B.A. Harvard) and his work experience have good balance between production, sales, and general management. In each assignment he has made definite, measurable impact with his achievements leading, in each case, to promotion and wider responsibility.

He has outgrown his current position and is unable to find the challenge he seeks within this company.

> Sincerely,
> Alex Lee

Now a thumbnail resume of another job candidate:

FACTS AT A GLANCE

Name: Thomas E. Grange
Personal: Age 34, weight 5′11″, weight 180, health excellent
Family: Wife, two sons, one daughter
Education: B.S. (Mechanical Engineering) Purdue; M.B.A. Columbia Graduate School of Business Administration
Present Earnings: $22,000 including bonus, plus stock options
Present and Recent Titles: Director, Special Planning Group; Product Manager, Assistant to the President
Industries Known: Appliances, Aircraft Manufacturing, Radio and TV
Location: Roby, Indiana, but willing to relocate as needed anywhere

Following is a resume made up by the individual it represents, but names have been changed for the sake of anonymity. The form used is an example of the *functional* resume. The backup pages, not reproduced here, provide detailed information under the headings of jobs held with employers named below.

Chris Anders, Sales Executive
901 West Oak Street
Los Angeles, California

Age—42
Marital Status—Married, 4 children
Health—Excellent; height 6 ft; weight 185.

Marketing—Developed and supervised a continuing series of research projects throughout the United States. Developed sales-potential measurements for given areas. Summed up findings in the form of written reports, and made recommendations for sales improvement in covered areas, programs for new territories.

Sales Promotion—Worked up sales-promotion programs for a broad range of products, with heavy concentration on toys and adult games. Helped plan newspaper and trade-journal advertising and point of purchase promotions. In many instances, succeeded in raising the volume of sales 20 per cent within a year's time. (This statement documented in backup pages of this resume.)

Sales Management—Hired, trained, and supervised sales staffs ranging from ten to one hundred ten men, on national basis. Developed communications network between field and H.O.—call reports, regular summary letters, and so on. Particularly successful in starting new products.

Sales—Heavy experience in wholesale selling to department stores. Also, have sold at retail.

Order Clerk—Received, processed, and expedited orders. Worked with the head of the department to develop an order control system that was eventually adopted, and considerably increased efficiency.

Present and Previous Employers

1959–Present	F & L Sales Company	Sales executive
1951–1959	Sales and Marketing Corp.	Sales promotion manager
1946–1951	J. K. Adams Toy Company	Salesman and sales manager

Education—University of Pennsylvania—B.S. 1935

References—as indicated on last page

Following is a resume that uses the standard *reverse chronological* presentation. Reproduced here is the first page of the form. In the original, four pages were used to provide the details of the highlights given on the one-page summary.

David Towne	General manager
75 Patriot Square	Executive assistant
Boston, Mass.	

General Background: Have had twenty years of business experience, the last eight as general manager of a custom molding shop. In this position, carried entire responsibility, under the owner, for the policies and operation of the company. Accordingly, have set up office and production procedures, developed a small sales staff, and succeeded in getting the corporation to show an increasing level of profit over the last three years. Change of ownership of the molding company impels the search for a new position.

Experience

1957 to present: Trade Plastic Molding Company, Needham, Mass., General manager.

Started as assistant to the owner. A year later, ill health forced him to give up active participation in the management of the company, and the top job was given to me. Since the company had run down due to the owner's failing capabilities, it was necessary to start rehabilitating the organization from the ground up. Planned and implemented an efficiency program that, in the words of the owner, "boosted efficiency 50 per cent" in two years' time. In this period, gross output rose from $300,000 to more than $600,000 without any increase in workforce. At this point, an "inside man" was brought in, and my efforts were switched to sales.

1951–1956: All-style Plastics Manufacturing, Utica, N.Y., Assistant to president. Started in as a member of the production-control staff, then promoted to head of molding-powder division. After a year's time, was again promoted to a sales engineering job. After two years, made assistant to the president, with a 20 per cent increase in salary. Decided to leave company because of company policies that I felt were hurting the company competitively.

1946–1951: XYZ Chemical Company, Salesman
Coming out of the Army as captain, enrolled in a cadet training program just being started by one of the largest manufacturers of plastics in the country. Learned the plastics business from all angles—production, sales, sales engineering. In my last year with the company, I was among the top three of a twenty-five man sales force. Left the company when All-style Plastics made an offer too attractive to turn down.

1941–1946: U.S. Army. (Service record detailed on subsequent pages).

F. Comprehensive Candidate Presentation

For a comprehensive picture of a candidate, his work record, background, and so on, the job done by the executive-research consultants is generally most complete. Here is an example of one such presentation, made by George Fry & Associates, of Chicago, New York, and Los Angeles. The material is submitted to the client toward the end of a search, and is made up only for the final two or three candidates.

CANDIDATE PRESENTATION
XYZ Company

Subject: John H. Jones, Jr.
Position: Vice-president, marketing

Personal Information

Age: forty-five   July 8, 1917
Residence: First Avenue and 34th Street
                New York, New York

Telephone: UN 6 4750
Marital
Status: Married; three children, ages one, four, and six years
Height: 5'9"
Weight: 158 lbs

Educational History

Received B.A. degree from the University of California, Los Angeles, in 1941. Received M.B.A. degree from Stanford University, Palo Alto, California, in 1943.

Military History

Served in the United States Army from September, 1941, to June, 1946. Held the rank of captain upon discharge.

Employment History
(As related by subject)

September, 1961–Present   ABC Corporation
                                                 New York, New York
                                                 General–products
                                                     manager
                                                 Salary: $40,000–$45,000
                                                     including bonus

Supervises the creation and execution of complete marketing plans on brands doing a total gross sales of $273 million. Has 34 men in brand management reporting to him. Responsible for all plans, advertising, promotions, and new products. Successfully launched three new products in 1962 and has nine others in test market at present.

January, 1959–September, 1961   EFG Company
                                                 Chicago, Illinois
                                                 Marketing director
                                                 Salary: $32,000

Complete responsibility for profit and loss on brands showing net profit of $15 million. Supervised grain buying, production, packaging, pricing, advertising, sales promotion, personnel, sales incentives, trade relations, and commercial and consumer research. Was responsible for launching of Z brand, and concept testing three other new items. Had biggest profit year in the history of the company.

March, 1955–December, 1958   LMN Company
                                                 Dallas, Texas
                                                 Vice-president and general manager
                                                     New Orleans Office
                                                 Salary: $30,000

Built the office from one account to seven accounts, quadrupled the billing, and increased the staff. Brought the operation out of the "red." Supervised all accounts, made most of the creative contributions, trained account executives and handled all agency administrative work. Product experience included beer, bananas, lumber, milk and ice cream, television station, a corn-chip product, and an architect.

September, 1952–March, 1955   OPQ Company, Inc.
                                                 Chicago, Illinois
                                                 Account supervisor
                                                 Salary: $18,000

Was responsible for the Folger coffee account group. Guided all creative, research, and merchandising. Also supervised and prepared new-business presentations for other companies.

September, 1950–September, 1952   TTSW, Inc.
                                        Chicago, Illinois
                                        Account executive & mer-
                                            chandising manager
                                        Salary: $12,000

Worked as Merchandising Manager on XYZ accounts. Also worked on CCF appliances and Verni cosmetics. Coordinated the research and marketing departments, participated in creative sessions and special promotions.

May, 1946–September, 1950   Swift and Company
                                        Chicago, Illinois
                                        Assistant to
                                            advertising manager
                                        Salary: $7,500

Was a product man working on Allsweet, Pard, Meats for Babies, soap products, and industrial oils. Administered budgets totaling over $4 million. Had new product experience on Swift's cleanser and Swift'ning. Worked with the company's four advertising agencies.

May, 1939–September, 1941   California Oil World
                                        Los Angeles, California
                                        Continuity writer
                                        Salary: $3,000

Worked on technical articles and scouted oil fields for this trade publication.

Summary of
Psychological Evaluation

As indicated by a series of psychological tests and an interview with a staff psychologist, Mr. Jones's personal qualifications are well-suited to the position of Vice-president–account supervisor.

His principal psychological characteristics are:

Excellent mental adaptiveness and originality.

Possesses a high level of intellectual ability and can use it in an adaptable and flexible manner. Strives for new and better solutions; is resourceful and imaginative in the creative and artistic aspects of work expression. Is quick to grasp new situations and see the important and significant facts surrounding a problem. Copes with the unexpected situations and can deal competently with complex and abstract problems. Mental talents are highly attuned to the functional problems and challenges of the advertising industry.

Strong professional satisfactions and interests.

Enjoys the challenges and variety found in imaginative and demanding advertising problems. Areas of high interests that are both work and avocationally related are found in artistic expression. Furthermore, he enjoys the direct, face-to-face relationships of his work and situations where independent contributions are required for success. A strong interest in the biological sciences appears to be a condition of early educational exposure. Has little interest in, or patience for, computational routine. Does not enjoy the specificity of numbers, but can use such information when required in his work. Interests appear highly appropriate for one directly concerned with the creation and production of advertising.

Considerable desire for personal challenge in the work situations.

Is a hard-working, competitive person who sets high goals of achievement for himself. Is energetic and forceful in action, especially under pressure. Is conscientious and determined in meeting his responsibilities, and drives in a single-purposed manner to get action and movement on his projects. Holds high standards of quality achievement, and is annoyed by sloppy effort. Has the ability to get caught up in his work in an enthusiastic and intent manner. Occasionally oversells himself and others on programs and ideas that have generated interest and challenge. Makes decision quickly and with good ability. May, on occasion, make hasty or overly optimistic decisions.

Forceful and direct in communications.

Although capable of being diplomatic and tactful, his usual approach is frontal. Puts his thoughts and ideas into terms easily understood by others, and makes a conscientious effort to be objective and clear in expression. As noted earlier, he can, through his enthusiasm, oversell his position; however, he guards against doing this. Understands and considers the viewpoints expressed by others, and can incorporate their ideas into his own thinking. Is not highly discriminative in critically analyzing others' ideas, perhaps in an effort to not discourage initiative and creativity, and occasionally buys a bad suggestion. This requires occasional reevaluation of programs and plans at a later point.

Friendly and pleasant in interpersonal relationships.

Enjoys and respects others, and works cooperatively with associates. Is poised and mature in behavior and shows emotional stability. Can get good acceptance and cooperation from others; however, resists imposing demands and controls upon them. Feels that they should have the same sense of dedication and enthusiasm for their work as he has, and needs to be more firm and specific in supervisory action. An ability to adapt quickly and flexibly to a variety of interpersonal situations is shown. Is objective and insightful about himself, and projects confidence and assurance in his dealings with others.

APB: JGE: npj
April 30, 1964

REFERENCE DEVELOPMENT
John H. Jones, Jr.

Mr. Allan Zero, Senior vice-president, XYZ Company.

"I knew John Jones over five years ago when we were both with Clark and Clark. Although I did not directly supervise him in his work, I feel safe in saying that:

He is a very bright man.
He is highly analytical.
He has an engaging personality and is an excellent salesman.
He is imaginative and an excellent marketing man.

My overall impression of him was that he had a good deal of potential and would go far in the agency business."

Mr. William Potter, Director of advertising and promotion, LMN Corporation.
"I knew John Jones when he handled our account at Clark and Clark some five years ago. At that time, he was beginning to show considerable capability for account management. His major assets—he is very bright, conscientious, quite good on detail and follow-through. All in all, I think he is a very able man who is going a long way. His basic approach is marketing in nature—he thinks in marketing stratagems and always tried to inject that thinking into our conversations and possible solutions to our problems.

"While he was working with me he went through a fairly messy divorce which was not of his making. He is a devoted family man and is extremely loyal and, I am sure, this affected him for a brief period. I understand that his present marriage is a very happy one and that things are going well for him at Foote, Basey, and Shilham on the East Coast. This man is one of the very best."

Mr. Kenneth Smith, Executive vice-president, advertising, Ralph P. Thomas Company, Inc.

"I remember John Jones very well indeed, and I worked very closely with him when we were at Clark and Clark. He worked for me on Procter & Gamble and Bordo's and was one of the brightest and best marketing men I have ever seen. He is creative and imaginative—the kind of man who is full of ideas. When he left Clark and Clark it was immediately after his divorce which affected him very deeply. He is the kind of man you would think of as being a family man, and his marriage to a girl from a small town in Maine who was attached to her family was an impossible situation. Shortly after his divorce, an old army friend of his, a sort of entrepreneur with his finger in every pie, asked him to join him on the West Coast to set up an agency. His friend spread himself too thin, and John was forced to sever the connection. The film operation of which you make mention was a temporary arrangement until he could get an appropriate assignment with a major agency.

"He appeared to have considerable managerial potential when he was with us, and I understand he has developed considerably along these lines. He has an excellent personality, is highly articulate, and is a hard worker. All in all, he is a damn good man—so good that I hope he will not be responsible for a product that competes with us. He is extremely loyal, absolutely honest, and highly capable. He is one of the three best marketing men I have ever met."

Michael Westen, Vice-president, Clark and Clark

"Hearing you describe this agency spot, I can think of no better man than John Jones. On all counts—personality, creative imagination, and marketing savvy, he is one of the best men we have lost in recent years. I know John would like to come East, and it is interesting that you should call me about him because I have in mind getting him together with one of our clients for a top advertising spot. He is a fine guy that I would like to see back in this part of the country."

Index